# SLIP,
# STITCH &
# STUMBLE

Celebrating 35 Years of
Penguin Random House India

# SLIP, STITCH & STUMBLE

## THE UNTOLD STORY OF INDIA'S FINANCIAL SECTOR REFORMS

RAJRISHI SINGHAL

PENGUIN
BUSINESS

An imprint of Penguin Random House

PENGUIN BUSINESS

USA | Canada | UK | Ireland | Australia
New Zealand | India | South Africa | China | Singapore

Penguin Business is part of the Penguin Random House group of companies
whose addresses can be found at global.penguinrandomhouse.com

Published by Penguin Random House India Pvt. Ltd
4th Floor, Capital Tower 1, MG Road,
Gurugram 122 002, Haryana, India

First published in Penguin Business by Penguin Random House India 2023

ISBN 9780670092116

Typeset in Garamond by MAP Systems, Bengaluru, India
Printed at Replika Press Pvt. Ltd, India

www.penguin.co.in

*To my conscience keepers:*
*Teetash and Mekhala*

# Contents

# Chapter 1

## In the Beginning

On the afternoon of 24 July 1991, as Finance Minister Manmohan Singh stood up to present his maiden Union budget for the financial year ending 31 March 1992, a packed visitors' gallery in Parliament held its breath. There was a palpable sense of expectation. The visitors had somehow guessed that they were witnessing history in the making. On a normal day, the visitors' gallery held the usual complement of curious onlookers, visiting delegations from overseas, a scattering of diplomats, representatives of various lobbies and the sundry curious citizen. This was a different day, marked by a sense of impending change; there was an expectant air of watching history being made on the fly. The press gallery was packed. So was the visitors' gallery. Among the throng of spectators in the visitors' gallery was a prominent banker who headed one of Bombay's (the city is now called Mumbai) three leading private investment banks. His presence, in some senses, marked the change that this historic budget would achieve.

And, as it happened on that day of July 1991—at a time when the economy was smarting from a severe balance-of-payments (BoP) crisis—Manmohan Singh's speech changed the trajectory of the Indian economy, especially its financial sector. His budget measures infused the Indian financial sector with a competitive element, sketching out a roadmap for it that promised a somewhat level playing field for both the state-owned and private financial intermediaries.

From then to now, the journey of India's financial sector has been long and arduous. It has been unreservedly momentous with many high points, punctuated by some embarrassing moments too. The radical overhaul of India's capital markets, for example—involving the transformation of an antiquated and corrupt equities trading platform into a technology-led transparent and fair market—has been a model template for many developed and developing economies. But at the same time, the reforms momentum seems to have faltered in resolving the nagging problem of bad loans in the banking system; even a prolonged series of different regulatory measures, stretching over three decades, has been unable to root out the problem.

The reasons for such uneven outcomes perhaps lie in India's political economy, with many of its disagreeable pre-reform characteristics resisting change even after the onset of economic reforms, despite expectations to the contrary. The political economy's influence on public policy is a given in any society, but the extent to which it affects an economy lies in how authorities across jurisdictions manage to minimize its baleful influence. The motivation to pursue economic reforms or institutional reforms depends, to a large degree, on how the costs of reforms—or the benefits from the status quo—are distributed. When a few entrenched interest groups—with incommensurate political influence—enjoy large rents from status quo policies, they will have little incentive to pursue economic reforms.

Former bureaucrat and current Congress leader Jairam Ramesh's book *To The Brink and Back* provides an object lesson on the impact of the political economy. It describes the adrenaline-pumping tumultuous period between 20 June and 31 August 1991, when the newly elected Congress government of P.V. Narasimha Rao was trying to implement the economic reforms programme. Jairam Ramesh highlights how the draft of the new industrial policy had to be chopped and changed to assuage the reservations of the many ministers in the cabinet who had been drip-fed on the old economic dirigiste state and were ever suspicious of foreign investment.

The 1991 economic crisis and India's brush with near bankruptcy had invested the leadership of the new government—with Narasimha Rao as prime minister, Manmohan Singh as finance minister and P. Chidambaram as commerce minister—with popular trust, and there was a general sense of anticipation that things could only get better from here. The economic crisis had helped provide an inflexion point to the Indian economy. The new leadership—supported ably by the country's central bank, Reserve Bank of India (RBI), and its governor C. Rangarajan—was able to press home some of the economic ideas and concepts that had been swirling around in the system but had failed to gain momentum in the absence of popular support from either the entrenched political class or the industrial lobby. Importantly, the crisis proved to be a tipping point by setting the template for the future of financial sector reforms. As numerous events have decisively demonstrated over the past three decades, significant and consequential financial sector reforms—implying a complete systems overhaul and not just procedural changes or marginal tinkering with existing systems and processes—did not occur organically but were influenced by critical events. Meaningful reforms took place only when there were economic crises or scams.

In essence, reforms were initiated only when the political costs of not pursuing them had become prohibitive.

The crowd that had gathered in Parliament on 24 July 1991 had been keen on change and was hoping for a step-change in the system. So was the banker in Parliament we mentioned earlier. He helmed an investment bank which had morphed out of his family-owned, seventy-to-eighty-year-old stockbroking firm. This banker had graduated from south Bombay's well-known elite institutions and had joined the family's firm in 1962 after a brief stint with a London-based stockbroking firm. In the years immediately after 1973, his family's firm was among the first batch of home-grown broking companies that had decided to branch out into investment banks to help India's fledgling corporate sector raise capital. Indian companies, having lived precariously amidst a chronic shortage of capital and resources since Independence, had tentatively started spreading their wings, enthused by a growing domestic economy and an Indian polity focused on developing an indigenous private sector.

The timing of this private investment bank's birth was both propitious and serendipitous. A 1973 amendment to the Foreign Exchange Regulation Act of 1947 mandating, among other things, a 40 per cent ceiling on all foreign investments was promulgated in the backdrop of a severe foreign exchange shortage. Many multinational companies (MNCs) operating in India were 100 per cent owned by their overseas parent outfits and would repatriate a bulk of their profits as dividend. This situation rekindled visions of the old colonial regime. The foreign-owned companies were using Indian labour, raw materials and natural resources, including domestic working capital, but transferring the surplus from their operations to headquarters back home, somewhat reminiscent of the colonial surplus-extraction model. The MNC argument that the government should not overlook their contribution to the Indian economy—in the form of capital investment, technology transfer, labour wages and various government taxes—failed to convince the authorities.

It was hoped the foreign investment ceiling would reduce currency outgo in the form of the large dividend payments that foreign companies routinely made to their headquarters. Many MNCs left the country in protest, the most famous among them being IBM and Coca-Cola. But equally, many MNCs chose to stay on, despite being forced to dilute their shareholding in their Indian subsidiaries. And when the dilution happened in the form of the sale of shares to the Indian public, three private investment banks—all located in Mumbai—were close at hand to act as midwives to the process.

But beyond that first flush of business opportunity, growth options for private sector players in the finance industry were limited. Until the 1991 reforms, the bulk of India's private financial sector survived by mining the grey zone that existed at the tri-junction of an administered regime, an underdeveloped regulatory framework and what was considered legitimate. While some private players' proximity to the political economy and familiarity with campaign finance anomalies gave them unique access to power and the attendant benefits of business opportunities, most of the private institutions in the financial sector were made to compete with the state-owned commercial banks and development financial institutions[1] with their hands and legs tied.

To be fair, the private sector also brought unique expertise to the industry. When some companies wanted to explore alternative, but legal, funding opportunities in the late 1970s, JM Financial's Nimesh Kampani was at hand to market the country's first convertible debentures to retail investors. Kampani leveraged his company's nationwide stockbroking and distribution network to sell these bonds, creating not only a financing alternative for companies looking beyond ossified and straitjacketed public-sector banks to raise money but also catalysing the use of distribution networks for marketing financial products to retail investors, a tool that many institutions would use to great effect in later years. The second competitor in this arena, Hemendra Kothari, who was the fourth-generation member to join his family's old stockbroking outfit D.S. Purbhoodas, had also launched his investment bank, DSP Financial Consultants, in 1975. The third company was

Champaklal Investment and Financial Consultancy Ltd (CIFCO) and its head, Bhupen Dalal, was also an early investment banking maven. He was probably the first to realize that the non-resident Indian population in Western economies was a potential source of capital for Indian companies looking for new funding sources. CIFCO, like all other contemporary investment banks, was the result of family-owned stockbroking operations diversifying to take advantage of the changes occurring in the Indian corporate sector's legal framework.

All three—Kampani, Dalal and Kothari—had their offices within a square mile of each other's in south Bombay's financial and commercial hub, Nariman Point. The slow-burn reforms of the 1980s (and the accelerated opening of the economy after 1991) had catalysed many other emerging boutique investment banks and finance companies (such as Kotak Mahindra Finance Company), to also try and break into the big league. There was hope all around that Manmohan Singh would eliminate some of the shackles that had restrained many of these private enterprises.

One of these three investment bankers was present in Parliament in July 1991, which was somewhat symbolic and, in many ways, seemed to indicate that changes to the status quo were imminent.

Even outside Parliament, there was widespread expectation that this was going to be a landmark event, especially after the two or three years of domestic political instability and the external crisis which had enveloped India in the wake of Iraq's invasion of Kuwait on 2 August 1990. A brief explanation of the crisis might be necessary to understand the trigger for the 1991 economic reforms.

## The Gulf Spark

The unprovoked invasion and seven-month occupation of Kuwait by Iraq was widely criticized globally (and by India too), forcing the US to respond with an armed assault on Iraqi forces in mid-January 1991, in what was popularly known as the first Gulf War. This geopolitical conflagration in West Asia resulted in a global oil price spike, which bled India's meagre foreign exchange reserves and pushed the country's economy to the edge of bankruptcy and loan defaults. Worse, worker remittances from the Gulf region, a critical input for the country's BOP,[2] were also affected adversely, further aggravating the external account crisis. The Indian economy was already suffering from a number of infirmities, including an overwhelming amount of foreign debt, and the Gulf War exacerbated these vulnerabilities. By November 1990, India's foreign exchange reserves amounted to only $1.9 billion, just about enough to finance three weeks of imports.

The problem had been building up for over a decade, and the Gulf War just happened to be the last straw. An August 1991 memorandum from the World Bank[3] summed up the developing crisis:

India is in the midst of an economic crisis. The oil shock of 1990 was the proximate cause, but the crisis has been a long time in the making. Several years of unsustainable fiscal and balance of payments deficits have left little room for maneuver. In 1990/91 prolonged political uncertainty, policy shortcomings, internal conflicts, and other unforeseen economic problems compounded India's difficulties. Reflecting growing concern in international capital markets about the continuing deterioration of India's macroeconomic balances, mounting external debt, and political uncertainty, three credit rating services downgraded Indian issues in 1990. Further downgrading took place in 1991, and India's access to commercial credit markets has been effectively cut off. International reserves declined by $1.8 billion in 1990/91 after cumulative losses in 1988/89 and 1989/90 of $2.3 billion; notwithstanding drawings on the IMF of $1.8 billion in January 1991, reserves (excluding gold) stood at barely one month of imports on March 31, 1991. Since then the external liquidity position has remained extremely precarious.

India's 'extremely precarious' economic position forced the government to borrow $777 million in January 1991 from the multilateral agency International Monetary Fund (IMF) for three months, under a window with minimum conditionality. This was quickly followed by the borrowing of another $1009 million from the Compensatory and Contingency Financing Facility for oil imports, which was also a low-conditionality window. Clearly, as the World Bank memorandum noted, these stop-gap financing modes were not enough because the country's foreign currency reserves continued to deplete, dropping precipitously to $1.1 billion in June 1991, just about sufficient to meet two weeks of imports. The Indian economy was staring down a steep cliff without any accessible parachutes. In all, India had borrowed roughly $4.3 billion from the IMF under its various windows during 1991–93.

In May 1991, India sold 20 tonnes of gold from the government stock (accumulated through confiscations from smugglers) to the Union Bank of Switzerland, with an option to buy it back. Again, this rearguard action proved to be an insufficient, stop-gap solution. Soon thereafter, India was forced to mortgage its gold reserves of 47 tonnes with the Bank of England and the Bank of Japan in return for a $600-million loan, hoping to replenish the rapidly depleting foreign currency reserves. Trust in the Indian economy had reached such a low point that both the Bank of England and the Bank of Japan had insisted that the gold be physically shifted to the London vaults of the two central banks. In March 1991, the international rating agencies downgraded India's credit rating, further jeopardizing its ability to borrow from the international markets.

It might be instructive to pause for a moment to understand how the Indian economy had reached such a precipice.

## The Backstory

The seeds of the crisis were sown during the pivotal decade of the 1980s during which the annual growth rate in gross domestic product (GDP) was able to escape its two-decade restrictive trap of 3.5 per cent and touch 5.7 per cent. The prolonged phase of the slow, non-accelerating growth rate of the 1960s and 1970s had invited derision from many academics, including the disparaging term 'Hindu rate of growth' from the economist and Planning Commission member Raj Krishna. India was essentially a closed economy marked by severe restrictions, which included a stifling industrial licensing policy and a straitjacketed financial sector dominated by public-sector banks.

The 1980s decade helped India leave that embarrassing episode behind. After the October 1984 assassination of former prime minister Indira Gandhi, her son Rajiv Gandhi won the general elections and succeeded her as India's prime minister. He started easing some of the decades-old curbs on industry and trade (including some licensing constraints on imports, such as by introducing the Open General Licence). For example, the broad-banding industrial policy—under which companies with licences to produce certain kinds of products (such as trucks) were allowed to produce similar products (such as cars)—had a salutary impact on growth, even though it benefited only a select clutch of companies and industries.

Former NITI Aayog vice chairman and Columbia University professor Arvind Panagariya[4] acknowledged the impact of broad-banding in a paper for the IMF:

> Broad banding, which allowed firms to switch production between similar production lines such as trucks and cars,

was introduced in January 1986 in 28 industry groups. This provision was significantly expanded in the subsequent years and led to increased flexibility in many industries. In some industries, the impact was marginal, however, since a large number of separate product categories remained due to continued industrial licensing in those products.

In a podcast series titled *Ideas of India*,[5] political scientist and Ashoka University professor Vinay Sitapati also mentions the beneficial impact of these hesitant reforms during the 1980s:

> In the '80s . . . there's a number of committee reports, whether it is deregulating cement, deregulating sugar, how we think about tariffs. It's in the air. And then of course, we have this open general license. We have broad banding. Something as simple as broad banding managed to unleash so many percentage points of growth in the GDP is remarkable. That's how shackled India was.

Other economic parameters—such as per-capita income or merchandise exports—also looked encouraging. Yet, under the cover of these years of higher growth lay another story of exigent politics and profligate economics. The source of this growth lay primarily in public expenditure, which was being funded by government borrowings. The cost of this fiscal stimulus was soon reflected in the growing fiscal deficit, which grew from close to 6 per cent at the start of the decade to over 9 per cent by its end.

A large part of the government's expenditure was sourced by commandeering private savings. This was done through tax-saving instruments issued by public financial institutions (such as insurance companies) or through regulatory fiats compulsorily diverting private savings in government-owned financial institutions to investments in government bonds. Over the years, as the deficit grew, this became unsustainable and began to put pressure on interest rates, inflation and the external account.

During the decade, public-sector savings dropped as a result of the government's preference for revenue expenditure over capital expenditure and poor public-sector performance. Thus, despite a rise in private-sector savings (including households), rising public expenditure necessitated increased overseas borrowings. The current account[6] deficit increased from 1.7 per cent of GDP in 1980–81 to 3.1 per cent of GDP by 1989–90. External borrowings (which included deposits solicited from non-resident Indians at higher interest rates) expanded from $20.6 billion to $63.1 billion during the same period, growing roughly by over 20 per cent every year.

Former RBI governor C. Rangarajan recounts those times in his recent memoir, *Forks in the Road*:

> The steady rise in the fiscal deficit was also happening at a time when the Government of India had put out a long-term fiscal policy aimed at improving the tax structure and administration and setting long-term goals to ensure the stability of tax rates. It was the drive to grow fast at any cost that bore the seeds of a crisis that finally bust (*sic*) a few years later.

The book narrates how the crisis ballooned. As explained earlier, high government spending and a concomitant increase in domestic demand led to rising current account deficits during the 1980s decade, which could only be partially met through external sources of financing. The balance had to be met through the drawdown of foreign exchange reserves.

India was almost pushed over the edge of this unsustainable economic position when the Gulf crisis erupted. With oil prices reaching stratospheric levels during those months of 1990–91—moving rapidly from $34 to $77 per barrel—India's oil import bill also raced past the country's ability to pay. Caught literally on the wrong foot with an over-leveraged book, India's credit rating was downgraded in 1990, and thereafter again in 1991, effectively shutting it out of the global credit markets. Nobody wanted to lend to a country with an onerous loan burden, made even more vulnerable by its rapidly diminishing foreign exchange reserves.

The Indian government promised to behave itself while availing of the loans from the IMF. The IMF annual report for 1991[7] stated: 'The Government has announced it intends to reduce sharply the fiscal deficit and implement a wide range of policies to improve the Indian economy's efficiency and competitiveness, including policies to strengthen the financial position and performance of public enterprises.'

The BOP situation was just a symptom, the manifestation of a deeper and more structural malaise. India's broader economy— and, of course, the financial sector—had been struggling to deliver its twin objectives of sustainable growth and poverty reduction. Ironically, the policies designed to reduce poverty were precisely those which hobbled growth (and, in many cases, even created rent-seeking opportunities).

Many reports and academic tracts authored in the 1980s pointed out the systemic flaws in India's economy. In his book *Backstage*, Montek Singh Ahluwalia has quoted from his late wife's academic work to highlight the problems with the policy regime of those times:

> There was surprisingly little support from academic economists for either domestic decontrol or external liberalization. However, empirical research was pointing to the need for a policy rethink. Isher's book, *Industrial Growth in India: Stagnation Since the Mid-60s*, showed that many conventional explanations for the low rate of industrial growth in India, such as worsening

income distribution and shortage of wage goods, did not stand up to empirical scrutiny.

Economist Isher Judge Ahluwalia, who passed away in September 2020, had worked extensively on industrial development and productivity growth in India before focusing on urbanization and urban infrastructure in her later years.

The broader Indian economy was characterized by a command-and-control structure, with the state assuming a large role. Industry had to depend on government licensing for creating or expanding manufacturing capacity. The government decided what entrepreneurs could manufacture and where they could manufacture it, including how much of it and, occasionally, even where they could sell it. For example, fertilizer manufacturers had to submit to a price-and-distribution control system as part of a policy to ensure fair prices and equitable distribution of fertilizers. Even the supply of raw materials was controlled: coal and steel were rationed out to industry, and the power supply was unpredictable. This shackled the entrepreneurial spirit and gave rise to inefficiencies, low productivity, corruption and restrictions on the level of industrialization in the country.

The financial sector, in lock-step with the real economy, was also marked by high levels of repression under which credit was rationed, interest rates administered and the private sector shackled. Starting with the two-stage nationalization of commercial banks—first in 1969 and then again in 1980—the Indian financial sector was progressively hamstrung by restrictive rules, eventually becoming a handmaiden to public finance. The nationalized banking sector, in particular, became a convenient platform for aggressive resource mobilization. These resources were then channelled towards reckless government spending or diverted to targeted lending schemes at concessional interest rates. The government's profligacy, financed by means of automatic monetization of the deficit, led to surges in the money supply. The RBI, tasked with ensuring price stability, among its other mandates, was then forced to use statutory reserve instruments to mop up the excess liquidity to stave off inflationary impulses in the economy. As the deficit and money supply increased in tandem, so did the reserve requirements, forcing banks to part with a larger proportion of their funds for investing in government bonds and cash deposits with the RBI. This left banks with little resources for commercial lending to industry.

The entire banking system was controlled by means of a complex web of administered deposit and lending rates. Banks were told how much they could lend to industry, and at what rates. The banking sector was dominated by government-owned banks and financial institutions, thereby limiting competition and efficiency. The capital markets were equally stunted. The primary equities market was artificially constrained and tightly controlled, with the government deciding who could raise money, how much money, when, and at what price. The secondary equity markets were largely unregulated, controlled by a cabal of brokers and completely opaque in their operations. With both the banking sector and the capital markets skewed, the result was inefficient allocation of capital. The bond market was non-existent, with government bonds mopping up most of the private savings through a rigid and impenetrable market, antiquated in its structure and inefficient in its processes.

The preface to the fourth volume (covering the 1981–1997 period) of the RBI's history—titled unimaginatively *The Reserve Bank of India* (henceforth referred to as *RBI History*)—sums up the tsunami of woes that assailed the economy:

The decade of the 1980s remained broadly as the continuation of a mostly inward-looking, planned and administered era of central direction, though several initial attempts were made at liberalising certain segments of the economy. During this period, the country faced many uncertainties including, *inter alia*, a severe drought in 1987, causing supply constraints; erosion in the profitability of banks on the back of the introduction of populist political measures such as the loan *melas*, which engaged the attention of the Reserve Bank towards safety and prudential issues in the commercial banking system; administered interest rates that limited the scope of transmission and efficacy of monetary policy besides the fiscal dominance that further constrained manoeuvrability of monetary policy actions; and the fixed exchange rate regime with limited external sector opening up, leading to build-up of external imbalances.

The entire structure made for an economic sandcastle, vulnerable to the gentlest of shocks. The economic crisis, which was occasioned by the 1990 Gulf War, came on top of the prevailing internal political turmoil and globally shifting sands.

## The Political Imperative

In India, the May-June 1991 general elections (during which former prime minister Rajiv Gandhi was tragically assassinated) had ended a chaotic two-year rule by a rag-tag coalition—ironically, supported by both the right- and left-wing parties—which had prioritized social engineering over economic development, especially through caste-based reservations. Prime Minister V.P. Singh, who had made his mark as a reformer as Rajiv Gandhi's finance minister in 1985, had become a 'messiah of the backward castes'[8] by 1991. The Congress party made a comeback in the 1991 elections, riding on a sympathy wave generated by Rajiv Gandhi's brutal assassination. The incoming government found the economy in tatters, industry stagnant and the nation in hock to various lenders.

Externally, the Berlin Wall had fallen in 1989 and the Soviet Union had begun to disintegrate. On the east of India's borders, China under Deng Xiaoping had adopted an experimental economic model with many features of capitalism and a clutch of South-east Asian nations was embracing an export-led economic development model. This gave Indian planners some pause, having styled the Indian economic edifice since Independence on centralized Soviet-style planning, making it a command-and-control structure that privileged a dominant role for government, rather than private capital, in the economy. Resource allocation for the entire economy was centralized through the state, and the markets had no role in allocating the factors of production—either capital or other resources—resulting in endemic low productivity, corruption, inefficiencies and stunted economic growth. The internal political and economic crisis and the global winds of change necessitated a drastic economic reset.

After winning the 1991 general elections, the Congress party selected P.V. Narasimha Rao, a scholar-politician from Hyderabad in Andhra Pradesh, to lead the country at this critical juncture. A lawyer by training and a polyglot, Rao had earlier served in both the Indira Gandhi and Rajiv Gandhi cabinets in various capacities. Rao, in turn, selected Manmohan Singh—a former bureaucrat who had helmed some of the country's most important economic portfolios (chief economic adviser to the finance ministry, finance secretary, governor of the RBI, deputy chairman of the Planning Commission)—as the finance minister. A soft-spoken man, Singh wore his erudition lightly but was widely respected as an able and righteous officer.

Interestingly, neither Rao nor Singh were automatic choices. Rao was selected only after the Congress party's first choice, Shankar Dayal Sharma, turned down the offer of the post of prime minister (he was India's vice president at the time). Similarly, Rao's first choice for finance minister, I.G. Patel (former RBI governor and director of the London School of Economics and Political Science), was also unwilling to take on the responsibility.

There were extraordinary expectations invested in Manmohan Singh, whom people saw as an encouraging and enabling amalgam of critical skills. These he had picked up from three different roles he had assumed in his career—as an accomplished economist, a former central banker and a seasoned bureaucrat. Born into a family of modest means, Manmohan had excelled in academics, winning scholarships to some of the best educational institutions (University of Cambridge and University of Oxford) globally. And, though a surprise choice for the finance minister's post in P.V. Narasimha Rao's cabinet, his selection as finance minister still generated a groundswell of hope and goodwill. He was viewed as an honest and upright officer who could provide the right direction to the Indian economy, a marked change from some of the unethical or incompetent politicians that had preceded him in that role.

Singh's budget speech on 24 July 1991 was expected to provide the long-term solutions to the stasis that had beleaguered the Indian economy for decades. The task was two-fold: first, to initiate measures to stave off the immediate balance-of-payments crisis; and second, to implement sweeping structural reforms that would put the Indian economy on a sound footing for future growth.

A fortnight earlier, on 9 July 1991, Prime Minister Rao had provided a foretaste of things to come in an address to the nation on Doordarshan and All India Radio: 'Desperate maladies call for drastic remedies . . . We believe that a bulk of government regulations and controls on our economic activity have outlived their utility . . . We believe that India has much to learn from what is happening elsewhere in the world. Many countries are bringing in far-reaching changes.'

Even Manmohan Singh's budget[9] speech did not lose time in conveying the urgent need for change:

There is no time to lose. Neither the Government nor the economy can live beyond its means year after year. The room for maneuver, to live on borrowed money or time, does not exist anymore. Any further postponement of macroeconomic adjustment, long overdue, would mean that the balance of payments situation, now exceedingly difficult, would become unmanageable and inflation, already high, would exceed limits of tolerance. For improving the management of the economy, the starting point, and indeed the centre-piece of our strategy, should be a credible fiscal adjustment and macro-economic stabilisation during the current financial year, to be followed by continued fiscal consolidation thereafter. This process would, inevitably, need at least three years, if not longer, to complete. But there can be no adjustment without pain. The people must be prepared to make necessary sacrifices to preserve our economic independence and restore the health of our economy.

Singh also underscored the need for structural reforms beyond the immediate need for crisis management through macroeconomic adjustments and exchange rate interventions. He summed it up as follows:

The thrust of the reform process would be to increase the efficiency and international competitiveness of industrial production, to utilise for this purpose foreign investment and foreign technology to a much greater degree than we have done in the past, to increase the productivity of investment, to ensure that India's financial sector is rapidly modernised, and to improve the performance of the public sector, so that the key sectors of our economy are enabled to attain an adequate technological and competitive edge in a fast changing global economy.

## The M Document

So, there it was, the core two-pronged reform process: the unchaining of the industrial and financial sectors. Both sectors were considered interdependent: if the industrial sector had to really expand and realize its 'animal spirits', a critical component for achieving that end objective would be a truly efficient financial sector which could freely and capably allocate capital at economic prices to deserving projects. The industrial sector liberalization process principally involved abolishing the prevalent licensing regime, including the restrictive practice of reserving numerous industries for only the small-scale sector or the restrictive and pernicious monopoly regulatory framework called the Monopolies and Restrictive Trade Practices (MRTP) Act.

A rough draft of the core strategy had already been in circulation for a while. In June 1989, then prime minister V.P. Singh had asked the Special Secretary to the Prime Minister's Office, Montek Singh Ahluwalia, to prepare a note on the kind of economic reforms India needed. A thirty-four-page note on reforms required in the macroeconomy (especially on the fiscal economy), the industrial policy, the trade strategy and foreign investment was prepared for formal presentation to the Committee of Secretaries. The note was not translated into action or policy though it did find many supporters. But, mysteriously, it was leaked to the *Indian Express* newspaper, which carried it in full. The note's authorship was not disclosed by the newspaper, but it was widely suspected that the author was Montek Singh, and it came to be known as the 'M Document', a moniker that has refused to go away. The M Document became one of the guiding roadmaps for the reform process.

In his non-memoir, *Backstage: The Story Behind India's High Growth Years*, Montek summarizes the contents of the note:

. . . although a gradual process of liberalization had been
underway for some time, most other developing countries had
gone much further, and even the former Communist countries
of Eastern Europe had started adopting market economy
concepts. We could not expect to compete internationally if
our industry continued to operate in an environment that was
much more restrictive and less congenial for various types of
international linkages . . . The note also emphasized we needed
to articulate a clear medium-term strategy in which the different
but interconnected components of the reforms are identified.

Interestingly, the motive behind the leaking of the M
Document to the media is not known but can be speculated
on. Long before stakeholder consultation became de rigueur
for policy formulation, it was an established practice in Delhi
administrative circles to 'float balloons' to assess public opinion.
Ministers or senior bureaucrats would often leak select portions
of confidential documents, policy briefs or discussion notes to
favoured journalists or publications. Occasionally, even outlandish
suggestions (such as abolition of capital gains tax) would be
floated. Public response to the news would become an important
source of feedback. This practice continues to a limited extent
even today.

The response to the publication of the M Document in
the newspaper was predictable: it was both supportive and
truculent. What was, however, more important than the individual
suggestions in the M Document was its attempt to present an
integrated medium-term economic strategy in which different
parts of the economy intersected and influenced each other. There
were reforms suggested for five key areas: the fiscal economy,
public-sector operations, industrial controls, trade restrictions and
foreign investment rules. Some of these ideas endured and found
favour with subsequent governments, albeit in slightly different

shapes and forms. These ideas and their variants even found subsequent expression in the Congress party's manifesto for the 1991 elections or in various notes drafted for the Narasimha Rao government.

In short, there was no getting away from the fact that the Indian economy needed a radically new strategy, one that was aligned with the hopes of millions of Indians. As Manmohan Singh articulated it in his maiden Budget speech:

> I do not minimise the difficulties that lie ahead on the long and arduous journey on which we have embarked. But as Victor Hugo once said, 'No power on earth can stop an idea whose time has come.' I suggest to this august House that the emergence of India as a major economic power in the world happens to be one such idea. Let the whole world hear it loud and clear. India is now wide awake. We shall prevail. We shall overcome.

## Pre-Budget Reform Moves

The Rao government had, in fact, initiated three radical moves even before presenting the 24 July budget of 1991.

The first was a two-step devaluation of the Indian rupee. The first devaluation of the rupee against all the major currencies (between 7 per cent and 9 per cent) took place on 1 July 1991. The second devaluation, of about 11 per cent, was initiated two days later before the markets had time to adjust to the first devaluation. This two-step feint allowed the government and the RBI to first gauge market (and political) reaction with a smaller devaluation before pushing ahead with the second, and more substantial, step. The overall 18–19 per cent devaluation had become necessary after months of high inflation, which, given that inflation in India's major trading partner countries was much lower, had effectively resulted in the rupee's real effective exchange rate appreciating, thereby adversely affecting exports. Volume Four of *RBI History*, covering the period 1981–97, describes the devaluation step:

> The devaluation took place in two steps. On July 1, 1991, the Finance Minister wanted to 'test the waters' before effecting any large change in the value of the rupee. Only when the markets reacted positively, a second devaluation was permitted on July 3, 1991. The two-step downward adjustment in the value of the rupee worked out to 17.38 per cent in terms of the intervention currency i.e., pound sterling and about 18.7 per cent in US dollar terms. Further, to counteract any inflationary impact, the Bank increased the Bank Rate, term deposit rates and the lending rate for large borrowers.

The second step, facilitated by the rupee devaluation, was a radical trade policy that was announced on 4 July 1991. The subsidies paid to exporters were abolished first. Next, building on the M Document's recommendations, imports were linked to export performance through a new instrument called Eximscrips, which could be traded freely in the market. This effectively abolished import licensing for a wide range of products.

The third measure was an industrial policy, which was placed in Parliament on 24 July, just a few hours before the presentation of the budget, without any fanfare. This was ironic because the policy was truly far-reaching in its scope and sought to upend a policy structure that had been in existence for almost four decades. The new industrial policy's avowed objective was to unleash the economy's competitive energies and was focused across five key areas: industrial licensing, foreign investment, foreign technology agreements, public-sector policy and the MRTP Act. The policy's most significant decision was the abolition of industrial licensing (except in a few critical areas, such as defence), which had become a way of life for Indian private enterprise for forty years and a continuing source of institutional corruption, apart from inefficiency and low productivity. Foreign investment of up to 51 per cent, especially in high-priority industries requiring large capital outlays and advanced technology, was allowed. Automatic approval was accorded for foreign technology transfer agreements. Accordingly, a new organization came into being— the Foreign Investment Promotion Board (FIPB), which was located in the prime minister's office. Public-sector investment was henceforth limited to only a few areas that were considered strategic, essential for India's economic development and did not traditionally attract private sector capital, such as infrastructure (which was opened up to private investment much later), defence or railways. Finally, huge changes were also made to the MRTP Act, which was originally crafted in 1970 to guard against the concentration of economic power but had subsequently become a hurdle to industrial growth and expansion.

## Pulling on Strings Attached

The government's economic reforms programme, a radical pivot from the established economic model, was not acceptable to many within the political establishment. The Left was concerned with the nature and beneficiaries of the reforms programme. The old socialists from the Congress party saw the new regime wresting away their powers and privileges. There was also a degree of apprehension, somewhat legitimate, about how an abrupt pivot to a market-led economy would impact the large section of the population which had no access to any safety net, especially if the state's historic, and unprincipled, proximity to industry was carried forward from the licensing era into the reforms era. Industry, cocooned from competition for decades, was anxious about competition and survival. As is natural in such circumstances, a sustained drumbeat of allegations and insinuations, primarily about external influences thrusting the package of reforms on unsuspecting Indian citizens, began informing the general public's perception about the nature of reforms. The bogeyman in this case, and one that seemed credible, given the institution's somewhat dodgy history and its policy rigidity, was the IMF.

The common refrain was that the IMF had attached conditionalities to the loan package, especially that part of structural reforms focused on narrowing down the fiscal deficit, lowering import duties and welcoming foreign investment. In reality, the attaching of conditionalities was a standard operating procedure for the institution, and it had thrown up mixed outcomes during its chequered history, thereby generating some element of apprehension about the outcomes.

However, available documents suggest that the Indian authorities had themselves suggested a revival package that resembled a putative IMF package of conditionalities. The Indian economy had reached such a critical juncture that it limited the options available to it. Jairam Ramesh recounts in his book an interview the renowned economist K.N. Raj had given to the magazine *Frontline* around the same time, in which he had asserted that the leftists would have also adopted the same solutions framework had they been in power and were confronted with a similar economic crisis.

In his letter[10] to the IMF managing director Michel Camdessus on 27 August 1991 requesting for an eighteen-month stand-by arrangement for about SDR[11] 1656 million (equal to roughly $2.25 billion then), Manmohan Singh had also attached a note, 'Memorandum on Economic Policies', outlining all the structural adjustments the government proposed to make, including stabilizing the fiscal position, tightening the monetary system and re-aligning the external economic policies to ensure a sustainable current account deficit and a manageable balance-of-payments situation.

The new Government that took office on June 21, 1991 inherited an economy in deep crisis . . . The new Government, recognizing that there was no time to lose, immediately adopted a number of stabilization measures that were designed to restore internal and external confidence. Thus, monetary policy was tightened further through increases in interest rates, the exchange rate of the rupee was adjusted by 18.7 percent, and a major simplification and liberalization of the trade system was announced. It is the Government's intention, as announced in the Budget speech to Parliament on July 24, 1991, to complement these initial measures by a comprehensive program of economic adjustment. The centerpiece of the economic strategy will be a substantial fiscal correction in the remainder of the current fiscal year and in 1992/93, to be followed by continued fiscal consolidation thereafter. The reduction in fiscal imbalances will be supported by reforms in economic policy that are essential to impart a new element of dynamism to growth processes in the economy. The thrust will be to increase the efficiency and international competitiveness of industrial production, to utilize foreign investment and technology to a much greater degree than in the past, to improve the performance and rationalize the scope of the public sector, and to reform and modernize the financial sector so that it can more efficiently serve the needs of the economy. During the inevitable period of transition, it is the Government's firm intention that the poorest sections of society are protected to the maximum extent possible from the costs of adjustment.

Many authors of books and papers on India's economic reforms have pointed out that through the 1980s, New Delhi had managed to attract a constellation of market-friendly advisers, experts and academics who were continually pointing out the flaws and the growth-restraining elements of the policy framework through a steady output of notes, internal memos, academic papers and policy briefs. These academics

included Jagdish Bhagwati, Padma Desai, T.N. Srinivasan and
Ashok Desai. Even among economic administrators, a new
breed of professionals was constantly holding up a mirror to the
political class, and that cohort included Montek Singh Ahluwalia,
Rakesh Mohan (then economic adviser to the Ministry of
Industry), C. Rangarajan, Bimal Jalan (chief economic adviser),
P. Chidambaram, Shankar Acharya and Vijay Kelkar.

In his book *Political Economy of Reforms in India*, the academic
Rahul Mukherji argues that the 1991 crisis was like a tipping point,
with a steady build-up of ideas having preceded the real event.

> Economic change in India can be likened to an ideational
> tipping point. India's gradualism can be frustrating. But
> it works through a process by which the government
> changes its mind, building over decades of policy failure and
> experimentation. Crises often highlight these failures but what
> looks like a discontinuous change has an ideational past which
> has been building up over a long period. The reason why India
> responded differently to the BoP crisis in 1991 than the one
> in 1966 cannot be understood in terms of external pressure. It
> needs to be understood in terms of the dominant idea of the
> day in 1966 and in 1991. India was prepared for globalisation
> and deregulation in 1991, but not in 1966.

This is not an isolated view. Even Vijay Kelkar and Ajay
Shah in their joint authorship of *In Service of the Republic* have
made exactly the same point: 'The reforms of 1991 are linked,
in the minds of many, to the balance of payments crisis and
consequential IMF conditionality. A closer examination of that
period, however, shows the policy pipeline that was established
through the 1980s made this possible.'

These arguments are constructed to refute the notion
that the 1991 loan had come with strings attached, because
available documents, especially the Manmohan Singh letter to

Michel Camdessus and the argument of similar ideas having reverberated around in the Delhi policy circuit since the 1980s, seek to demolish the view that the IMF had indeed imposed structural adjustment conditionalities to their loans.

In all fairness, though, it could well be possible that Manmohan Singh's letter to Camdessus was to pre-empt any political backlash arising from suspicions of external compulsions behind the loan and compromise with India's sovereignty. Rahul Mukherji also posits that industry—an important political constituency, protected and cossetted till then—also did not resist the government's approaching the IMF because the foreign exchange scarcity at the time had affected their import plans. And many of the industrialists had earlier enjoyed preferential access to industrial and import licences. Given the close links that many policy wonks and economic administrators enjoyed with the Fund-Bank senior officials, some of them having spent a part of their professional lives employed with these institutions, it is quite possible that they knew exactly what remedial measures the IMF would have proposed, and pre-empted that.

Manmohan Singh faced an unending stream of questions in Parliament about the IMF's involvement. In his budget speech[12] for 1992–93, he clarified that the reforms programme being implemented was exactly as his letter to the IMF had outlined:

It has been alleged by some people that the reform programme has been dictated by the IMF and the World Bank . . . I wish to state categorically that the conditions we have accepted reflect no more than the implementation of the reform programme as outlined in my letters of intent sent to the IMF and the World Bank, and are wholly consistent with our national interests. The bulk of the reform programme is based on the election manifesto of our Party. There is no question of the Government ever compromising our national interests, not to speak of our sovereignty.

Former IMF staffer, James M. Boughton, who has documented the institution's history over multiple volumes, seems to support the notion[13] that India charted out its own reforms path:

> The working relationship was a little unusual, in that the authorities knew full well what they needed to do to qualify for the Fund's seal of approval and financial support. The decision to devalue, for example, was not made at the insistence of the Fund, but on the understanding that the Fund would approve it and that both sides believed it was necessary and was in India's interest . . . Over time, it became clear that the government would carry out these reforms in a heterodox way and on its own terms. For example, in March 1992, the authorities temporarily introduced a dual exchange rate scheme as a way to finance subsidies to imports of essential goods (notably petroleum products and fertilizer) while shifting to a market-determined rate for most transactions. As a multiple currency practice, the dual rate violated the terms of the stand-by arrangement. The staff, however, chose not to object to it, and the Fund readily granted a waiver so that India could continue to draw on the arrangement. The underlying premise throughout this time was that no one seriously doubted the government's commitment to the ultimate objective of liberalizing the economy, especially foreign trade and payments.

But whatever scenario we assume to be the reality, it does indicate that the policymakers were already seized of a sense of the task ahead. The 1991 crisis and the electoral lottery provided the perfect opportunity for the posse of economic administrators and advisers who had been waiting since the 1980s to overhaul the decades-old economic model. They were also aware that introducing reforms came with the added responsibility of having to sell the reforms concept and package to the political class, including hardened and wizened Congress stalwarts.

## Financial Sector: The Pivot

Manmohan Singh's budget speech briefly mentioned the reforms initiated in all the relevant areas: industrial policy, exchange and trade policy and foreign investment policy, among others. A necessary adjunct to these policy shifts was the accompanying reforms in the financial sector. In a sense, the two were inextricably linked; reforming one without reforming the other would not have been possible. The message was explicitly stated in the speech: 'The objective of reform in the financial sector would be to preserve its basic role as an essential adjunct to economic growth and competitive efficiency, while improving the health of its institutions.'

The formation of a committee was announced. It would examine the existing structure, organization, functions and processes of the financial sector and recommend necessary changes to improve the sector's viability and health without jeopardizing the basic principles of a sound financial system. The committee, which was set up under the chairmanship of M. Narasimham, former RBI governor, recommended far-reaching changes. Another committee was set up, under the chairmanship of another former RBI governor, R.N. Malhotra, to examine the steps required to open up the Indian insurance sector to private, including foreign, investors.

The second, and important, move related to freeing interest rates in the system. The complex and convoluted multi-tier interest rate architecture which was administered had become a hindrance to credit operations or loan recovery. It had made loans not only exceedingly expensive for commercial borrowers, thereby making them uncompetitive, but also rendering the loans unpayable from the get-go. The government and the RBI started by partially freeing lending rates, first by prescribing a floor rate above which banks and term-lending institutions were free to charge any interest rate, depending on their risk perception.

Manmohan Singh then took the reforms campaign to the capital markets by first arming the regulator, the Securities and Exchange Board of India (SEBI), with legislative teeth and announcing a comprehensive reforms package for the stock exchanges, including the setting up of a central depository as well as a national settlement and clearing institution. The finance minister then turned his attention to mutual funds by allowing private-sector and joint-sector mutual funds as investment vehicles for households.

All this got financial sector reforms in the country off to a start. But it has been three decades since then, and financial sector reforms still appear to be a work in progress. This book focuses on the trajectory of financial sector reforms in India, given that they became the foundational basis for many other economic reforms. The strategy behind the financial sector reforms, and their design and structure, thus had a direct bearing on the outcome of reforms in other segments of the economy. While this book does not purport to present a history of financial sector reforms, it demonstrates that many key reform initiatives were by no means part of a long and planned series of measures or integral components of a grand design. They were, instead, inspired by some immediate event, like a crisis or a scam. Except for some broad issues that had often been raised by past expert committees (such as the Sukhamoy Chakravarty Committee, which brought out a report on the working of the monetary system in 1985) or were related to some glaringly misaligned financial variables (such as an over-valued rupee exchange rate), many components of the first burst of financial sector reforms were perhaps influenced by exogenous factors, such as the revelation of a systemic scam in the Bombay equity and money markets.

While Manmohan Singh was presenting his maiden and historic budget on that late afternoon of July 1991, preparing India for a new century by unleashing its animal spirits, another drama was unfolding in distant Mumbai which would also force Singh's hand and the future course of reforms. A scam, which would exert additional influence on the design of financial sector reforms, was surfacing in the country's commercial capital. An interloper named Harshad Mehta had drilled holes into the artificial levees erected between the government bonds market, the banking system and the stock market. He leveraged the flawed settlement system in the government securities markets through the banking system and took out funds to ramp up select stocks in the equities market. He did this till the daisy chain snapped and left a large number of banks out of pocket, forcing the RBI to review its gilts settlement system.

The Harshad Mehta securities scam uncovered the vast inefficiencies, malpractices, short-cuts and corrupt principles that had been embedded in the Indian financial system in the absence of regulatory capacity and regulation or even a fundamental understanding of how control had distorted the financial system, rendering it ripe for exploitation by smart traders willing to push the envelope. A few years later, in 1996, a finance company called CRB Financial collapsed under the weight of its fraudulent promises to investors and bondholders, triggering another round of reforms. At the turn of the millennium, another stock market operator, Ketan Parekh, exposed some more chinks in the capital market armour, sparking off yet another energetic round of reforms.

Our spectator in Parliament on budget day, the investment banker mentioned in the opening paragraphs of this chapter, also got caught in the subsequent wide-ranging investigations into the

1992 scam and other associated malpractices in the bonds and
equities markets. A number of criminal cases were filed against
him, resulting in protracted trials, some lasting over twenty years.
He was eventually exonerated of all charges after twenty-seven
years of legal battles.

There is another example of how the 1991 crisis enabled a
decisive and ground-breaking change in fiscal-monetary relations,
one that the RBI had been pleading with the government for many
years but without any progress. This related to the government's
short-term borrowings from the RBI for meeting its revenue-
expenditure mismatches. Whenever the government needed
short-term finance to meet its immediate expenditures, it would
issue what were known as ad hoc treasury bills, and the RBI was
obliged to subscribe to them. The name 'ad hoc' was exactly how
the government used the instrument: outside the pale of a targeted,
predetermined borrowing programme. These ad hoc T-bills were
not only always unplanned but also contributed to the automatic
monetization of the deficit, since the RBI's subscription to any
Central government security almost always results in the creation of
fresh money to buy the bonds. This leads to an increase in money
supply and puts pressure on the price line. The practice of issuing
ad hoc T-bills made it difficult for the RBI to meet its primary
legislative mandate of ensuring price stability. Former RBI governor
Y.V. Reddy once described the phenomenon[14] in a 1997 speech to
the Hyderabad-based Administrative Staff College of India:

> The ad hoc Treasury Bills, which were meant to be temporary,
> gained a permanent as well as a cumulative character. Indeed,
> it became an attractive source of financing Government
> expenditures since it was available at an interest rate pegged at
> 4.6 per cent per annum since 1974, i.e., actually at a negative
> real interest rate.

The RBI had been seeking to bring some order to this
madness by requesting the government to introduce some

discipline in its spending programmes. Former RBI governor
R.N. Malhotra (1985–1990) wrote to successive finance
ministers about this but to no avail. For example, in January
1989 he shared[15] his concerns as a central bank governor with
then finance minister S.B. Chavan:

> Over the years the practice has grown by which the entire
> budget deficit of the Central Government is taken up by
> the Reserve Bank of India through the acceptance of ad
> hoc Treasury Bills issued in its favour. Since these budget
> deficits are not temporary, the huge amount of Treasury
> Bills outstanding is being continuously rolled over. A part of
> the outstandings has recently been converted into long-term
> securities at the rate of interest applicable to Treasury Bills.
> In addition, the Reserve Bank continues to provide support
> to the Central Government's market borrowing programme.
> The automatic monetisation of large and growing budgetary
> deficits has led to excess liquidity in the system with serious
> inflationary implications.

We do not know whether or how the finance minister
responded to Malhotra's concerns. All we do know from
available documents is that Malhotra persisted with his request.
He subsequently wrote to the next finance minister, Madhu
Dandavate, in December 1989, providing him with some historical
context as to how the issue of ad hoc T-bills had become an
accepted practice and how many previous RBI governors had
warned about the collateral damage from over-reliance on them
by the government for meeting its current expenditure. He even
provided the minister with an alternative solution:

> While the longer term needs of the Government should be
> met from the market, the Reserve Bank should provide only
> temporary accommodation to the Government. This question
> was also addressed in the Report of the Central Board of
> Directors on the working of the Reserve Bank of India for

the year ended June 30, 1989, wherein it was argued that an effective monetary policy would require the avoidance of the automatic monetisation of the budget deficits and that over the medium term, beyond a mutually agreed Ways and Means accommodation from the Reserve Bank, Government should aim at placing its entire debt in the market at appropriate interest rates.

The 1990–91 BoP crisis, in a fortuitous turn of events, brought home the frightening spectre of sovereign bankruptcy, thereby shining a light on all the past elements of fiscal mismanagement, including the abhorrent government practice of issuing ad hoc T-bills. It is precisely the immediacy of this crisis that impelled the government to reconsider this practice. One of the ardent advocates of ending the practice was former RBI governor C. Rangarajan. He even dealt with the issue, along with the prickly question of central bank autonomy, at great length in his landmark tenth M.G. Kutty Memorial Lecture[16] in Calcutta (now Kolkata) on 17 September 1993. He writes in his latest book that there was no resistance to ending the practice:

> Formally, I took up the issue with the finance minister (Manmohan Singh). I had no problem in convincing the finance minister. He readily agreed to bring to an end the earlier agreement. Discussions only centred on the time period over which the system should be phased out and the alternative arrangement that must be put in place to enable the Central government to tide over temporary mismatches between receipts and payments.

Manmohan Singh announced the end of the arrangement in his 1994–95 budget speech. It can be persuasively argued that the RBI and the finance minister were able to reach an understanding because both sides of the table had two capable economists who not only understood each other but had a shared, innate sense of what was good for the Indian economy, which included fiscal discipline. But it is also difficult to ignore the fact that had the balance-of-payments crisis not occurred, it might have been difficult for either Manmohan Singh or P.V. Narasimha Rao to sell the deal to the other ministers in the cabinet or, in a broader sense, to the rest of the legislative, which had frequently voiced apprehensions of reforms eating into the subsidy bill or other social-sector schemes.

The unavoidable role of external factors in influencing financial sector reforms is also made evident by the patchwork progress in the different markets. The reforms process was most pronounced in the equity markets, given the succession of scams in it and perhaps, importantly, because of the absence of the government as a player in that market. In the broader scheme of things, the reforms process required a capital market that would intermediate transparently and efficiently between the economy's gross savings and investments. Also, given the key role envisaged for foreign portfolio investors, the equity markets needed to be brought up to speed. Conversely, the presence of foreign investors also acted as a catalyst, providing enough motivation to keep the reforms process moving ahead and not allow it to get derailed by the legacy rent-seeking class.

The same attention was not paid to the debt markets or to some of the other markets (such as commodities). The debt market, for example, continues to be overshadowed by one big borrower, the government. Even though the private sector's borrowings from the debt market have gone up significantly over the past three decades, the lion's share of borrowings in the debt market still belongs to the government. Many reports and papers have been authored over the past three decades on how to animate the Indian corporate debt market, but the needle has moved only marginally. The dramatis personae in the Harshad

Mehta scam exploited gaps in clearing, settlement and record-keeping segments of the government securities market to access funds illegally. This scam did give rise to a payments crisis and the RBI had to institute remedial measures post-haste. But given the visible absence of defrauded middle-class investors in this sector, the government lacked a credible raison d'être to take the reforms momentum to the debt markets.

Political scientist and Brown University professor Ashutosh Varshney feels that one has to look beyond 'economic logic' to understand the administration's penchant for reforms in one sector over another. In his contribution[17] to a book of essays on India's economic reforms (which he has also co-edited), Varshney writes:

> Reforms that touch, directly or primarily, elite politics have gone the farthest: a large devaluation of the currency, a restructuration of the capital markets, a liberalization of the trade regime, and a simplification of investment rules. Reforms that are economically desirable but concern mass politics have been of two types: those that have positive political consequences in mass politics (for example inflation control) and those that have potentially negative or highly uncertain consequences in mass politics (labour laws, privatization of public sector, agriculture). The former have been implemented with single-minded determination; the latter have either been completely ignored or pursued with less than exemplary policy resolve (fiscal balances).

It's been more than a quarter of a century since Manmohan Singh pressed the switch on financial sector reforms, which have changed and (in many ways) undone a wobbly architecture that had been designed and erected in another era. Singh's adoption of a twin-track reforms process—targeting industry and finance—was logical. If Indian industry had to be made productive and competitive, it needed access to an equally productive financial services sector which could efficiently allocate capital as well as provide a cost-effective pool for capital accumulation.

Interestingly, the reforms process has endured through different political regimes, even if it's been somewhat episodic and haphazard in sequencing. The subsequent chapters explore the grand design or overarching strategy behind the financial sector reforms in India. It is this book's thesis that even if there was indeed a master plan, many of the changes and reforms processes were induced by one or other crisis; and in areas where there were close to no crises or where scams affected people only marginally, reforms have remained half-hearted.

This book does not purport to be a laundry list of all the reform measures implemented in the past three decades, but attempts to examine some of the main reform measures in the financial sector to understand the external factors impacting the reforms impulse; it also tries to discern the kind of stimulus provided to financial sector reforms by the broader political economy.

The pace of reforms implementation has also witnessed its share of debate and dissent. In Montek Singh Ahluwalia's paper for the *Journal for Economic Perspectives* in 2002, titled 'Economic Reforms in India Since 1991: Has Gradualism Worked?', he castigated the slow progress of economic reforms and India's inability to extend the reforms ambit to other areas of the economy:

> Critics often blame the delays in implementation and failure to act in certain areas to the choice of gradualism as a strategy. However, gradualism implies a clear definition of the goal and a deliberate choice of extending the time taken to reach it, to ease the pain of transition. This is not what happened in all areas. The goals were often indicated only as a broad direction, with the precise end point and the pace of transition left unstated to minimize opposition—and possibly also to allow room to retreat, if necessary. This reduced politically divisive

controversy and enabled a consensus of sorts to evolve, but it also meant that the consensus at each point represented a compromise, with many interested groups joining only because they believed that reforms would not go "too far." The result was a process of change that was not so much gradualist as fitful and opportunistic. Progress was made as and when politically feasible, but since the end point was not always clearly indicated, many participants were unclear about how much change would have to be accepted, and this may have led to less adjustment than was otherwise feasible.

The fourth volume of *RBI History* counters the impression of reforms being gradual:

On the issue of integrating the Indian financial markets with the global financial system, India has chosen to proceed cautiously and in a gradual manner, adjusting the pace of liberalisation with the underlying macroeconomic developments, the state of readiness of the domestic financial system and the dynamics of the international financial markets. This stand was not only because of its inherent preference for gradualism but also because of its recognition of the distinctive institutional and legal features.

Even C. Rangarajan has refuted the allegation of gradualism about India's financial sector reforms in *Forks in the Road*:

It took exactly six years to put through the reforms. It was this which helped the system to move smoothly to a new regulatory regime. The banking system had to work through a period in which changes were being made simultaneously in the monetary sector, exchange rate regime and in the regulatory and supervisory system. I do not think that the pace could have been accelerated without causing serious disruptions in the system.

In her influential paper[18] *Political Economy of Reforms*, World Bank staffer Stuti Khemani outlines two conditions for successful reforms. One, reforms should be more beneficial and less costly than maintaining the status quo; therefore, calling any and every type of policy or institutional change a 'reform' is 'not consistent with how economics research examines reforms'. The second condition for successful reforms requires the existence of independent and non-partisan think tanks and research agencies that can provide non-ideological technical evidence to support reform measures. However, interest groups are often able to scupper the reforms process, even after the two conditions have been met, when they perceive the loss of future rents to be large. Disinformation is often the weapon of choice to throw the reforms process off course, either by convincing actual beneficiaries of the reforms process that the entire exercise is not in their interest or by insinuating that the reforms process is inherently flawed, or influenced by external agents.

Financial sector reforms in India too experienced its share of disinformation campaigns. Opponents to the reforms process generated multiple strands of false narratives which also included the claim that reforms would inevitably lead to a greater number of scams. It is true that the spate of scams and frauds in the financial sector seems to have accelerated after the onset of financial sector reforms. But it is also true that scams inhabited the Indian financial sector even in the 1960s. However, what additionally needs to be questioned is whether the higher frequency of scams post-1991 was due to reforms or due to some other reason. It is this book's contention that the scams and scandals accelerated as a result of the political economy of reforms, the incomplete design of reforms and the close links between many financial-sector operatives and the political apparatus, notably through the instrument of campaign finance.

Another feature of the reforms blueprint—and this applies to all segments of the economy and not just the financial sector—seems to be the notable absence of a proper sequencing of reforms. In many sectors, the floodgates were thrown open before an independent regulator was established or before the setting of ground rules. This is evident from how SEBI, over the past decade, has had to continuously improvise and tighten the regulatory framework for trading in equity derivatives, given the unbridled speculation in that market segment which threatened to disrupt overall financial sector stability. In many cases, regulators had serious capacity deficit issues. Consequently, this provided free rein to crony capitalists, scamsters, plutocrats and oligarchs, who played havoc with public trust and resources. The spectre of the political economy continues to loom large over reforms, in the form of resistance from the political class, which has been accustomed to a certain economic system, as well as in the form of obstacles erected by select economic agents (especially the Indian corporate sector) who had enjoyed privileged access to resources and markets because of distortions in India's campaign finance system.

In an essay on the sequencing of reforms, economist Deena Khatkhate wrote: 'The sequencing of financial reforms which take into account the institutional imperatives have a better chance to succeed.' Economist and former RBI deputy governor Rakesh Mohan argues that financial sector reforms in India were well sequenced, while Montek S. Ahluwalia has wondered whether 'gradualism' slowed down their progress. Both are right, and both are also slightly off the mark: even within the financial sector, reforms in some segments, such as monetary policy, have been somewhat more methodical than in the rest.

Strangely, the arc of financial sector reforms takes a curious turn after 2014, with the Central government's decisions demonstrating a certain random, ad hoc characteristic, such as the demonetization episode. Economic reforms are generally pursued with the hope of improving the lives of citizens but the demonetization episode, in contrast, visited hardships on a large section of the population by withdrawing 86 per cent of currency from the system overnight. Another characteristic of financial sector reforms after 2014 is the marked emphasis on ensuring that financial sector players are not too inconvenienced or wanting for pathways to growth. However, one key trait remains unchanged from the beginning of financial sector reforms in the country, and that is the disproportionately large influence of crises or scams on reforms. The decisions taken during the post-2014 period once again seem to suggest the lack of a grand design or strategy for the reforms, but the strong influence of realpolitik on it. The relatively short time taken for the initial euphoria over the formation of an Insolvency and Bankruptcy Code to dissipate into cynicism indicates how a few interest groups with outsized political influence continue to skew the incentives for financial sector reforms.

The subsequent chapters will deal with various segments of the financial services sector, the process of reforms initiated in each of them, the proximate triggers for these reforms, the current stage of the reforms process and what is left to be done.

# Chapter 2

## Recurring Scams in Pre-reforms India

It has been argued that the story of the Indian financial sector reforms is actually the story of a succession of scams. While that might be partially true, it is equally fallacious to equate reforms with granting financial and other players a licence to scam. It is indeed true that the frequency of scams did seem to increase after economic reforms were initiated, but this could perhaps be attributed to the fact that regulatory structures and regulations had not kept pace with the state of reforms. But if we are to disregard the frequency of scams for a moment, the thing to remember here is that the Indian economy is not new to scams, which have happened both in the pre-Independence and post-Independence days.

These scams not only affected commercial banks and the central bank, the RBI, but also exercised the executive and legislative pillars of the newly democratized republic which was still trying to find its economic feet and was grappling with the dilemma of jettisoning colonial structures in favour of newer ones that were appropriate for India.

The post-Independence Indian economy had a mammoth task at hand, especially in managing the ravages of a century-long colonial exploitation, exacerbated by two world wars that found India as an unwilling participant, fighting somebody else's battles in distant lands while incurring heavy loss of life and suffering economic deprivation. Life in India, both pre-Independence and post-Independence, was marked by famines, droughts, border incursions, reorganization of states and internal boundaries, capital scarcity, emergency food imports, employment crises, all-round economic scarcity and poverty.

In the midst of this, scams continued to rock the Indian Parliament, and most of these fiddles were centred around banks. Of course, not all bank failures were directly linked to frauds or scams. Many of them were the natural outcome of normal business downturns or extreme climate episodes involving excessive rains or floods, or even earthquakes, playing havoc with assets and impairing repayment capacities.

The RBI came in for some heavy criticism after the 1938 failure of Travancore National and Quilon Bank, formed from the merger of Travancore National Bank and Quilon Bank the previous year. The RBI also had to take direct financial action in the failures of the Exchange Bank of India and Africa in 1949 and the Nath Bank in 1950. The central bank had made emergency advances to these two banks in an unsuccessful attempt to save them. Some banks also went belly-up because of regulatory failure. The Palai Central Bank failure of 1960 in Kerala, or that of Laxmi Bank in Akola (Maharashtra), where the management had misappropriated depositors' funds, strengthened the central bank's inspection and regulatory powers.

The *RBI History* notes in its first volume how repeated bank failures necessitated legislative action:

> The matter of bank failures received considerable attention at the hands of the Central Banking Enquiry Committee. After analysing the principal causes, such as insufficient capital and reserves, inadequate liquidity of assets, payment of exorbitant interest rates to attract deposits, injudicious advances,

speculative investments, and dishonest and incompetent management, the Committee recommended that a special Bank Act be passed, incorporating the existing provisions of the Indian Companies Act in regard to banking and including new provisions relating to (i) organisation, (ii) management, (iii) audit and inspection and (iv) liquidation and amalgamation. This object was not, however, accomplished till 1949, though efforts in this behalf were made from 1939 onwards.

This Act, first passed as the Banking Companies Act in 1949, was renamed the Banking Regulation Act 1949 in 1966. This is the same Act which governs and regulates all commercial banking operations in India even today, though it has been amended from time to time to cope with the developments in the industry. But even before this Act could be legislated in 1949, the RBI had been implementing interim or stopgap measures that helped bank failures come down from 119 in 1939 to only twenty-seven in 1945. A total of 207 banks went out of existence between 1946 and 1950, with failure more prevalent among the larger banks. Even after the passage of the 1949 legislation, banks continued to collapse: fifty-three in 1949 itself, forty-five in 1950 and sixty-two in 1951.[1]

The Dhiren Mitra Committee set up in 1952 to examine bank liquidations provided a despairing picture of the seventy-eight banks under liquidation in West Bengal. The committee had reported that the liquidators had found it impossible to disgorge benami assets from corrupt officials who had misappropriated depositor funds.

The spate of bank failures impelled the RBI to introduce deposit insurance in 1962. The government also nationalized banks in two tranches, in 1969 and 1970, but that did not completely stop the frauds. The enduring narrative was about how regulation and supervision were always trying to play catch-up with frauds.

A good example of this was the fraud committed on Central Bank of India's London branch by its staffer Sami Patel, who, without the knowledge of any senior bank officials, provided the bank's guarantee and endorsement to fraudulent trade bills, running into millions of pound sterling and Deutsche marks, raised by the bank's customers. These bills were fraudulent because they were not backed by any real or tangible business operations or trade transactions. Typically, sellers of goods raise a bill on the buyers, get these bills endorsed by their bank and then discount them with other banks without waiting for the full credit period to collect proceeds directly from buyers.

Suppose A sells goods worth Rs 100 to B, who is supposed to pay the proceeds after the usual credit period of ninety days. A, without waiting for the ninety days to lapse, takes the bill raised on B to any bank that is willing to discount the bill and is confident of B's ability to pay. So, A gets Rs 99 now instead of waiting for 90 days to get Rs 100. The discounting bank recovers the full Rs 100 from B on expiry of the credit period. These bills are usually guaranteed or endorsed by the sellers' banks, ensuring the discounting banks that buyers will pay up the proceeds on the due date. In the London Central Bank of India case, some of the bank's clients were raising bills against non-existent transactions, getting them discounted, deploying the funds in the market and repaying on the due date. In essence, these companies had access to free money to deploy in the share markets.

The RBI's investigations found that Central Bank had not earned any fees for providing the guarantees or endorsements, implying that Patel had gained pecuniary benefits by misusing the bank's name. In 1973, Central Bank had to pay over 7,50,000 pounds sterling in an out-of-court settlement with three German banks. The incident and the resulting liability drove home the need for increased vigilance on the part of the RBI over Indian bank branches overseas. It also helped the authorities structure some kind of policy framework for Indian banks' overseas operations and allowed both the finance ministry and the external affairs ministry to have a say as to which bank could open branches where.

*RBI History* says:

> The magnitude of the fraud created ripples in the banking industry and became a subject of active debate in India, in the Lok Sabha, Rajya Sabha and the media. The role of the head office of the Central Bank of India as well as that of the Reserve Bank of India in supervising foreign branches of Indian banks came under scathing criticism.

*RBI History* also notes how the legislative was unsettled by the spate of frauds in the banking system:

> On 25 June 1971, Finance Minister Y.B. Chavan wrote to Governor Jagannathan: 'I have been very much perturbed over the spate of frauds in recent weeks in some of the public sector banks. You will agree that what is at stake in these bank frauds is not merely the large sums of money involved, but also the reputation and the image of public sector banks in general and the trust and confidence reposed by the public in the banking system of the country.' Chavan went on to add that one common feature in these frauds was the direct involvement of bank employees, largely facilitated by the non-observance of the instructions laid down for safeguarding banks' funds.

S. Jagannathan was the RBI governor from June 1970 to May 1975.

Post-Independence, as the economy grew, slowly but also steadily, scamsters slowly expanded their operating net to encompass a wider swathe of the financial system: banks, insurance companies, the corporate sector and stock markets. Three characters stand out.

## Haridas Mundhra

A post-Independence scam involving a businessman called Haridas Mundhra sent such strong ripples across the system that it not only forced then finance minister T.T. Krishnamachari to resign in 1957 but also ended up smearing the reputations of Finance Secretary H.M. Patel and many other senior officials, including Life Insurance Corporation (LIC) Chairman L.S. Vaidyanathan. It did not even spare RBI Governor H.V.R. Iyengar.

Mundhra's was a classic rags-to-riches story. He came out of nowhere and acquired a string of companies in a short time. Using bank debt and leverage to acquire companies, he would mortgage his controlling interest in cash-rich companies to acquire more companies, use borrowed funds to drum up the share prices of his companies and thus raise even larger loans to purchase more companies. This financing cycle hit a speed breaker one day, as such financial cycles are usually wont to do, requiring Mundhra to pony up additional funds to finance the difference between the initial value of the stocks he had mortgaged and their reduced market price.

Mundhra then issued duplicate and forged shares, which he pledged with the banks as additional security. The four-volume *RBI History* has a special appendix dedicated to the Mundhra episode. It says:

> It was clear by the end of 1956 that Mundhra had overreached himself. Large borrowings from banks and falling share prices were together narrowing his room for manoeuvre. Mundhra began buying his own shares back from the market to steady them but with only limited success. Nor could he, for want of the necessary resources, take delivery of shares from brokers who largely financed their operations on Mundhra's behalf with loans from banks. As the prices of his shares continued to

slide, brokers began demanding additional margins from their principal. It is not clear when Mundhra began raising bank finance against bogus shares, but by spring 1957 his affairs were in a state of crisis and were said to be a major cause of the gloom hanging over the Calcutta stock market.

Life insurance had just been nationalized in 1956 and the rules required LIC to form an investment advisory committee to channel investments into the right areas. In violation of these rules, LIC invested in shares of six companies in which Mundhra was already a significant shareholder: Richardson and Cruddas, Jessop and Company, Smith Stanistreet, Osler Lamps, British India Corporation and Agnelo Brothers. The move was viewed as helping Mundhra prop up the value of his holdings in these companies.

Kanpur-based Haridas Mundhra's misdemeanours were exposed first in Parliament when members raised questions about LIC's propriety in buying shares in Mundhra's companies in violation of the corporation's investment principles and ground rules. Questions about Mundhra's dealings were first raised by Member of Parliament Feroze Gandhi. As then Prime Minister Jawaharlal Nehru's son-in-law, Feroze Gandhi's expose was embarrassing for the administration.

The RBI appendix on the scandal documents it in detail:

The collapse of his (*Mundhra's*) industrial empire and the many civil and criminal cases lodged against him arose because of the dubious methods Mundhra adopted to raise money for his activities. But public and Parliamentary concern, if not necessarily interest since the judicial fate of this unsuccessful adventurer continued to feature regularly in the newspapers for the next few years, was mainly evoked by the efforts of the government and the life insurance monopoly owned by it to rescue Mundhra, and the financial losses that the LIC sustained as a result.

In his book on India's post-Independence history, historian Ramchandra Guha writes:

> Known initially as the Mundhra affair, it was soon promoted to become the Mundhra scandal. Until it erupted, the ministers of Nehru's government were widely held to be fond of power, yet above financial impropriety. A halo of Gandhian austerity still hung around them. The Mundhra affair made the first serious dent in this image. It was a dent as deep, and as damaging, as those made by political parties leaning left or right.

## Ramkrishna Dalmia

Feroze Gandhi, who exposed Mundhra's derring-do in Parliament, was also instrumental in exposing Ramkrishna Dalmia and the diversion of funds from his group's insurance companies and banks for personal purposes.

Dalmia was a leading businessman of his time and had invested across the country in a number of industries: cement, sugar and paper, among others. Business historian Dwijendra Tripathi describes the man:

> Ramkrishna Dalmia, a Marwari from Rohtak, in Punjab, who would have a meteoric rise in the Indian industry during and after World War II, made his debut in industry shortly before the war broke out with the establishment of five sugar mills in Bihar. He later set up Dalmia Cement Company with factories in Bihar, Punjab, Sind, and Madras, all functioning as part of a diversified group known as Rohtas Industries. Having made his money in speculation and trade, this highly individualistic Marwari refused to join the selling syndicates formed to meet the problem of overproduction in sugar and cement. He kept his company out of the Indian Sugar Syndicate and refused to merge his cement enterprise with ACC, to which he gave a

stiff competition. He was also among the first Indians to start manufacturing paper.

Dalmia also started a bank, called Bharat Bank. He acquired a Lahore-based insurance company called Bharat Insurance and became its chairman in 1936. He resigned in favour of his brother Jaydayal Dalmia in 1942 and shifted the bank's headquarters to Delhi in 1947. He was re-appointed chairman in 1949 when his brother resigned. It is this insurance company that led to his downfall.

Dalmia allegedly siphoned off funds from this insurance company's cash flows, essentially accrual of insurance premium, to finance his speculation and margins elsewhere.

Dalmia was imprisoned and fined for misappropriating funds from Bharat Insurance Ltd and Punjab National Bank. Dalmia, incidentally, had to borrow money from his son-in-law Shanti Prasad Jain to pay off the monetary penalty and, in exchange, transferred control of two companies—Bennett, Coleman and Co. Ltd (publishers of the *Times of India* and the *Economic Times* newspapers) and Rohtas Industries, which had since gone sick and had shut down—to Jain.

## Rustom Sohrab Nagarwala

The Nagarwala scam has all the elements of drama, and the mysteries and unanswered questions surrounding it refuse to die down even today.

On the hot Delhi morning of 24 May 1971, the chief cashier at the Parliament Street branch of the State Bank of India received a strange call. The caller stated that Prime Minister Indira Gandhi wanted Rs 62 lakh in cash as part of the war efforts in Bangladesh and that the cash was to be delivered upon an exchange of code words. There are many accounts of what Nagarwala, the alleged caller, actually said, including one in which he is purported to have credibly impersonated Indira Gandhi's voice, thereby compelling the cashier to deliver the money.

Once the cash was delivered, the cashier sought a receipt from the prime minister's office, whereupon he was told that no such instructions had been issued. A complaint was lodged with the Delhi police and Nagarwala was arrested in twenty-four hours. He confessed to having taken the money. A speedy trial was conducted and he was sentenced to four years' imprisonment. The trial, surprisingly, lasted only ten minutes.

So far, so good. The mysteries began soon thereafter. Nagarwala kept requesting for a retrial, but his pleas were rejected. The fact that Nagarwala had suffered partial facial paralysis earlier, rendering him incapable of mimicking someone, and his background as an intelligence officer tasked to coordinate Bangladesh operatives triggered many questions. These doubts further gained ground upon the inexplicable death of the police officer who had investigated the case, followed by Nagarwala's sudden collapse and demise.

The only certainty in the case was that the police recovered the entire amount of defrauded money when they arrested Nagarwala.

## Why/How Scams Succeeded in the Pre-reforms Era

Many of the scams of the pre-reforms era occurred because the hucksters were able to take advantage of yawning regulatory gaps in the market. Some of these scams and dirty trades spilled over into the post-reforms era too.

One good example is the Harshad Mehta-led securities scam, which is analogous to the tip of the iceberg. Below that tip sat a myriad of other malpractices, which were essentially arbitrage plays between different instruments and markets, funded in a manner that skirted the existing rules and approved processes. Many of these transactions and deals were outright illegal, while many existed in the grey areas of legitimacy.

An example of the 'grey zone' scams was the trading in units issued by the government-owned mutual fund, Unit Trust of India, which was set up by an Act of Parliament. These units were popularly called US-64, after the year of their launch. The idea behind a government-owned mutual fund was to create another means for channelizing household savings to the capital markets. The fund's net asset value, or NAV, was never declared, but its sale and repurchase prices were announced at the beginning of the fund's financial year (June). The two prices could also change every month and there was a secondary market for these units, the price of which fluctuated within the sales-repurchase band. The funny thing is that these prices often had no connection to the fund's real, intrinsic value, which the NAV ideally represents. The fund also declared a dividend every year, which kept rising every year and helped create the illusion of assured returns, thereby leading to higher inflows of household savings.

Savvy traders always bought units from the open market before the fund's annual declaration of dividend and sales-repurchase prices. These units, pregnant with dividend, would be available at a premium. Once the dividend was declared, the price would readjust downwards, whereupon the trader would sell them at a lower-than-purchase price and book a loss. This trading strategy allowed traders to adjust their dividend-based taxable income against the capital loss arising from their unit purchase-sale transactions. Plus, the overall capital loss also helped in setting off other tax liabilities incurred during the year.

Traders were, essentially, adjusting one kind of income against another kind of pecuniary loss. While this was not strictly illegal, it was still bad accounting practice because it involved the adjusting of apples against oranges. However, traders indulged in it because the tax laws did not explicitly forbid the dodge. In fact, Manmohan Singh stopped this rampant practice in the historic 1991 budget speech:

> The present provision for offsetting short-term capital losses against income leads to tax avoidance. I, therefore, propose that any loss on transfer of a capital asset will be set off only against gain from transfer of another capital asset. This is only logical. It should also stop the practice of buying short-term capital losses being resorted to by some unscrupulous tax payers.

But some of the other scams of the later years made this tax-arbitrage trade—which, by the way, was legitimate—look like child's play. As has been illustrated in this chapter, the pre-reforms Indian financial system often played host to scams, frauds, funds misappropriation and forgery. The frequency and nature of these mishaps may have been varied, but they have been a regular feature in the Indian financial system.

It might be tempting to think that scams and crises are unique to the Indian financial system. It is not; all financial services industries across the world, whether in the developed economies or the emerging markets, have seen scams and frauds. Here are two examples.

Former chairman of the stock exchange NASDAQ, Bernie Madoff, was considered an investment guru and his promises of high returns enticed investors—from individuals to even pension funds—to entrust their savings to him. In the aftermath of the 2008 financial crisis, when investors started asking for their money, Madoff was unable to repay. It eventually transpired that the investments were not yielding the outlandish returns he had promised and that he was using fresh investor inflows to pay back existing investors. It is estimated that Madoff lost about

$20 billion of investor money and was sentenced in 2009 to 150 years of prison time. He died in April 2021.

The second example relates to US-based bank Wells Fargo, which was reputed for its prudent management, emerging unscathed from the 2008 financial crisis even after acquiring failed bank Wachovia. In a complete reversal of fortunes, news emerged in 2016 that Wells Fargo had fraudulently opened millions of savings and checking accounts in the names of the bank's existing clients without seeking their consent, transferred money surreptitiously from existing accounts to the new ones and sold credit cards and other financial products to these fake accounts. The ostensible reason for this underhand activity was to demonstrate growth in the bank's sale of financial products. On complaints from some customers, regulators cottoned on to the fraud in 2016 and fined the bank $165 million; the bank faces additional damages of $3 billion in civil and criminal suits.

One of the enduring themes in all these Indian scam episodes has been that of hucksters exploiting regulatory deficits or artificial barriers between different markets or instruments with varying yields. Money, like water from a higher level to a lower one, will flow from low-yielding financial instruments to high-yielding ones. If artificial barriers are stopping this flow, people managing this money will always find ways to side-step the rules or even break them outright.

# Chapter 3

## The Securities Scam of 1992: A Brief Anatomy

There were many proximate causes for Indian politicians and administrators to consider abandoning the prevalent dirigisme model of economic management in favour of a completely new architecture. One was, of course, the 1990–91 balance-of-payments crisis. That event capped multiple layers of economic detritus that had accumulated over decades of economic mismanagement. The most visible manifestation of this corrosion was the crumbling regime of industrial licensing and monopoly control. The second reason was the visible decay of a dominant politico-economic model which had held India in thrall for well over four decades and whose redundancy—symbolized by the Berlin Wall collapse and dissolution of the Soviet Union into Russia and numerous independent states—must have also forced deep introspection. The administrators had probably realized that the dominant economic model of post-Independent India was past its sell-by date and needed reviewing. The Indian political class had no choice but to embrace economic reforms and push for liberalization of the industrial and financial sectors.

But, beyond these external influences, another home-grown crisis—the 1992 stock market scam—forced the government to closely examine the micro-structure of the markets, their inefficient functioning and the malpractices this reforms-resistant institution had bred over time. As mentioned earlier, and it merits repetition here, efficient and productive capital and credit markets were necessary and sufficient conditions for Indian industry to become efficient and productive.

As Manmohan Singh completed his landmark budget speech of July 1991 and got down to the hard work of averting a looming economic crisis and re-energizing a jaded economy, the equity markets were euphoric. The Bombay Stock Exchange's benchmark index, the 30-scrip Sensitive Index (Sensex), rose giddily, deceptively conveying the impression that the stock market had endorsed the sharp turn in India's economic philosophy and ideology. The index shot up from close to 1000 points in February 1991 to 4500 in March 1992, a rise of 350 per cent in a year. Looking solely at the market index, or trusting in the cliché that the stock market is the economy's true weather vane, the ordinary citizen would have misread the signals, believing that the country was past the BoP crisis and all was well. The rise actually hid the rot in the capital markets, specifically in India's leading stock exchange, the Bombay Stock Exchange, which exploded in a major scam a few months later.

The bull operators, or those betting on stocks rising in the future on the Bombay Stock Exchange—the largest bourse among the dispersed, independent and seemingly unconnected twenty-two exchanges in the country—often did not buy their shares outright. The market settled, or squared, outstanding trades between brokers only once a fortnight. But brokers were also allowed to carry over their transactions in certain scrips from one settlement cycle to another, provided they paid a finance charge. The brokers had to pay either the seller or the financiers (who would step in and take delivery from the seller and agree to hold the shares on behalf of the buyer) a charge, more like an interest charge, for agreeing to postpone delivery.

Brokers would need finance to pay this charge. In fact, in the din and hoopla surrounding the dizzying rise of the BSE index, the existence of a corollary was ignored: the rising stock indices would require an equal, if not greater, need for financing this activity.

Brokers would, often, also need liquidity to finance their speculative urges, depending on their calculations of the residual gains after paying off both the principal and interest. Borrowing in the informal market was prohibitively expensive, the interest rate ranging between 35 per cent and 40 per cent on an annualized basis but also known to shoot up to 100 per cent in times of tight liquidity. The next best option was to hit the banking system—not legally, but through subterfuge and regulatory deception. Banks were operating out of state-imposed straitjackets and were desperate to show some profits. This, then, represented the fundamental conditions that gave rise to the 1992 securities scam.

A number of factors had been coalescing for a few years prior to 1992, the year when the scam was eventually detected, creating a critical mass that finally upset the finely balanced house of cards constructed by the broker-banker nexus. The widely prevalent malpractices involved stockbroking firms, commercial banks (domestic, cooperative and foreign), public-sector companies, stock exchanges and some private companies. The regulators and the government either knew and looked away or, worse, were blissfully unaware of the subversion of the financial system occurring below their noses.

## The Scam

The 1992 securities scam, apart from everything else, highlighted the futility of erecting artificial walls between different markets—in this case between the money market and the stock market—and demonstrated how ineffectual it is to try and stop money flowing from low-yielding to high-yielding assets. The 1992 scam was essentially a story of funds diverted from the banking industry, specifically the inter-bank bond market, to the stock market.

Extant regulations of the period prohibited banks from lending to stockbrokers, which forced the brokers to rely on the informal money markets which, predictably, charged a scarcity premium. As a result, the interest charged in the informal markets was almost double the rate in the inter-bank market, where banks lent to each other against the collateral of government securities. IIM-Ahmedabad professors Samir K. Barua and Jayanth R. Varma have estimated in a paper[1] that the differential in yields between the two markets was anywhere between 17 per cent and 20 per cent. This, then, encouraged some unscrupulous operators to create breaches in the contrived, man-made barriers between the two markets.

However, a distinction needs to be made here. Most of the brokers who diverted money from the inter-bank market to the stock markets can be slotted into two camps: One lot that resorted to the method out of desperation and therefore would have been in a minority, occasional in their endeavours; and one lot that would have sensed the opportunity for arbitrage—especially where the differential in interest rates was so wide. Arbitrage, always a breeding ground for greed, is an investment strategy in which investors take advantage of a price differential between two different markets and are often willing to take extraordinary risks to exploit that differential. As an extension, regulatory arbitrage is when investors exploit gaps or differences in the regulatory frameworks issued by different regulators to sidestep inconvenient barriers to profits or higher yields.

Three developments had come together to push the capital markets towards a precipice.

The first consisted of the changes taking place in the Indian banking system. While a detailed analysis of the sector follows in the later chapters, it is worth pointing out that Indian banking at that point was inefficient and the existing regulatory framework had made banking exceedingly unprofitable, with most of the banks sitting on a mountain of camouflaged losses.

The regulatory framework had left Indian banks with very few avenues for generating revenue. For example, banks were left with little to no chance of making money from the core business of accepting deposits and lending. Their other alternative was to exploit treasury operations, which included the active buying and selling of government securities or foreign exchange. This is where the brokers entered the picture.

The second development arose from the huge overseas borrowings made by public-sector companies, especially oil companies, which needed to be deployed. Many of these companies had raised these foreign currency resources at the government's behest, without a specific project in mind. These were borrowed funds, and hence the companies needed to earn a return on them to service the interest outgo. Banks, in partnership with their brokers, played suitable handmaidens here. This became another source of liquidity for the broking community.

The third development that precipitated matters consisted of the three increases in the interest rate offered by government bonds. Between September 1991 and June 1992, the interest rate offered on government bonds went up from 11.5 per cent to 13 per cent. As is common knowledge, bond coupon rates and bond prices move in opposite directions. The result of the three interest rate hikes was an approximate 10 per cent drop in bond prices, which added complications to the existing convoluted bonds trades opened up by brokers across various counter-parties.

These developments were transacted through a few trading mechanisms that winked at accepted banking practices, bending a few rules here and there, and even leaving space open for outright fraud. This web of deceit was strengthened by the special relationship developed between brokers, banks, public-sector companies, bureaucrats, regulators and politicians.

One of the mechanisms involved a straightforward transaction that is common across markets globally, known commonly as a repo transaction. It was given the special moniker of ready forward (RF) trade in India. This form of trade was legitimate among banks and allowed them to overcome temporary liquidity shortages. The deal would go like this: Bank A, say, in need of some funds for meeting the RBI's mandatory regulatory reserve requirements and finding itself short on reporting day, would approach Bank B, which would agree to lend it money for fifteen days, but only against the security of government securities. Bank A would get the money for fifteen days but would have to keep some government securities with Bank B for that period. At the end of fifteen days, Bank A would return the money, with some added interest, to Bank B and would get its government bonds back.

So far, so legit. But then, banks and brokers distorted this trade in multiple ways to allow brokers to use this route to access finance to pay their carry-forward charges on the stock exchanges. What was a routine bilateral deal between two banks was now being intermediated through a broker. The broker would not only play matchmaker between the borrowing and lending banks but also receive both the bonds and the cheques and move them to the respective counterparties. This simple process was further distorted, and sham RF deals were created between consenting banks to allow brokers to access the funds during the intervening period.

This meant cheques issued by one bank in another bank's favour were actually credited to the broker's account. This was the first step of the massive scale of the fraud perpetrated: cheques issued by Bank B favouring Bank A would actually end up in the broker's current account. This involved the active collusion of the banks. Every prominent broker in this market had his pet bank, which ranged from State Bank of India to ANZ Grindlays Bank to Citibank.

There were two other steps in the fraudulent transactions.

Since the sham transaction was created to enable brokers to access bank finance, this implied that the broker had to provide the security for the finances obtained. This was because, unlike in a plain-vanilla RF trade, the borrowing bank (say Bank A in the earlier example) was only lending its name and would not part with government bonds. It thus became incumbent upon the broker to provide the security. Occasionally, his intermediary role would allow him to divert the securities being exchanged between two other banks represented by the same broker. But what if that was not possible and the broker had no security to provide?

The first step was to conduct the sham RF with the bank with the backing of other securities, and not necessarily government bonds. The instruments of choice in this case were units issued by the government-owned monopoly mutual fund, Unit Trust of India, or bonds issued by public-sector companies. This was in direct contravention of the existing RBI rules, which prohibited banks from entering into RF deals with non-banks for UTI units or PSU bonds. Also, with the volume of transactions multiplying rapidly, brokers started providing fake sureties of securities owned by them. They adopted the simplest route, creating a sham receipt called the Bank Receipt, or BR.

The Janakiraman Committee appointed by the RBI to investigate the scam highlighted this point in its first interim report of May 1992:

> The major device by which the transference of funds to brokers' accounts has been achieved has been through the issue of BRs which were not supported by underlying securities and by payments being diverted to brokers' accounts either directly or through counter-parties named in the transactions. This appears to have been made possible by a significant lack of internal control in the banks and presumably by collusion between the concerned officials

and the concerned brokers. There is prima facie evidence of
fraudulent misrepresentation.

Banks used to issue BRs to each other as a stand-in for the
real securities for short periods. The reasoning was that transfer
of the physical securities or their ownership was a lengthy process
and the RBI's antiquated systems did not help matters. So a
convention developed, in which banks issued BRs to one another,
which were broadly respected and honoured. That is, until the
brokers intervened and decided to also issue BRs to raise money
for their stock market transactions.

The Janakiraman Committee's investigations continued to
excavate layers of transactions in the scam. Its first interim report
of May 1992 revealed that four parties (one financial institution and
three banks) had paid out Rs 1795.66 crore for securities they did
not own and for which they did not even possess BRs; by the time
of its sixth and final report of April 1993, this figure had jumped
to Rs 2262.57 crore. The number of organizations involved had
also gone up to one financial institution (National Housing Bank),
two commercial banks (Standard Chartered Bank and State Bank
of Saurashtra)[2] and two investment bank subsidiaries (SBI Capital
Markets and Canbank Financial Services).

On the matter of BRs too, the first interim report said that
two puny banks—Bank of Karad and Metropolitan Cooperative
Bank—had issued BRs worth Rs 1282.97 crore for securities
they did not own, the amount being in multiples of their capital.
By the final report of April 1993, this amount had increased to
Rs 1473.47 crore. Predictably, both banks ceased to exist after
their indiscretions were discovered.

There was one small detail that further proved that banks acted
in collusion with brokers in creating bogus deals: the embedded
interest in RF deals was mostly lower than the interest rate charged
on the stock exchange for carrying forward a long trade.

When the scam was discovered, all hell broke loose. Post-mortem reports found that the regulators had been lax, having issued circulars prohibiting banks from entering into RF deals with brokers or the indiscriminate issue of BRs but failing to follow up with supervision, inspections or punitive follow-up actions.

A period of introspection and hectic remedial action followed. But, like everything else in India, the reforms process and policy contours were influenced by vested interests who abhorred transparency and had a motive in continuing with the earlier opacity. Their contribution to campaign finance gave them access to politicians, and their wealth and circle of influence got them closer to bureaucrats. In an era when policy was crafted without stakeholder feedback, the market reforms process after the 1992 debacle also remained incomplete, allowing the key accused in the scam to briefly reprise his actions. Incomplete market-level reforms left the grounds fertile for another scam in 2000, with the emergence of another market manipulator leveraging the unreformed parts of the capital markets. This gave further credence to the belief that reforms were attempted only when a crisis broke through the surface, forcing the hands of regulators and government officials. The reality is that policies to reform the financial markets were designed reluctantly, with lots of latitude afforded to certain sections of the market.

The two dramatis personae and their actions discussed in the following paragraphs were like two large pointers to the governance fault lines in the markets, giving rise to suspicion that a nexus existed between the government and capital market operators.

The scam personalities are dealt with in chronological order. The starting point is a news break in hot, muggy Bombay that set the proverbial cat among the clichéd pigeons.

In April 1992, the *Times of India* reported that there was a discrepancy of Rs 574 crore in the government security holdings of India's leading commercial bank, State Bank of India (SBI). This was the difference between what SBI had recorded in its books and what the RBI had in its. An internal investigation by the bank had shown that some of its staff had attempted to fraudulently cover the gap. SBI was, and continues to remain, India's largest bank, handling not just commercial banking but also some critical government transactions. This news about missing securities in a bank such as SBI was like the setting off of a firecracker in an ordnance depot. Parliament was up in arms, the markets unravelled and India's premier investigative agency, the Central Bureau of Investigation, was pressed into action, following which arrests were also made.

The news also highlighted the pitiable state of the government securities market. SBI's own securities ledger showed that it owned government bonds worth Rs 1744.95 crore. But in the books maintained by the RBI, entries against SBI's name showed bonds worth only Rs 1170.95 crore. In effect, SBI's books claimed it owned Rs 574 crore of securities which were not backed up by the RBI, the issuer and manager of government bonds.

There were other startling discoveries. Somebody in SBI had tried to cover up the RBI's periodic statement to the bank by clumsily trying to overwrite Rs 1170.95 crore as Rs 1670.95 crore. The short answer to what happened is this: certain SBI officials had given the bank's money to some market intermediary for buying government bonds which were never delivered but were fraudulently included in the bank's asset portfolio.

A word about the state of the government securities market might be in order here. Lack of vitality and reforms marked the state of the market. Any market is considered robust and efficient when there is a mix of players with heterogeneous investment objectives and differing time horizons, allowing for rich interplay and genuine price discovery. In the Indian bond market of that era, there was only one issuer (government) and one uniform set of bond purchasers (banks) with identical investment objectives (fulfilling statutory reserve requirements). One of the probable reasons behind this market's dullness of character was that both the principal and agents lacked incentives for reforms; which is perhaps why all the market functions had remained manual and trading restricted to a tiny clique of bankers and private brokers. The RBI—as the government's manager for issuing, monitoring and accounting for its debt securities—had an office called the Public Debt Office, or PDO. This office maintained something called the subsidiary general ledger (SGL), in which all trades and ownership changes in government bonds were recorded. Entries in these ledgers were made manually, by hand.

The problem was that it took anywhere from a fortnight to a month for a trade between two banks buying and selling bonds through a select and tight band of brokers to be reported to the PDO and finally reflect in the SGL. A particular broker-scamster found this gap suitable for exploitation: between selling non-existent bonds to a clueless bank with the help of corrupt and colluding officers, receiving the funds and delivering the securities, the speculator had felt he could utilize the funds in the stock market and square up the unreconciled trades later. Apart from perfecting the art of exploiting this technical gap, this person's web of deceit encircled a large number of banks, both Indian and foreign. This man was Harshad Mehta.

## Harshad Mehta

In popular perception and media portrayals, Harshad Mehta came to personify the scam and the rot in the equity markets, even though the investigations and post-mortem reports had pointed to the involvement of many other personalities. This diverse cast of characters had perpetrated a scam not just in the equity markets but had spun a multilayered web of underhand deals at the tri-junction of the bond, money and capital markets. Harshad, by some twist of fate, became the central figure, the man who stood out; it was on his shoulders that the entire 1992 securities scam was pinned. There were many reasons for this.

Harshad had, for one, broken into the cosy clique of brokers who helped the government bonds market chug along. The gilts market was basically a telephonic market, and all trades between banks were facilitated by these brokers. In fact, even if banks themselves struck a bilateral deal without the help of brokers, they would still route the transaction through these brokers for settlement. The market was near-soporific, dull, and rarely merited newspaper headlines. Harshad managed to subvert this coterie, offering banks—especially bank managers who were tasked with securities operations—superb deals, showing them hidden yields and helping sluggish bottom lines discover new territory.

Harshad also broke one cardinal rule of the Bombay Stock Exchange: he spoke publicly and unabashedly about his woolly financial theories and was not embarrassed to display his wealth. He had some favourite stocks (such as the cement company ACC Ltd) and poured money into ramping up these scrips.

Harshad Mehta was an extremely ambitious and impatient interloper who discovered and exploited loopholes in the market system. He leveraged the systemic infirmities of the government bonds market and diverted funds from there to speculate in the stock market, driving up prices of select scrips to unsustainable levels. What was unique about him was his ability to move funds from one segment of the financial system to another; till then, government-imposed artificial restrictions had acted as walls between the systems, and money rarely flowed from one market to another, adding unnecessary costs to money's pursuit of yields.

Harshad's drive and unrelenting ambition sprang from the ordinariness of his background and upbringing. He was born to a small trader family, which moved to Raipur (then part of Madhya

Pradesh, before the state was bifurcated, leading to the creation of a new state, Chhattisgarh) when he was young. Harshad was not academically inclined (he was rusticated from his Raipur school for a series of misdemeanours and had to complete his schooling privately) and barely managed to scrape through his bachelor of commerce exams from Lala Lajpat Rai College in south Bombay. His father had a small but faltering yarn business and had to struggle to raise his four sons and a daughter. Harshad was desperate for an alternative life, a better lifestyle, but his qualifications were misaligned with his aspirations.

He was able to secure a clerk's job at the government-owned general insurance company, New India Assurance Company. The fixed work timings and lax work culture of a public-sector organization allowed Harshad to moonlight, and he explored various side businesses. This included speculating in the stock market during lunch hours. He even tried and failed at diamond trading. But it was the lure of the financial markets that finally seized his fancy.

Back then, trading in the stock markets was conducted inside a ring, through a system of outcries and hand signals. Broking houses engaged jobbers to make markets (match quotes on both sides of a trade) in select scrips and trade in the ring.

Harshad convinced a broker to allow him to become a jobber and resigned from his insurance job. His beginning was not promising, and he incurred frequent losses initially. Faced with the threat of dismissal, he hung on by a slender thread, learning his lessons in double-quick time. Harshad also realized that his path to stock-picking and trading success lay via better quality of information, something that would give him an edge over his competitors. It was a crummier and tawdry version of what is known as equity research in the advanced markets, often bordering on collecting and acting on inside information. He plunged headlong into the trading life, gaining confidence as he got a better grip on the business, taking bolder bets and building up courageous positions. And while his financial position had definitely improved, something still gnawed inside Harshad. He was still playing in the minor leagues; he wanted to be among the big guys.

Two pivotal events changed his trajectory.

The first was a stock market crash in March–April 1982, when the Bombay Stock Exchange, the country's premier trading bourse, had to be shut down for three trading days. The market had entered a phase in which some prominent bear operators had formed a syndicate and were trying to beat down the prices of some stocks they felt were overpriced. Bears are usually pessimistic about either the economy's future or some specific stock; they then bet that either the market index or the price of a specific stock will decline in the future and try to profit from this insight. In this particular crash, the bears were selling without owning the shares, in what is known as naked short-sales, and were trapped by bulls who had bought shares en masse and demanded delivery from the bears.

The market in those days settled outstanding trades once a fortnight, and traders were even allowed to carry forward their positions into the next fortnight on payment of a small interest, called 'badla'. Fortnightly settlements were the established market practice those days, and the custom of carrying forward trades from one fortnight to another without settling them was among the root causes of the scam, as we shall see soon.

Back to Harshad, who was scarred badly from the market shutdown . . . His open positions were in the red and the family had to rally around and bail him out. A few months later, his father passed away, presenting him with the second pivotal event in a few months. After all the last rites were over, Harshad and his brother Ashwin reconnoitred their father's office—actually a cubby hole—from where he had conducted his business.

Harshad decided to try his luck with that shabby space. He had been toying with an idea for a while, and the availability of this space, perhaps, provided the impetus for what was to follow.

Harshad had already created a company called Growmore Consultants a few months earlier. He decided to set up his own broking firm, solicit both wealthy and retail investors, and sell them stock ideas based on research. He started in a small way, selling ideas and running a portfolio management scheme. In a year he had enough earnings and by October 1983 Harshad moved out of his hole-in-the-wall office to a larger office. He also bought a membership card at the Bombay Stock Exchange a few months later, in December 1984, thereby making substantial savings on brokerage fees and margins.

It was around this time that Rajiv Gandhi was elected as India's prime minister, following his mother Indira Gandhi's assassination by her bodyguards. Rajiv Gandhi brought a whiff of freshness to Delhi's shop-worn economic management style, promising liberalization of key sectors. Rajiv Gandhi was a young pilot, wary of India's stifling bureaucracy and keen to introduce new technologies, especially computer technology, in the country. He appointed V.P. Singh as his finance minister, who began the gradual task of relaxing India's infamous industrial licensing regime. The markets were excited and Harshad seemed to have timed his new office and membership card well.

In the years leading to 1992, Harshad grew more aggressive, taking bolder positions in the market and increasing his risk appetite. He faced near bankruptcy once but managed to extricate himself, at great personal cost. His aggression couldn't be dimmed and his risk-taking grew even more breathtaking. He believed in buying stocks and then pumping them up to dizzying heights, following it all up with a healthy and loud dose of braggadocio. He courted the media assiduously, spewing his unproven theories about the markets and corporate finance, and showing off his wealth and acquisitions. He had acquired a sea-facing 15,000-square-foot apartment and a fleet of cars. He was featured on magazine covers, posing with his new, gleaming Toyota Lexus.

There was no shortage of enemies either. He was an upstart, not belonging to any of the old families which had monopolized market policies and institutional positions for well over fifty and sixty years. Harshad's ostentatious show of wealth was found to be repugnant by many of his peers; for some, it militated against their sense of refinement, but for some others, it was as if his antics were focusing the arc-lights on some of the underhand practices they had managed to keep hidden all these years.

His relentless buying and pumping up of stocks became a threat to the cabal of bears who had ruled the roost till then. It weakened their economic model; Harshad had wrested the market initiative from their traditional grasp. He came to be known as the Big Bull, with a dedicated fan following. He had a list of favourite scrips—such as Apollo Tyres or the cement manufacturer ACC Ltd—and would periodically exhort his supporters and acolytes to invest in these stocks. True to character and form, he also built aggressive—and speculative—positions in these stocks on his personal account.

Increasing sums of money were required to feed Harshad's aggressive stock-buying spree and that became the root of the problem, which manifested itself in amplified forms across different markets in the financial system.

On the stock market, two problems arose. The first was the steep margins imposed by the exchange authorities on share purchases between 1991 and 1992. Brokers had to submit either cash or securities to the exchanges for safekeeping, as a percentage of their trade. Many exchanges around the world use cash margins as risk management tools to dampen excessive speculation from both excessive bullishness or bearishness in the market.

There were murmurs that the steep margins were the handiwork of a bear cartel at the Bombay Stock Exchange, which had managed to embed some influential members in the managing committee and was eager to bring down the ascendant bulls and the stock market rally by a notch or two. But these were just rumours and none of the investigative agencies or reports provided any supporting information in the form of proof. On 29 May 1992, SEBI issued a circular[3] to all stock exchanges asking them to step up monitoring and inspection of brokers and not restrict risk management to the imposition of margins:

> You would be aware about the recent revelations about the alleged involvement of a few member brokers of the stock exchanges in the reported unauthorised practices adopted in the market for Government Securities which in turn enabled them to influence trading in and prices of shares in the stock exchanges. In this connection you would recall that the stock exchange authorities are required to closely monitor the market and maintain a close watch on price movements in scrips and volume of business transacted therein, both in aggregate and individual broker-wise, so as to ensure that the market works in an orderly manner. This function of stock exchange authorities assumes greater importance in the context referred to above and especially when it was reported that a few groups of persons could raise the prices of certain scrips which were far out of alignment with their fundamentals and future prospects. The investors were tempted to enter into bargains at the higher levels and subsequently found themselves in quandary as the price levels at which they entered the market could not be maintained. The exchange authorities have however taken a limited view of their role and confined their management of the exchange to monitoring margins, payment and delivery. They have not looked into malpractices like price rigging and market manipulation.

The second problem arose when Harshad wanted to roll over his positions from one fortnight to another without taking delivery of the stocks he had bought. He had to pay a small interest, which needed financing. In some cases, the financiers were brokers who would charge usurious rates of interest, higher than the ruling interest rates on bonds or bank deposits. Banks, by regulation, were prohibited from lending to stockbrokers. This was when Harshad decided to hit the commercial banks, gaining access to their funds at very low interest rates.

There were ways to do this. One way was to insert himself into the money markets, which included a separate market for government bonds. Here he found ready patronage from the foreign bank ANZ Grindlays, which was looking at ways to counter the growing but insidious influence of another foreign bank, Citibank, which had cultivated its own set of brokers. These banks were joined by a number of public-sector banks looking to exploit the profitable but banned business vertical of lending to stockbrokers. Under this route, Harshad would act as a broker between a bank that wanted to sell a government security and another bank that needed to buy one. But this route was slow and the earnings were not commensurate with his market positions unless he took the initiative to speed up this market.

So he combined that activity with another innovation that other brokers had devised in the market to access cheaper bank funds, a subterfuge known as the portfolio management scheme. The central bank had allowed commercial banks to invest in these schemes in their hunt for higher profits. The charade run by brokers had a simple modus operandi: banks 'invested' funds in the sham portfolio management schemes run by these brokers. The banks' money would be parked with the broker for a short term against the security of government bonds furnished by the broker for a fixed period. This exchange would be reversed after a designated period, with the brokers paying an assured return, which was nothing but the surrogate interest masquerading as investment growth.

All this was fine, except for one fundamental problem. Harshad did not own government securities. This was when he used his access to the bonds market and exploited the sloth in the RBI's debt management cell, the PDO, to finance his positions in the market.

Banks trading government bonds in rapid succession would issue BRs in lieu of the real security, given the prolonged turnaround time at the RBI. These pieces of paper were tradeable, and every market participant honoured them on trust. These instruments derived their legitimacy from the absence of any specific regulatory framework banning them. If there was no detailed RBI circular explicitly proscribing their use, or expressly banning them, then they were kosher to use. Remember, these were the days when the RBI decided everything. This is what the Joint Parliamentary Committee, a thirty-one-member committee headed by Ram Niwas Mirdha and officially entrusted with inquiring into 'Irregularities in Securities and Banking Transactions', said about the use of BRs:

> In the inter-bank market, a large number of transactions in securities were being concluded by means of BR deliveries (instead of physical delivery of securities sold); however, there was no uniformity in the format of the BR and there were also no set guidelines for its usage. BR does not find a place in the Banking Regulation Act, 1949. It was only on the 6th May, 1991 that IBA issued a circular prescribing a format and laying down certain broad guidelines and recommending its adoption by member banks and other financial institutions like IDBI/ IFCI/ ICICI/NABARD etc. The RBI for the first time inter alia issued instructions to banks in this regard in their Circular of 26–7–1991.

As the broker in many trades, Harshad would often divert these BRs to raise funds from other banks and finance his positions on the stock market. He would then use BRs from other banks to replace the earlier lot of BRs. This layering of one deal over another continued merrily. Harshad and many other brokers in the system were also known to have issued fake BRs. The RBI-appointed Janakiraman Committee had confirmed the use of fraudulent BRs:

> The major device by which the transference of funds to brokers' accounts has been achieved has been through the issue of BRs which were not supported by underlying securities and by payments being diverted to brokers' accounts either directly or through counter-parties named in the transactions. This appears to have been made possible by a significant lack of internal control in the banks and presumably by collusion between the concerned officials and the concerned brokers.

Harshad's close relationship with certain banks, such as the State Bank of India, definitely helped him. The Janakiraman Committee's first interim report had found that SBI had undertaken trades in government securities worth Rs 17,000 crore through Harshad in a period of just nine months, between June 1991 and April 1992.

The merry-go-round had to stop one day as Harshad kept increasing the size of his portfolio and the stock market officials started imposing heavier margins for brokers carrying forward their trades. As the margins went up, so did the interest required to be paid for the rollovers. Strangely, Harshad seemed confident that the markets would keep rising and that he would be able to square up all his outstanding positions in the stock and bond markets. But, as with all pyramids built on false hopes, Harshad's unsteady edifice also came crashing down when the news of

SBI's missing government bonds spooked the capital markets. Harshad was arrested, interrogated and charged with twenty-seven offences, of which he was convicted for four. The man died in 2001 in police custody from a sudden heart attack.

But in his arrest and investigation, a large-scale scam was exposed. Numerous committees were set up and many voluminous reports were compiled. What showed up was the dark and dirty underbelly of India's financial system, ignored and side-stepped by regulators and government authorities. Many of the brokers involved in the scam were close to senior political figures and even played an intermediary role in campaign finance.

One would think the scope and depth of the scam would invite drastic remedial measures that would comprehensively change the core genetic architecture of the system, especially to deter any repetition of it. But once again, politicians and regulators seemed reluctant to press home the opportunity presented by the 1992 scam—after some initial moves, they relaxed their grip on the reins.

The Big Bull, in fact, attempted a comeback which was driven, perhaps, by an abiding faith in the authorities' inability to completely overhaul the market system. Harshad, having spent some time in jail, tried to have another shot at the markets in 1998, once again using mysterious sources of funds to ramp up the prices of a few select stocks—Videocon, BPL and Sterlite. He had been battling numerous cases in relation to the 1992 scam and was barred from the market, but that did not seem to slow him. He mined the novelty of the Internet and started his own website for stock tips. He deployed a large number of front companies to rig up the prices of his select stocks. Some of his select companies also lent money to these front companies to rig their own share prices. The prices of these shares spiked by 100–300 per cent in a span of three or four months. The breakneck upward spiral in their prices was halted in the aftermath of Pokhran-II in May 1998, when India tested its nuclear capability for the second time, and was immediately subjected to economic sanctions by the US and Japan. The markets crashed, and then the cracks representing the incomplete market reforms showed up once again. The BSE president influenced the BSE administration to reduce margins and kept the exchange's trading system open past midnight on 12, 17 and 19 June 1998, to help select brokers square up their open positions and tide over the payments crisis. He ostensibly took all these actions without informing the BSE governing board. SEBI, after completing its investigations, cracked the whip a bit harder this time. First, in November 1998, the regulator asked Vice President Rajendra Banthia to resign and step down from the governing board after his broking company was allegedly involved in price rigging. Then in February 1999, it sacked then BSE president J.C. Parekh. But its harshest step came in 2001 when it barred Harshad from the securities market for life.

Watching this unfolding drama in two acts from the sidelines were Harshad's adherents, waiting for the right moment for their opportunity. Surprisingly, one of them initiated a similar modus operandi as Harshad's during 1999–2000. This was also another Big Bull.

## Ketan Parekh

Ketan was distinctly a Harshad acolyte, having watched from the periphery, as a Growmore employee, how the Big Bull operated. Ketan learnt a lot from Harshad, but there were two crucial and distinguishing differences between the guru and the student. Ketan was a qualified chartered accountant and came from a family of stockbrokers, NH Securities being the name of his family-owned broking firm. He was able to put these two qualifications to good use. Harshad, on the other hand, had had none of these early advantages. The other lesson Ketan learnt was about the benefits of operating under the radar and not drawing attention to himself, unlike Harshad. Ketan had also innovated on Harshad's signature financing ploy—of diverting bank money. It was going swimmingly well till it all came crashing down one fine day, as it invariably does, leading to his arrest, breathless media revelations about his modus operandi and the usual hand-wringing by politicians and regulators.

Ketan Parekh's style was starkly opposed to his mentor's. He remained media-shy and hardly spoke in public. Ketan had probably learnt this particular lesson after observing the animus that Harshad's public profile generated. Ketan's stock-picking also differed from Harshad's. Ketan chose to identify low-traded stocks, conduct his personal research and then go at them full tilt, buying up large quantities of his chosen scrips, which would cause their prices to spike. He preferred stocks in the media-telecom-technology space. The timing was fortuitous: he chose to press on the accelerator around the same time that the world was witnessing a boom in technology stocks, which would come to be known as the dotcom boom. For example, he chose to lavish his attention on the second-rung software stocks that were bypassed by institutional investors for reasons of the companies' doubtful provenance or dubious governance practices. Ketan's preferred mode of operation involved spotting undervalued or illiquid stocks, borrowing from the banking industry and ramping up the price of these shares. Eventually, he would offload these shares to either gullible or colluding financial institutions. Occasionally, with the help of financing from certain industrialists, Ketan would even resort to manipulating the share prices of their companies by indulging in circular trading (which involved buying and selling particular stocks repeatedly through a closed network of known brokers) in those stocks.

Another thirty-member Joint Parliamentary Committee, which was convened in April 2001 under the chairmanship of Prakash Mani Tripathi to investigate Ketan Parekh's market operations, had this comment to make at the outset in its 545-page report:

> The Committee note that Ketan Parekh who emerged as a key player in this scam received large sums of money from the banks as well as from the Corporate bodies during the period when Sensex was falling rapidly. This led the Committee to believe that there was a nexus between Ketan Parekh, banks and the corporate houses.

Ketan Parekh's pet stocks came to be known as K-10 stocks and included Zee Telefilms, Himachal Futuristic, Pentafour, Global Telesystems and Pentamedia Graphics. His emergence with a market strategy around 1998–99 coincided with the market preference for tech stocks in the US and the dizzying rise of indices at the NASDAQ. The first flush of dotcom companies was promising to change the world, and the new economy was guaranteeing a second industrial revolution, one that would reduce distance and time between tasks, lead to an unbelievable spike in productivity and radically transform the way people had worked, played and lived so far. The K-10 pick reflected some of that optimism, mostly through word-of-mouth and demonstration effect reflected by the unrelenting rise in their prices.

As a side note, it might be interesting to mention here that Ketan had also managed to convince Australian media tycoon Kerry Packer to invest in Himachal Futuristic, a company engaged in the manufacture of telecom cables. Packer's Consolidated Press Holdings invested about $238 million (close to Rs 1039 crore then) for a 10 per cent stake in Himachal Futuristic. The deal would also include two joint ventures focused on software services and B2B e-commerce. Packer was better known for having changed the course of world cricket by launching a parallel, unofficial cricketing series in 1977 that featured one-day matches played by cricketers in coloured flannels under floodlights. All of these were taboo in the world of staid cricket, but Packer managed to pull it off for a while, primarily to cock a snook at the Australian Cricket Board, which had denied broadcasting rights for international cricket matches in Australia to his media group's Nine Network. While all these rebel features have now become part of mainstream cricket, it is surprising that Ketan was able to convince the hard-nosed Packer to invest in Himachal Futuristic. There were jokes—memes had not made their mark yet—and speculation about what could have finally tilted Packer's decision to make the investment, and whether it was because both shared the same initials, KP.

Among the multiple banks Ketan touched to fuel his stock market operations, his mainstays were the Bank of India (BoI) and the Gujarat-based Madhavpura Mercantile Cooperative Bank (MMCB). Ketan and his associate group companies had multiple accounts in MMCB's south Mumbai branch. This branch would issue pay orders favouring Ketan, who would then get them encashed at the Bank of India. A pay order is like a prepaid banking instrument that can be encashed at another bank within the same city. The bank branch issuing the pay order usually gets paid by the beneficiary beforehand or deducts the amount from his account. But in Ketan's case, when the Bank of India presented the pay orders favouring Ketan to MMCB for reimbursement, they bounced. In essence, MMCB had issued pay orders favouring Ketan on the strength of love and fresh air: they were not backed by any funds but gave Ketan access to BoI's funds for a short while till the encashing banks presented the pay orders to the issuing branch. Ketan could manage to keep this cycle active until such time as his stocks were moving up. This would allow him to keep the stocks as collateral and borrow some more.

Ketan's downfall also came about as a consequence of his over-the-top bullish push into the market, forcing the bears to retaliate and cause a payments crisis, and forcing Ketan to tip his hand. The spark was finally lit on the Calcutta Stock Exchange, where some of his associates were caught in a trap, failing to pay up for their outstanding positions as the market started sinking.

The first signs of trouble were discerned when the benchmark BSE Sensex dropped by close to 180 points on 1 March 2001, only a day after Finance Minister Yashwant Sinha had tabled a market-friendly budget in Parliament. Around the same time, there were media reports about a private bank's capital market exposure exceeding the prudential norms, prompting the RBI to start looking into the entire banking sector's capital market exposure. It was also around the same time that a controversy arose around then BSE president Anand Rathi, with allegations that he had used his position to find out the outstanding positions of prominent bulls—which would give him some indications of their financial vulnerability—and had used that information to tip off the bear cartel.

It is interesting to note that the battle of wits between Ketan Parekh and his associates with a faceless, nameless bear cartel pretty soon became a contest about who could marshal what kind of financial resources in the pursuit of their endgames. Ketan Parekh's ability to re-route bank finance and money from the corporate sector has been well documented. But what got missed out in the din over his misdemeanours was the bear cartel's ability to sell an unending supply of shares in their endeavour to bring share prices down. This indirectly shone a light on their ability to borrow vast quantities of shares, because the operators were unlikely to have been in ownership of such large quantities, given the unremitting sale orders they executed to trap Ketan Parekh and his associates. All they needed was information about which shareholder—especially from among the large institutions—owned how many shares of which scrip. And it appears that they were able to access this vital information and borrow shares from these institutions. The unceasing sales of K-10 stocks forced Ketan Parekh to keep re-routing higher amounts from his favourite banks, till one day he had borrowed way beyond his capacity to repay.

It is indeed telling that after the dust had settled down, it was Ketan Parekh who emerged as the villain of the piece. This is not to exonerate him or to air-brush his misdeeds because he was clearly in the wrong. But no light was ever shone on the role of the bears, or on how they managed to obtain an endless supply of shares, or on who financed their campaign. There was also no punitive action against the many corporate sector executives who had provided Ketan Parekh with funds to manipulate the share prices of their companies or against numerous bankers who bent rules to allow for stock market manipulation. Even regulators, who remained inert when market manipulation sent stock market indices up but were quick to express concern when it inevitably crashed, only escaped with a mild rap on the knuckles. A single paragraph from the 2002 JPC report illustrated this bias among regulators and administrators:

> When stock markets were rising, there was general lack of concern to see that such a rise should be in consonance with the integrity of the market and not the consequence of manipulation or other malpractice. On the other hand, when the markets went into a steep fall, there was concern all over. Such dissonance in the approach to issues of regulation and good governance needs to be replaced with effective regulation which concentrates on market integrity and investor protection whether at any given point of time the market is buoyant or not.

In the end, though, it was Ketan Parekh who took the rap for the precipitous fall in the markets because he had certainly pushed the markets into this corner. It was his recklessness that had caused the tower of cards to first teeter dangerously and then collapse. He alone had to bear that cross. There were frequent interventions in Parliament on this scandal and SEBI was forced to submit a report. The Opposition members in Parliament demanded and got a Joint Parliamentary Committee to look into the scam.

So far, so indignant. As the next chapter will illustrate, in keeping with India's larger political-economic design, the regulatory response fell short. Sure, there were recriminations all around and some remedial action was also initiated in due course, but the regulatory response from authorities did not manage to fully utilize the opportunity to reform the market micro-structure.

# Chapter 4

## Equity Markets: A Historical Perspective

Commerce and trade were an integral part of ancient India and historians date its genesis back to the economy of the Indus Valley civilization (3500–1800 BC). In his book[1] *Trade and Commerce of Ancient India*, historian Haripada Chakraborti has written: 'The pre-historic Indus Valley culture shows India's connection with the land of Sumer. The Rgveda alludes to Iran and it runs parallel with the Avesta, the earliest document of the Iranians, showing thereby India's close relationship with the Western Asia.' Oxford University don and historian Peter Frankopan refers to overwhelming and rich archaeological discoveries from India in his book *The Silk Roads: A New History of the World*, which clearly point to flourishing trade with the Roman Empire of antiquity; he also mentions, among other archaeological finds, of coins found in Western India that date back to the reign of Roman emperor Augustus (27 BC–AD 14).

It can also be assumed, somewhat logically, that as the volume and value of trade (both inland and overseas) grew, so did the sophistication of financing instruments. According to the RBI publication *Payment Systems in India 1998*,[2] loan deeds in ancient India, called *rnpatra* or *malekhya*, would record the names of the debtor and creditor, the amount of loan, the interest rate, condition and time of repayment. These credit instruments kept evolving with time, changing from *adesha* during the Mauryan period to *dastavez* during the Mughal period. Similarly, there was another credit instrument that pre-dated the formal banking systems: traders would exchange local promissory notes (called *hundis*) to finance commerce. The RBI publication states: 'The most important class of credit instruments that evolved in India were termed **Hundis.** Their use was most widespread in the twelfth century and has continued till today. In a sense, they represent the oldest surviving form of credit instrument.'

The *hundis* were tradeable, and that act of congregating and trading in these scraps of paper perhaps sowed the seeds of the Indian capital market. These early, nascent capital markets were comparatively informal in form and modus operandi, and far removed from the sophisticated version that exists today. It's been a long journey from there to today's fully automated bourses, which measure up to the best international standards. This journey has been tumultuous, and its trajectory has affected many people (brokers, investors, managements of stock exchanges, regulators, among others), products (such as home-grown derivative products) and traditional ways of conducting business.

The country's largest and oldest stock exchange, the Bombay Stock Exchange (now known as BSE Ltd), was started in 1875, earlier than the 1878 formation of the Tokyo Stock Exchange, making the BSE Asia's oldest stock exchange. The BSE started off as a voluntary non-profit-making association but, over time, evolved into the country's premier stock exchange. Historically, the BSE enjoyed the largest market share among all stock exchanges in India, followed by the Calcutta and Delhi stock exchanges. Consequently, this became a double-edged sword: while the BSE became synonymous with the Indian capital market, its leadership position and invincibility bred arrogance and an aversion to change. As a result, things came to such a pass that the continent's oldest stock exchange started being identified with negative attributes: vested interests, opaque financial dealings, hostility towards retail investors and unwillingness to change.

To better understand how Harshad Mehta and Ketan Parekh were able to subvert established practices repeatedly while cocking a snook at the regulators, it might be instructive to revisit the state of affairs at the BSE, emblematic of most Indian stock exchanges, and understand how reform attempts were repeatedly sabotaged or undermined.

## The Old Boys' Club

The BSE traditionally used the 'open outcry' system of trading, a practice still in vogue only at the New York Stock Exchange (NYSE) and the London Metal Exchange. On NYSE, although over 80 per cent of the transactions are conducted through electronic means, a few stocks are still traded through the outcry mode. The practice involved traders using verbal and hand signals to negotiate, finalize and communicate trade orders with their fellow traders in the trading ring.

The structure of trading often allowed 'jobbers'—who were employed by brokerage firms to participate in the outcry system to cut deals on the floor of the trading ring—to manipulate spreads (the difference between a bid and an offer rate). For ordinary investors, this frequently meant hidden costs. For example, investors rarely got the rates quoted in the financial papers, since these figures represented the rates at which jobbers cut deals with other jobbers. Investors had to pay a margin over these published quotes, which was in addition to brokerage. Investors, ironically, had no voice or representation, nor recourse to restorative justice. It was a one-sided relationship, with the stockbroking community having all the power. The arbitration structure at the level of the stock exchange, which is usually the first-level regulatory authority, was also loaded against the investor.

At the organizational end, the BSE (and most of the other major stock exchanges, such as the Delhi, Calcutta and Ahmedabad bourses) was operated by something akin to a medieval cabal. It was run by brokers, for brokers. In 1981, the BSE's daily turnover was Rs 40 lakh, contributed by 517 brokers. A decade later, in 1991, its daily turnover had gone up to Rs 2.3 crore a day, but the number of brokers had increased to only 550. This data point alone illustrates the irony of how a stock exchange, the frontline symbol for free-market and competitive forces, was manipulated to keep competition at bay. Membership was through the purchase of cards, but the BSE administration rarely issued new cards. Consequently, a thriving secondary market grew for existing membership cards. And, while the BSE did periodically auction off some cards that belonged to defaulting members, it rarely issued new cards.

Not surprisingly, the prices of these cards were steep, which too acted as an unnatural barrier for competition.

The clubby nature of the organization created its own drawbacks. Regulation was the biggest casualty. Regulation was the responsibility of the stock exchange's governing board, but that was only on paper. Conflicts of interest trumped good governance: brokers of the exchange elected other brokers to the board, creating extensive networks of favours and obligations. The stock exchange's regulatory regime remained effete, making it impossible to punish or penalize transgressors. The rules mandated that the government appoint or nominate an executive director to the board of each stock exchange. The original purpose behind this mandate was to ensure government oversight and to create an effective, morally constraining force in the stock exchange management. But, unfortunately, most of these nominees had limited powers because they had to nominally report to the board. As a result, the investor had nowhere to go to complain.

BSE brokers remained stubbornly inimical to any change and resisted any semblance of a corporate structure for years. Most of the broking-member firms on the stock exchange were proprietorship or partnership firms and were very thinly capitalized. The notion of stockbroking as a financial activity, based on adequate capital to cover risks, was non-existent. Membership cards were handed down from one generation to the next as family heirlooms. Corporate broking firms were not allowed, and competition was limited. Getting these small firms to invest capital was next to impossible, which meant that while these firms lacked adequate capital, they still engaged in brokerage for amounts that were several multiples of their size. This presented a huge risk to the market, especially in the event of a default.

The potential for default, in turn, was also very high, given the nature and volume of risks these firms undertook. But what kept these stockbroking firms from injecting additional capital was precisely the clubby nature of these exchanges, the belief that any misstep or wrongdoing would be overlooked, that the other members would ring-fence the extent of damage or would bail them out. It is also interesting to note that these community-like rescue acts had almost universal buy-in because most of the brokers knew that they were all equally fragile and vulnerable to defaults and that they would also have to turn to the stockbroking community in times of trouble. Although there are no recorded events, apocryphal stories of some of these rescue acts are now part of the BSE's oral legends.

There are, of course, exceptions too. There is anecdotal evidence (again, possibly apocryphal) about a powerful bear on the BSE who put downward pressure on the shares of an equally influential, emerging corporate behemoth. The company's promoter shareholders—who had built strong political-industrial patronage links and were beneficiaries of the 'licence raj'— stepped in to stem the 'rot'. They were able to thwart the bear's onslaught and, as the legend goes, created a severe financial squeeze for him. Importantly, this once-powerful broker found himself isolated once he decided to take on this large post-1970s industrial complex, which was then beginning to be considered all-powerful in the markets. Stockbrokers, who usually sprang to the defence of their community members, abandoned this bear once the realization sank in that he was up against a stronger and more influential adversary. The moral of the story is that in a universe where everybody is an influence peddler, rules can easily be broken or reset only by the largest among them.

The fault lines in market institutions did not stay hidden for too long. SEBI, which carried out inspections of the Bombay, Calcutta, Ahmedabad and Vadodara stock exchanges, and a few others too, was scathing about the findings in its annual report for 1992–93:

> The inspections revealed several inadequacies and deficiencies in the functioning of the stock exchanges. It is noted that the stock exchanges were not functioning as effective self-regulatory organisations and not regulating their own members effectively through enforcement of the bye-laws, rules and regulations of the Exchanges. The mechanism for enforcing discipline amongst the members was also found to be inadequate and the attention to redressal of investors grievances minimal. There were several instances of long pending arbitration cases, resulting in great inconvenience to investors. It is in the interest of the development of the securities market and investor protection that the stock exchanges function efficiently and effectively. It is therefore important that the stock exchanges take steps to rectify these deficiencies.

BSE trades were kept open for fifteen-day settlement cycles, which meant that if a broker bought or sold shares on day one, he had the luxury of fifteen days before having to pay up the required funds or part with the shares, as the case may be. This system engendered huge risks, such as the possibility of one of the parties involved in a transaction going bankrupt in those fifteen days. The buyer or seller was thus very vulnerable to their transactions going sour.

The other risk could be the share price moving to the disadvantage of one of the parties. Suppose Person A had contracted to buy 100 shares of Company X from Person B at Rs 10 per share on day one of a settlement period. Now suppose, for some unforeseen reasons, on day seven the share price plummets to Rs 6. Despite the shares being available in the market at a lower price, A would still have had to fork out a higher price. In a shorter settlement system, this risk is obviated to a large extent. In fact, even as stock exchanges around the world were moving to shorter settlement cycles, the BSE stubbornly stuck to its fifteen-day cycle. The reason for this was a speculative instrument, unique to the Indian market, which the BSE brokers were loath to jettison.

## The Practice of Badla

This unique instrument was called badla and was available on the BSE, inspired by the deferment products available on the London Stock Exchange (LSE).[3] Badla was a financial cost for carrying forward a contracted trade into the next settlement period. To go back to the example mentioned above, had Person A not wanted to accept delivery of the shares of Company X, he could roll it over to the next fifteen-day settlement period. All A needed to do was to pay badla or compensate for B's cost of holding on to the stock. This rate, much like a rate of interest, would be fixed on the floor of the stock exchange through an open outcry system of bidding, like stock trades, also in a completely non-transparent manner. This interest rate could be quite high—ranging from 24 per cent per annum to as high as 70 per cent or 80 per cent per annum when money got tight.

The opening paragraph of a paper[4] on the Milan Stock Exchange's *riporti* system, which was similar to the badla system, describes a scene that could resemble any Indian stock exchange in the 1980s:

> One morning in the middle of every month in Milan, before the main trading session begins, some thirty brokers gather round one of the rings on the floor of the Stock Exchange to arrange riporti contracts. An auctioneer, taking each issue in turn, calls out interest rates, trying lower ones until reaching equilibrium. This auction is the most visible part of a larger market, in which these and other brokers negotiate riporti contracts directly with clients or with banks. The participants, as is typical, see nothing novel in the day's procedures; to outsiders, the significance of the riporti market is far from obvious.

Many scholars and market observers have pointed out repeatedly that badla became an instrument for perennial future deferment, thereby embedding an unattended risk element in the market system. Assume that Person A and Person B kept deferring their positions for many successive settlement periods. Now, suppose B suddenly goes bankrupt or dies, leaving A with a huge bill—A having paid interest on successive carry-forwards—A would still have no shares. The process for acquiring B's shares in either case would be so lengthy and cumbersome that A would have to close the transaction without owning the shares. Now, A's predicament is bound to have ripple effects on the rest of the market as he would be in no position to pay up his badla commitments, setting off a chain reaction across the length and breadth of the bourse. Now, multiply the A–B dynamic across multiple contracts in the market and you have the perfect mix for a market meltdown.

Given the magnitude of risk involved, it became obligatory for the stock exchanges to install stringent risk containment measures, especially as the volume of transactions had been growing every year. Yet, mysteriously, regulation on this score remained non-existent, leading to numerous defaults and abuse of the badla system. In the absence of a strong regulatory framework, brokers had every incentive to keep increasing their over-bought positions.

The 1993 JPC report highlighted how the BSE operated outside the pale of any regulatory gaze:

> . . . the BSE, which accounts for more than 2/3rds of the total turnover in securities all over the country, is clearly the market leader in all irregularities noticed in the Stock Exchanges at large. It is also noticed that this Stock Exchange was inspected for the very first time, by a regulatory authority, after more than a century of its coming into existence, and that too only in February, 1993, almost a year after the major banking and securities transactions scam had taken place. What has been revealed is that irregularities have been committed not just by the member-brokers but also by the members of the Governing Board themselves.

According to some estimates, only 20 per cent of the market trade volume during 1991 was for delivery; the balance was done under badla. An inescapable question then arises: what could have inspired the stockbroking community to blatantly violate the rules and regulations? Which wellspring of indiscretion did they draw their intransigence from? The only plausible response—and perhaps speculative response, to some degree—could be the stockbroking community's proximity to power, greased by campaign finance.

Two incidents witnessed by this author testify to that hypothesis, though they are mostly anecdotal and can by no means be considered empirical or authoritative confirmations. N.D. Tiwari, during his tenure as Union finance minister in 1987–88, was asked to respond to a highly speculative news story in a leading business publication about duty restructuring in the auto industry. He shook his head and said he could not comment because huge short positions had been built up in certain auto stocks and the operators were just waiting for him to officially deny the story so they could beat down the price of those stocks and make profits. Remember, this was 1987–88, when real-time data on outstanding positions was difficult to obtain. But Tiwari was on top of the development, displaying close government knowledge of some market practices.

The second incident occurred a couple of years later, when a senior finance ministry bureaucrat came to visit the Calcutta Stock Exchange. The day of his visit also happened to be settlement day and the brokers were openly transacting badla rates in the trading ring through the open outcry system while the ministry official was doing the rounds of the exchange building. What was extraordinary about this incident was that badla had officially been banned but the Calcutta brokers decided to conduct an auction for badla rates openly in front of the government official, on the official trading floor. The official happened to be part of the ministry's capital markets division and, given his position, it is unlikely this senior government secretary would have been unaware of what was taking place under his nose.

Badla became symbolic of the market's open contempt for rules and regulations. How did badla go from being a mere financial instrument to acquiring the stature of an institution, fiercely protected by brokers, exchange authorities and regulators? It is quite likely that the absence of hedging opportunities and hedging products gave rise to badla in India. Like most other perversions, the badla practice perhaps started with good intentions but soon degenerated into a distortion.

There were three kinds of deliveries in the Indian stock markets: spot delivery, hand delivery (which meant delivery in fifteen days) and trading in securities through the clearing houses of the stock market, the last of which gave birth to the badla system. This last kind of delivery was banned in 1969, when the government outlawed forward trading of every kind in the country. The prima facie reason was to stop speculation in essential commodities, which were witnessing an unusual rise in prices. Since all forward trading in India was regulated through the Securities Contracts (Regulation) Act, the legislative changes wrought for checking excess speculation in commodities also, by default, applied to stocks.

Badla, however, went underground and thrived there. Then, in 1974, the government enacted the Foreign Exchange Regulation Act, which was aimed at stopping capital flight and also required listed multinational corporations (MNCs) doing business in India to offer part of their equity to the public. As a result, a large number of MNCs came to the market with share offers and the market boomed.

The equity markets anticipated this development and initiated a move to revive badla. The BSE—followed by the Calcutta, Delhi and Ahmedabad stock exchanges—created a workaround in 1974 to sidestep the ban. They would conclude the transaction at the end of the settlement period and then simultaneously enter into a new contract without any actual delivery taking place, but the difference between the contracted price and the market price was paid out and the contract was closed and re-entered into. This effectively allowed them to carry forward their trade position without technically violating the law. But then, this also led to recurring payment defaults during the subsequent share market booms. The government became aware of this trend and issued warnings to the stock exchange authorities to curb this speculative activity but to no avail. The government intervened by nominating additional personnel on the boards of stock exchanges, but even that did not help. Somehow, no firm action was ever taken, barring a couple of isolated instances.

The government made threatening noises from time to time but failed to crack down comprehensively on the practice of badla. Indeed, after having banned badla in 1969 and then allowing it to exist as a surreptitious system post-1974, the government finally allowed the official revival of forward trading in 1983 on a limited basis. Under this new system, the government allowed market players to carry forward their position for up to a total of three months. However, even this was blatantly disregarded. This prompted a former controller of capital issues, Nitish K. Sengupta, to acknowledge the existence of this kind of speculation in a 1991 public speech: 'For over a decade, forward trading was not recognized by law and yet [was] permitted in the major exchanges through extra-legal means over which our laws and regulations had no control.'

Badla was banned after the Harshad Mehta scam in 1992 but was re-introduced in different forms under pressure from the stockbroking community, and it continued to be practised till it was completely banned in 2001 following the Ketan Parekh scam. However, brokers had the final laugh when the market regulator subsequently decided to introduce exchange-traded futures and options derivative products, especially individual stock futures, which we shall discuss later in this chapter.

The blatant disregard for government rules probably reflected the enormous political bargaining power exercised by the broker-speculator lobby. It also reflected the diminished or non-existent bargaining power of investors, who did not have any significance as a political constituency. In fact, investors became a powerful constituency—but with varying degrees of influence between wholesale and retail investors—with significant lobbying powers only after the onset of economic reforms.

There is a counterpoint to be made in favour of badla, though, without necessarily endorsing the way brokers used it to build up unsettled positions. Many market players feel that badla did serve some purpose in a market that was hamstrung by overbearing laws and regulations. Many senior market experts had described badla as a product that rolled together the facilities of margin trading, hedging, stock lending and moneylending. These observers felt that its only shortcoming was insufficient or lax regulation and supervision. In an August 2022 article[5] for the *Hindu BusinessLine* newspaper, IIM-Ahmedabad professor Jayanth R. Varma had written: '. . . with all its faults, badla was the only mechanism for hedging, for short selling and for leverage in a market without derivatives. Similarly, badla provided a workaround for the worst inefficiencies of the paper-based settlement system. In an era when it took the buyers several weeks, if not months, to get the share certificate transferred to their names, badla allowed them to sell these shares before receiving those certificates.'

There might be a grain of truth in these observations. In an era of excessive government control and attempts to build dichotomous markets in which artificial walls were built to dam money's natural flow from low-yielding assets in one market to high-yielding assets in another, intrepid operators found ways to breach these barriers, and not legally all the time. Also, in a society driven by an economic philosophy that prioritized centralized pricing and allocation of all resources, it was almost second nature to be inherently suspicious of market mechanisms, thereby ignoring the need for hedging instruments or financing opportunities to improve the efficiency of market-led price discovery or asset allocation. With institutional structures and beliefs built on the premise of market inconsequence, it was only logical that regulatory frameworks also turned a blind eye to the market mechanisms or, perhaps, became oblivious to market malpractices. Strangely, but in keeping with the times, market regulation was orchestrated by the finance ministry in New Delhi and not by an independent regulator with domain knowledge or expertise. Consequently, it was a combination of both subject innocence as well as political priorities that eventually moulded regulation.

Naivety, political compulsions and speculative greed combined to convert badla into the monster it eventually became, leading to over-leveraged positions taken by speculators, which have occasionally created payments crises in the stock markets. A preponderance of over-leveraged positions gave birth to the securities scams of 1992 and 2001.

## The Side Problems

Many of India's capital market problems can also be traced back to the primary market level.

The primary market is where companies come to raise money and issue shares. However, in the period prior to the mid-1990s, a major problem was an overbearing government presence in this area. The government, through an entity called the Controller of Capital Issues (CCI), would control all aspects of new share issues—how much companies could raise from the market, through what kinds of instruments, and at what price. The CCI disallowed most initial public offerings (IPOs, in which companies raise money from the capital markets for the first time by offering shares) from offering shares above a notional face value of Rs 10 per share, considered as the par value. Later, after much prodding and many committee reports, it would allow some companies to offer their shares at a 'premium' to the face value, based on a synthetic formula and not what the market could bear.

This spawned an inefficient system which raised the cost of capital generation for most companies, which were often forced to sell paper below their fair market value. This made for a disincentive for companies to use the stock markets as a viable alternative for capital-raising.

In addition, the market also had its systemic inefficiencies. The problem began with what the companies chose to share with the investing class. The information they shared about themselves through their issue prospectuses was usually very sketchy, and most companies chose not to reveal much about their operations. In some cases, companies even made exaggerated claims which were not backed by adequate facts or suppressed uncomfortable truths about their financial or physical performance. This was particularly rampant in the new-issue market of the 1980s. Companies chose to make announcements which would help sell their shares and underplayed or held back information that could potentially harm the prospects of the new issue.

The usual practice also entailed applicants having to pay upfront all the money for the shares they were applying for. If Company A was offering its shares at Rs 10 per share, then somebody applying for 100 shares would have to pay the entire Rs 1000 to the company and wait for allotment. In times of market boom, companies would collect two to three times the money they wanted to raise through the share issue process.

However, once the money was raised from the market, companies were lax in returning the funds to unsuccessful applicants or even shares to successful bidders. Typically, companies would sit on the application money for four to six months before either refunding it or allotting shares to investors, and they didn't have to pay any interest on these funds. This gave the companies a clear float to enjoy for six months, which is akin to free money. Interestingly, the Companies Act had laid down a time limit of twenty days for a refund of this application money. But, as with most other regulations, this one too was observed more in the breach than in practice.

Apart from this being an unethical practice, it also created an inconvenience for investors. For an unsuccessful applicant, it meant locking up funds for more than four months without earning any interest on them. For the investor who was allotted shares, it meant a lack of liquidity till she had the physical share certificates in hand.

This was another risk plaguing the Indian stock markets and all investors who wanted to participate in it—problems linked to the physical delivery of shares. The transfer of shares was a laborious process, riddled with risks and uncertainties. Buyers of shares would have to fill out forms and then send them to the company to get their shares and have the ownership rights transferred to and registered under their names. And, if the investor was large, the paperwork would multiply. Companies would often refuse to transfer shares after a transaction on a number of excuses, and this would cause huge delays in the rightful owner of the shares actually coming to own them. This problem gave rise to fraud, duplication and forgery, and even theft of physical shares.

Often, buyers of shares would not get their physical shares even after receiving confirmed allotment letters. A nexus between the registrar and the transfer agents (third-party service providers responsible for maintaining a company's roll of shareholders), postal authorities and unscrupulous operators would intercept the physical shares and sell them to unaware buyers.

This abuse was common knowledge but came to light after two incidents involving Reliance Industries Ltd.

In the first, an ordinary shareholder of the company—one closely linked to the promoter family—requested the company to issue duplicate shares, claiming the physical certificates had been lost or misplaced, when her broker had actually sold those shares in the open market. The company issued the person duplicate shares, effectively leading to two sets of shares with the same distinctive numbers floating in the market. The incident came to light after a buyer of the shares from the open market lodged the shares with Reliance for their transfer to his name. When the company refused to transfer the shares, claiming there was a mismatch in the signatures, the buyer went in for arbitration to the BSE. A public sparring and exchange of words with BSE authorities ensued, which included the BSE suspending trading in Reliance shares and Reliance retaliating with a threat to delist from the BSE. After hectic back-channel negotiations and mediation, Reliance relented on its threat to delist from the BSE, but not before the entire episode helped shine a light on the perils associated with physical shares.

But this was only a curtain-raiser and a larger scandal was to follow which forced regulators to introduce another sweeping change in the equity markets.

In the second instance, also involving Reliance, it was the country's first mutual fund, Unit Trust of India (UTI), which was the victim. In November 1995, during the judicial process to determine the ownership of 15 lakh RIL shares claimed by Fairgrowth Financial Services (Harshad Mehta's company) and disputed by broker Pallav Seth, the special judge, Justice S.N. Variava, froze those Reliance shares and made the list of frozen shares public. When, as part of a due process, UTI tallied its holdings with the list, it was surprised to find those scam-tainted shares in its possession, even though it had not purchased them from either Fairgrowth or Seth. Apparently, RIL had, without informing UTI, switched the shares when UTI had submitted other shares it had purchased for transfer of ownership. Questions were also asked as to how Reliance came to be in possession of those disputed shares.

These two incidents provoked heated debates in Parliament and finally managed to focus regulator attention on market malpractices regarding physical shares. There had been numerous complaints in the past, especially from individual investors but, in the absence of a compelling scandal giving rise to collective outrage, key reforms in market infrastructure were ignored. The duplicate share certificate scam led to the introduction of share dematerialization, which reduced the misuse of physical shares.

This, then, was the imperfect state of the pre-1990s equity markets: decaying, decrepit, riddled with inefficiencies, and hugely self-serving. The markets were so complacent about their existence that they were oblivious to the changes that were occurring elsewhere in the world and were lapping against the Indian shores.

## The Triggers for Change

There were three watershed events in the early 1990s that changed the course of the markets forever. The first was the new Congress government of P.V. Narasimha Rao that was elected to office in 1991, with Manmohan Singh as its finance minister and a near-bankrupt treasury as its inheritance. This new government was forced to implement economic reforms across large parts of the economy, including the financial sector.

The second trigger for change was the securities scam that exploded in the markets in 1992, less than a year after the new government had taken over. And, the scam showed—and magnified a thousand times—all the chinks in the system. It showed how brokers were trading on the stock market using overleveraged positions for which they had no funds. And to finance these overleveraged positions, the brokers were siphoning off money from the government debt markets using fraudulent means.

To recap, the 1992 scam had three legs: the stock market, the government debt market and public sector units flush with money raised after issuing bonds.

The two reasons listed above—an economic crisis and a scam—forced the government to reform the equity market micro-structure. In addition, it also became clear to the new government that the country's prevalent economic system was actually impeding growth and capital formation. It was also clear that the government had no cash for new development, and industrial development would henceforth have to depend on private-sector capital. Thus, it not only had to vacate certain spaces in the manufacturing sector in favour of the private sector, but it also needed to nurture private-sector investment to accelerate growth in the economy. And, in order to grow, the private sector needed access to diverse sources of capital. This, then, necessitated changes in the capital market.

The focus shifted immediately to the equity markets, considered then as the best option for cheap capital-raising for the private sector. It was also realized that globalization was too strong a force for the economy to resist; the government had to allow the entry of private foreign capital, as both portfolio investments as well as direct investments. This was an added imperative to bring the capital markets up to speed.

Elsewhere in the world, the socialist model was being pulled down in some of the erstwhile Eastern Bloc countries. The Berlin Wall had come down, Czechoslovakia was in turmoil, the Soviet Union was breaking up, and Russia was adopting a free-market model. These developments also probably played some role in moulding the thinking of the Indian government and influenced it to take a hard look at the socialist economic model the country had followed for over forty years.

In the mix of reasons that were setting the stage for change, the biggest impetus for reforms, perhaps, came from the outbreak of the 1992 securities scam. At a time when India was opening up its borders to international investors, the government could ill afford to let such a scam go unattended. The scam threw up two things clearly. First, it was possible in the equities market to build up a pyramid of leveraged positions without paying adequate margin money, thereby putting the entire system at risk. This was a result of both inadequate understanding and regulation of the market. Second, a similar situation existed in the government debt market, which was used deceitfully by brokers to take out money from it to fund their positions on the stock markets.

In the public mind, the 1992 scam is usually considered an equity markets scam, although it actually germinated in the government securities market.[6] The state of the market was ripe for a scam. Deals in government securities were settled and cleared in the RBI, which acted as the clearing house as well as a depository for government securities. All government bond players had to open accounts with the public debt office (PDO) of the RBI—called subsidiary general ledger (SGL) accounts—to settle their trades in government bonds. The PDO was the main chink in the armour: it was slow, it settled trades between banks manually and entered or registered transfers of government securities to new bond owners after a considerable lag. Since this lag was detrimental to the market, many banks started an informal practice of exchanging unofficial IOUs—called bank receipts (BRs)—as a substitute for real securities or money in the interim.

The market exploited this lacuna in the settlement system. Many stock market players also doubled as brokers between banks for government securities. They would sell securities they didn't have, issue a BR for the security, use the money to play the equities market, and then route it back to the government securities market and settle the BR. Some of the more reckless players, fired by overconfidence and bravado, started building stacks of such deals, consisting of layer upon layer of false promises. Soon enough, this house of cards came falling down, exposing the prevalent practices in the government securities market. It also showed how vulnerable the government securities market was, given its over-reliance on manual operations and its antiquated systems.

The government thus decided to plug the holes—but surprisingly with greater gusto in the equity market than in the debt market. The reforms in the debt market were limited to blocking only the systemic leakages that the 1992 scam had exploited, proving once again that the government's capacity for reforms was tempered by crises to a large extent, and not perhaps by a belief in the larger need for reforms.

The reforms attempted in the government securities market were limited to largely institutional measures, such as price discovery through an auction method, introduction of primary dealers as market makers, an expansion in the range of instruments floated by the government (91-day treasury bill, zero coupon bond, floating rate bond, among others), and allowing foreign investors to buy government bonds subject to an annual limit. However, the market micro-structure remained largely untouched; it fell short of the kind of deep cleaning implemented in the equity markets.

## The First Change: Equity Markets Regulation

The first relic of the control era to go as a result of all the external and internal pressures was the office of the Controller of Capital Issues, which was abolished in August 1992. This gave companies the freedom to price their equity offerings. Earlier, in April 1988, the government had set up the Securities and Exchange Board of India (SEBI) for the express purpose of regulating the capital markets. The gazette notification announcing the formation of SEBI laid down the organization's key responsibilities:

1.  Development and regulation of the securities markets;

2.    Investor protection;
3.    Preparation of comprehensive legislation for the regulation and development of the securities markets

The notification also appointed S.A. Dave as the first chairman. A doctorate in economics, Dave had been the executive director at the Industrial Development Bank of India and chairman of the Unit Trust of India. He retired in 1990 and was succeeded by G.V. Ramakrishna, a career bureaucrat.

However, when SEBI was created in 1988, it had no powers and its legal standing was in question. In April 1992, the four-year-old SEBI was empowered with statutory powers under the Securities and Exchange Board of India Act. The powers under the Act were greatly enhanced in 1994, when many of the powers that had historically vested with the finance ministry were further transferred to SEBI under the Securities and Contracts (Regulation) Act.

Apart from the Harshad Mehta scam, one of the other large debacles to confront the newly empowered SEBI was an IPO scam, in which many fly-by-night companies took advantage of the regulatory hiatus between the abolition of CCI in 1992 and the granting of statutory powers to SEBI in 1994. Many dubious companies (including some well-established ones) rushed to raise money, exploiting the grey zone in the rules and regulations for new issues. The mad rush also witnessed many unknown companies come to the market, raise money and then disappear into the ether.

After the abolition of the CCI, SEBI was given powers to vet applications of companies that wanted to sell shares to the public and raise funds. Although it lacked the power to tell companies how to price their share offerings, it still could hold back a share issue on a variety of grounds. Increasingly, over time, SEBI relaxed its hold on the new-issue market and only made itself responsible for checking whether the company issuing shares had made adequate disclosures in its prospectus or not. Simultaneously, it also tightened regulation on how long companies could keep applicants' funds, and also the system of share allocation and norms for appointment of merchant bankers to manage the capital issue.

SEBI's powers of regulation were expanded to cover every agent in the capital markets, including mutual funds. The overriding aim was to protect the small investor and to ensure the orderly functioning of the capital markets. However, this could not be achieved to the fullest extent for three reasons.

First, the government decided to keep the country's oldest mutual fund, Unit Trust of India (UTI), out of SEBI's reach. As a result, the country's largest, oldest and most popular mutual fund, Unit Scheme 1964, did not have to report to SEBI on its practices, unlike the newer mutual funds that had to comply with SEBI regulations in everything they did.

It is necessary to pause here and reconsider the UTI case as symbolic of how the politics of markets and institutions in the country kept hobbling economic reforms at every possible juncture. The government established UTI in 1963 through an Act of Parliament, and its flagship scheme was called US-64. The original sponsoring entity was the RBI, and this sponsorship was later transferred to the Industrial Development Bank of India (IDBI) in 1978. In 1987, the government allowed public-sector banks and insurance companies to launch their own mutual funds, and it was not until 1993 that private-sector mutual funds were allowed. By the end of January 2003, there were thirty-three mutual funds registered with SEBI, with total assets of Rs 1,21,805 crore. UTI, which continued to remain outside SEBI's regulatory gaze, was still the largest, with Rs 44,541 crore of assets under management.

There is a reason for taking the January 2003 benchmark here rather than the March-end or December-end figures, as is the usual practice. The UTI Act was repealed the next month, February 2003, and the mutual fund was split into two entities. The lead-up to this landmark event showcased the rot that had set in at the institution. In 1999, the mutual fund institution had almost collapsed but was revived by a Rs 3300-crore government bail-out. But, displaying an extreme example of moral hazard, the fund's management accelerated its risky investment behaviour. The mutual fund had been buying all sorts of dubious stocks at inflated values, including stocks that had been pumped up by Ketan Parekh. The final denouement came when it transpired that UTI had bought over 3 lakh shares of a hollow company named Cyberspace Infosys Ltd at an exorbitant price of Rs 930 per share, persuaded perhaps by the political connections that this company's management flaunted. The 2002 JPC report, quoting an investigation by the Central Bureau of Intelligence (CBI), had observed that the UTI senior management had disregarded advice from the fund's equity research cell and subscribed to shares of the Lucknow-based Cyberspace Infosys. The report further stated that the Cyberspace promoters—primarily through a director named Arvind M. Johari—did not use the proceeds from the subscription as promised but diverted the funds to the stock market through circuitous routes to drive up the Cyberspace share price in the secondary market. The CBI, according to the JPC report, termed the deal between Johari and UTI officials a 'criminal conspiracy'.

Cyberspace was not the only investment made with mala fide intentions. UTI's senior management had been increasingly investing the fund's resources in questionable companies at inflated valuations through private placements, either under pressure from the political regime in Delhi or lured by illicit personal gains. In most cases, the shares of these investments would subsequently be available in the secondary market at a fraction of the original investment price, causing substantial loss to the fund.

The 2002 JPC was categorical about the reasons behind UTI's failings:

> The present state of affairs in UTI is a consequence of the negligence of its principal contributor, IDBI (which is also a public sector institution), the concentration of power in the post of the Chairman, UTI without adequate checks and balances to prevent its misuse, and the unwillingness of the UTI management and the government to make the necessary legislative and organizational changes to restructure the institution and bring it under the purview of the market regulator. Moreover, investment decisions in UTI were not always prudent or in accord with the interests of the investors . . . A combination of lack of urgency in successive governments, abetted by self-serving and negligent management in UTI and inertia in the Ministry of Finance undermined a public financial institution by directing its investment and lending decisions in favour of dubious private sector promoters in the name of reviving the capital markets, ignoring the fact that the purpose of UTI was to serve the interest of unit holders, specifically individual unit holders of small means. The UTI episode also focuses the need for improving the system by which statutory institutions can be made more accountable to Parliament and the public to ensure transparency in their functioning.

Finally, when the UTI Act was repealed in February 2003, the fund was split into two. One was the Specified Undertaking of the Unit Trust of India, encompassing the assets of the US-64 scheme and some others. This fund is managed by a special administrator under government rules and is exempt from SEBI's regulatory framework. The second entity—UTI Mutual Fund—was sponsored by public-sector banks and insurance companies and was brought under the rubric of SEBI mutual fund regulations.

A second reason why SEBI remained only partly effective was the slackness showed by the regulator itself in disciplining the recalcitrant broking community—especially the entrenched broking section of the BSE, which continued to oppose reforms in the capital markets, a reason for the continued outbreak of scams in the capital markets well into the new millennium. However, each scam brought in its train a fresh set of reforms, thereby forcing a major overhaul of the market micro-structure on the whole. For example, SEBI's reluctance to scrap badla or the extended settlement period continued well into 2001 before a major payments crisis on the Calcutta Stock Exchange forced the regulator's hand to ban badla and introduce rolling settlements.

The highlight of the antagonism between the broker community and SEBI was the face-off over payment of fees, which came in the midst of a payments crisis and the regulator procrastinating on banning badla. We will deal with it shortly.

The third roadblock to SEBI's achieving its full potential as a market regulator was the overlap of powers with the Department of Company Affairs (DCA, converted into the Ministry of Corporate Affairs in 2004) in the finance ministry. SEBI, as the market regulator, had no jurisdiction over companies that reported to the DCA. The Department also initially tried to block SEBI's attempts to introduce corporate and foreign stockbroking firms, but SEBI managed to prevail in the end.

SEBI's turf battle with the DCA was the most intense over the extent to which SEBI could regulate companies listed on the stock exchanges. DCA sought to limit SEBI's regulatory oversight of India's corporate sector, thereby forcing SEBI to use its powers over stock exchanges to bring some discipline in corporate sector disclosures. For instance, any company listed on any stock exchange in the country now has to disclose quarterly results. Also, the nature and content of balance sheet disclosures were enhanced greatly by SEBI to improve shareholder information.

However, beyond the disclosure norms, SEBI started off with limited powers to penalize erring companies, the powers expanding only gradually over time.

For instance, in the twilight zone after CCI was abolished and SEBI was yet to acquire its full suite of regulatory powers, a primary market boom in the early 1990s witnessed many fraudulent companies come to the market, raise money from the public and then vanish. Investigation into these companies was undertaken by the DCA but with marginal success.

SEBI had to lobby every inch of the way to expand its regulatory and legal ambit, with each crisis helping the shift in the balance of powers. For example, when the SEBI Act was first legislated in 1992, it mandated that the SEBI board would have two nominees from the RBI. Over the years, SEBI had to lobby hard with the government, arguing that the clause created an unequal hierarchy between regulators and that, in the spirit of reciprocity, SEBI should also be allowed to appoint its nominees on the board of the RBI. Eventually, the Act was amended to allow for only one RBI nominee on the board of SEBI without any reciprocal arrangement. This legislative concession, however, failed to flatten the regulatory hierarchy and, by default, accorded the RBI the distinction of being the senior regulator among all the financial sector regulators (the other regulators being the Insurance Regulatory and Development Authority of India and the Pension Fund Regulatory and Development Authority of India).

## The Second Change: Enter the Competition

Another interesting development took place in 1992, around the same time that SEBI acquired legal backing, which was crucial in changing the market structure: the birth of the National Stock Exchange (NSE). The idea of creating another exchange had been around for a while but was resisted by the entrenched BSE brokers. It took the 1992 securities scam to convince the government that the monopoly position of the BSE had to change.

The NSE was set up by a clutch of financial institutions, as had been recommended by a High-Powered Study Group on the Establishment of New Stock Exchanges, constituted by the finance ministry. The original idea behind launching such an exchange was to reach out to investors across the country, which the BSE had been unable to achieve. The BSE was limited in its geographical reach, which was confined to the municipal limits of Bombay, and therefore could access only a limited number of potential Indian investors. Also, a compelling reason for a new exchange was to seek an alternative, demutualized platform, where ownership of the exchange would be separate and distinct from its participants, which was seen as the root cause of the problems at the BSE.

However, the proposed nature of the NSE's parenthood stymied its birth for a few years. Since it was to be set up by financial institutions, all of which were public-sector entities, there were also doubts within the finance ministry about whether such an experiment would succeed, given the overall record of public-sector entities in the country. However, the outbreak of the scam forced the finance ministry's hand. At the same time, when the issue of introducing technology into the trading floor had become ever more compelling at exchanges across the globe, the BSE management kept resisting any introduction of technology. Also, it seems that an influential section of senior officials within the finance ministry was keen to set up the NSE and kept pushing the proposal. This proved to be pivotal in giving final shape to the NSE as we know it today.

The High-Powered Study Group on Establishment of New Stock Exchanges, helmed by former UTI chairman M.J. Pherwani, had originally recommended a rather limited role for the NSE in its 1991 report: that it be located in New Bombay (or Navi Mumbai, as it is now called) and its operations restricted to creating a corporate debt market and facilitating trading opportunities for mid-range stocks that lacked liquidity on main stock exchanges such as the BSE. Even this diluted form of an alternative exchange had met with tremendous opposition from the entrenched stockbroking community.

The team at the finance ministry, determined on fostering competition in the capital market space, hand-picked a team led by R.H Patil, an economist and former executive director with IDBI, who also became the NSE's founding managing director and CEO. This team, backed by the finance ministry officials and oblivious to the howls of protest from the existing stockbroking community, then went about implementing its grand plan of setting up another full-fledged stock exchange, which diverged from the Pherwani Committee's recommendations. The only committee proposal it accepted was the name: NSE.

The NSE was finally incorporated in 1992 and, interestingly, started its operations by first launching a wholesale debt market in June 1994, followed by equities trading in November 1994. The launch of a fully automated exchange, which in itself was no small ambition, in such a short time showed the urgency that the launch team invested in the project. Pulling together the best-in-class technology from across the world, the team also appointed Tata Consultancy Services to lead a consortium of software developers to adapt the technology to Indian specifications. Finally, the launch team's long arc of ambition relied on satellite connections to enable real-time trading for investors from across the country. The new trading system, National Exchange for Automated Trading (NEAT), democratized capital market access to a large extent by allowing any investor from any corner of India to access the full market in real-time and place orders directly, without having to go through layers of intermediaries as in the past or jump through multiple hoops. This was in sharp contrast to the situation prevailing earlier, when an investor in, say, Chandigarh, who wanted to invest in BSE-traded stocks had to go through multiple tiers of sub-brokers and then hope for the best.

This moment was, to use a shop-worn cliché, truly an inflexion point in India's capital market history. It not only changed the complexion of India's capital market but also transformed the political hierarchy of the markets by according greater agency to investors and other institutional intermediaries, by not only democratizing access but by also minimizing market and operational risk to a large extent. Apart from offering real-time trading, the NSE was also aware that its success would depend on how it could provide a clearing and settlement system that was materially many times better than the BSE's. The latter's broken systems, as discussed earlier, were loaded heavily in favour of speculative brokers and not investors.

The NSE launched a wholly-owned subsidiary in 1996 called National Securities Clearing Corporation Ltd (NSCC) for the clearing and settlement process. All the other large exchanges in the world, with the exception of the BSE, had already implemented something similar to contain risk. NSCC introduced something called novation, under which the institution placed itself at the middle of each transaction, thereby eliminating counter-party risk. It would make payments to the seller of stocks and receive payments from the buyer. Similarly, it would take delivery of shares from the seller and make delivery to the buyer. Consequently, the buyer's or seller's exposure was to NSCC and not to each other—the NSE being the seller of stocks for the buyer and the buyer of stocks for the seller—thereby reducing transaction risk to a large extent. This would ensure smooth settlement of trades without creating any hiccups in the market. NSCC managed its risk by levying a settlement guarantee fee from brokers. It also instituted a real-time position-monitoring and margining mechanism; the system automatically disabled anybody exceeding the risk parameters.

It can, therefore, be safely assumed that the NSE has never faced a single payments crisis in its thirty years of operations because of this remarkable risk containment design. The NSE's launch had an immediate impact on the BSE. In one year, by 1995, the NSE had overtaken the BSE, becoming India's largest exchange.[7]

The BSE—and later the Calcutta and Delhi stock exchanges—also switched to screen-based automated trading. Over the next few years, Indian stock exchanges went through a series of changes that have brought them on par with almost all the stock exchanges in the developed world. The global stock exchanges are all based on anonymous electronic trading, and not the traditional form of outcry-based floor trading. Today, large computers sitting somewhere in a back-room match orders on a time-price priority basis without any human intervention.

Emulating the NSE, all the other exchanges set up their own clearing corporations. The BSE set up a trade guarantee fund in 1997 to guarantee trades.

## Shares: From Physical to Electronic

A critical piece of reform was also triggered by a crisis. The problems of physical shares getting forged, stolen or lost in transit—not to mention the mounting problems in mailing them to the company for transfer of ownership and then waiting eternally for the share certificates to come back with no objections—had got to a point where they were lumped under the all-embracing term of 'capital markets infrastructure deficit'. This was not sufficient to induce an impetus to change and reform.

For example, this 18 December 1995 debate from the tenth Lok Sabha proceedings is illustrative[8], highlighting the government's initial perfunctory responses to mounting concerns over problems associated with physical shares.

PROF. K.V. THOMAS:
Will the Minister of FINANCE be pleased to state :

(a) whether duplicate share dealing is going on in many financial institutions like U.T.I.;
(b) whether this duplicate share dealing is likely to affect the stability of the stock exchanges; and (c) the steps taken by the Government to stabilise the stock exchanges in the country?

THE MINISTER OF STATE IN THE MINISTRY OF FINANCE (DR. DEBI PROSAD PAL) :

(a) and (b). Issue of duplicate share certificates is governed by the provision of Section 84 of the Companies Act, 1956 and the Rules made thereunder. Duplicate share certificates, which are genuinely issued after complying with the necessary legal requirements and procedures, are not illegal, and therefore, are not likely to affect the stability of the Stock Exchanges.
(c) The Securities and Exchange Board of India (SEBI), which is the statutory regulatory body for the securities market, is keeping a constant watch on the functioning of the Stock Exchanges for ensuring the orderly working of the Stock Exchanges.

But, as described earlier in this chapter, the twin Reliance episodes were like the proverbial last straw and forced the government to change tack in just three months. On 1 March 1996, the following pointed questions from a bunch of Parliamentarians in the Lok Sabha elicited[9] the exact information:

SHRI GEORGE FERNANDES
SHRI CHITTA BASU

SHRI ARJUN SINGH YADAV
SHRI HARI KEWAL PRASAD
SHRI SRIKANTA JENA
DR. S.P. YADAV:
Will the Minister of Finance be pleased to state:

(a) whether the Government have completed investigation into the printing of duplicate share certificates by Reliance Industries and some other companies;
(b) if so, the findings of the inspection/investigation; and
(c) the action taken or proposed to be taken by the Government in regard thereto?

THE MINISTER OF STATE IN THE MINISTRY OF FINANCE (DR. DEBI PROSAD PAL):

(a) Securities and Exchange Board of India assisted by officials from the Department of Company Affairs has been conducting an inspection of the books, records and other related documents of Ms Reliance Consultancy Services Ltd. (RCS) in connection with issue of duplicate share certificates of Reliance Industries Ltd. The Interim Report on this inspection has been submitted on 12.1.1996. This inspection is still continuing.
(b) The main findings of the inspection as contained in the Interim Report are given in the enclosed Statement.
(c) Securities and Exchange Board of India has recently appointed an Enquiry Officer under the Regulations on Registrar to an Issue and Share Transfer Agents for the purpose of issuing a show cause notice to Reliance Consultancy Services Ltd. It is also examining the desirability of making amendments to these Regulations in order to provide for an arms-length relationship between a company and its Registrar. Department of Company Affairs has also initiated appropriate follow-up action on the findings contained in the Interim Report.

STATEMENT:

(i) The Interim Inspection report has revealed that some duplicate share certificates had been issued while the original share certificates were in existence which fact was very much in the knowledge of RCS.

(ii) The Inspection report also reveals that the provisions of Section 113 of the Companies Act may have been violated.

(iii) The interim inspection report also reveals that the company has carried out reversal of the entries whereby there has been rectification of the register of members. It appears that the provisions of section 111 (4) (a) of the Companies Act have been violated.

The government enacted new legislation, the Depositories Act 1996, to overcome the problem of physical shares. However, the passage of the Bill into an Act was not smooth. It first fell victim to procedure—the Lok Sabha passed the Depositories Bill, 1995, in the winter session of 1995, but the Bill could not be passed by the Rajya Sabha before the tenth Lok Sabha was dissolved. Then, politics took over. In came a new but short-lived government headed by Atal Bihari Vajpayee of the Bharatiya Janata Party (BJP) which, with 161 of 543 seats, could last only thirteen days. Intense negotiations and back-room wrangling resulted in a coalition of thirteen political parties, with the Congress providing external support. So, when the finance minister P. Chidambaram re-introduced the depositories ordinance, it faced some resistance and delaying tactics, notably from some BJP members.

The depositories ordinance had to be re-promulgated on 21 June 1996 and was finally given the President's assent on 10 August 1996.

But then, the political economy of the capital markets once again asserted itself, with attempts made to tweak the legislation marginally. For example, the Act does not mention whether there should be one, two or more depositories in the economy. That decision was left to SEBI's discretion, which was fully exploited by BSE members who pushed the regulator to allow for more than one depository. Typically, around the world, markets make do with just one depository.

Consequently, the NSE set up a subsidiary, the National Securities Depository Ltd, to dematerialize shares and hold them in electronic form. The BSE also subsequently set up its own subsidiary, the Central Securities Depository Ltd. These depositories together hold more than 95 per cent of the shares in the market today in electronic form. Investors selling shares also automatically inform the depository to transfer the shares to the new owner's account with the depository, without any physical transaction taking place. This has eliminated almost all of the earlier problems related to the physical transfer of shares.

The transformation of the capital markets, once the depositories were set up and went operational, has been remarkable. According to data published by the National Securities Depository Ltd, the value of shares dematerialized stood at Rs 301.36 lakh crore, or $3.648 trillion as on 28 February 2023.

If the journey from paper and physical shares to dematerialized shares seemed rocky and fraught with multi-point pressures, the regulator's attempts to bring recalcitrant stockbrokers to heel, temper their speculative urges by introducing regulation, modernize the trading systems and abolish unethical trading practices turned out to be a multi-year process. Every time a scam occurred, the regulator tried a Band-Aid-and-patches remedy, expressly demonstrating an unwillingness to overhaul the system. The broker lobby's influence on both the regulator and the government worked overtime to leave grey zones in the regulatory framework which could then be exploited till the next scam was exposed.

The broker lobby would often threaten to go on strike, and the government or regulators would frequently buckle under that pressure. This raised issues of both asymmetric power display as well as an unwitting demonstration of irony. The brokers protesting against reforms or other crucial governance-related issues—or the broking firms that would have to spend on modernizing, recapitalizing and retraining staff to contend with competition—hardly numbered more than 300 but were able to exercise a political agency superior to that of hundreds of thousands of individual investors. Foreign portfolio investors had started investing in the Indian equity markets and the authorities were wary of letting something like a brokers' strike disrupt that equilibrium. Secondly, the stockbroking community usually stands for the spirit of a free market, the blunt edge of capitalism, but in India, it was not averse to indulging in industrial action, usually the preserve of trade unions, to protect its legacy privileges.

Badla in its myriad forms turned out to be the final frontier in SEBI's regulatory push to bring the Indian capital markets up to speed.

## Cresting the Badla Mountain

The market regulator, SEBI, had harboured the view for some time that badla as a trading practice should be discontinued. However, the lack of regulatory muscle and legislative powers enfeebled its desire. The 1992 scam provided some steam for that desire to be converted into action. The Joint Parliamentary Committee convened under the chairmanship of Ram Niwas Mirdha to probe the Harshad Mehta scam in 1992 observed in its final report:

> SEBI is currently examining the trading practices prevalent in the Indian Stock Exchanges, particularly carry forward of

transactions and badla system. SEBI is of the view that the carry forward/badla transactions should be disallowed and transactions conducted strictly on a delivery basis and trading in future and options be permitted in a separate market. According to SEBI, a notice of 6 months to the Stock Exchanges may be given to evolve the structure and the rules for operating trading in futures and options and the relevant section under the Securities Contracts (Regulation) Act be suitably amended. As an intervening measure, SEBI has suggested that badla can be prohibited on the exchange by allowing transactions to be carried forward at making up prices only subject to carry forward margins. The Committee would expect the SEBI, in consultation with the Ministry of Finance, to at least now enforce suitable and effective measures.

But before any steps could be taken, stockbrokers across all exchanges in the country had struck work and stopped all trading activity. This would not be the first time they would halt trading.

SEBI, once its legislative role was confirmed through the SEBI Act and it became a legal entity, in a communication on 10 April 1992, requested all stock exchanges to direct their stockbroker members to register with the regulator on payment of fees. SEBI was following the extant example of the practice followed in the US, Japan, Australia, Korea, Singapore and elsewhere. The brokers protested this, opposing any need for registration. They also complained about the fees being too high. SEBI responded by slashing the fees, which eventually worked out to Rs 1000 per Rs 1 crore of turnover, payable annually for the first five years. The brokers appealed to all authorities, including senior politicians, to intercede on their behalf. They even made representations to the finance minister and the SEBI chairman.

Responding to a calling attention notice in the Lok Sabha on 30 April 1992, Finance Minister Manmohan Singh[10] made it very clear that the government would not interfere in SEBI's decision, signalling to the stockbroking community that it was time to forget the past and acknowledge the primacy of the sectoral regulator:

> The brokers are important intermediaries in the primary and secondary markets and are expected to render services to individual and institutional investors. Exemption from the requirement of registration by the brokers, as requested by them will considerably diminish the role of the statutory authority in meeting its objectives of ensuring the healthy growth of the capital markets and also in ensuring that brokers provide adequate services to the small investors.

Brokers from fifteen stock exchanges who had stopped trading between 16 April and 24 April 1992 resumed trading on 27 April 1992. They had filed a writ petition in the Calcutta High Court challenging SEBI's 10 April communication to the stock exchanges. The case was admitted—it would grind its way through the legal process till a Supreme Court judgment in January 2001.

But there is another aspect of the strike, which often gets layered over by a bald reporting of the event. Chronology is vital here.

We come to the point in the Harshad Mehta scam when SBI and the RBI had discovered the Rs 574-crore discrepancy in its government securities holding, and Harshad Mehta, found responsible for promising securities for the amount and not delivering them, was asked to pay up. One must also keep in mind that there was a bear cartel waiting to cut Harshad down to size. It is here that the strike gets interesting. Harshad Mehta's only option for meeting SBI's demands was to sell some of his shares, but with the strike already progressing, he was unable to access the market and monetize his holdings. It is believed that the influential bear cartel prolonged the strike beyond the duration necessary to tighten the squeeze on Harshad Mehta. SEBI's decision to ease the fee structure was communicated on 20 April, but it was not until 27 April that trading resumed. It was, unfortunately, too late for Harshad Mehta . . . news of the hole in SBI's books was public by 23 April and all hell had broken loose by then.

It is rumoured that Harshad Mehta had apparently offered an olive branch to the bear cartel through a foreign bank intermediary by agreeing to sell his holdings at a discount, but met with rejection. So it is believed that the strike by the stockbrokers served a dual purpose: to pressure the government and SEBI to dim the regulatory arc lights and to squeeze Harshad Mehta into bankruptcy. In the end analysis, the bear cartel's operations had some unintended consequences: the can of worms that it opened went way beyond the story of just one broker and exposed the grimy underbelly of the entire Indian capital market. It was probably much more than what the broking community had bargained for.

But it is to the credit of these stockbrokers that they did not lose hope and kept chipping away, lobbying with the powers that be to retain their old practices. This is evident from tracking the practice of badla and its numerous lives.

In the aftermath of the 1992 scam, one of SEBI's first decisions was to ban badla and shorten the settlement cycle for non-active stocks—lumped under the category of 'non-specified shares'—to one week from fifteen days. By the end of November 1993, after consultations with SEBI, the exchanges took some scrips from the specified category, which were eligible for carry-forward, and put them on a cash-and-delivery basis. Brokers were also asked to reduce their outstanding positions by 25 per cent.

But on 13 December 1993, SEBI directed all the four exchanges where carry-forward trading was allowed—Bombay, Calcutta, Delhi and Ahmedabad—to transact all fresh trades on a cash basis. Brokers were asked to gradually square off their earlier outstanding positions and eliminate them by 12 March 1994.

The stock exchange representatives immediately went into overdrive and began lobbying in earnest with government officials and SEBI for reinstating badla. SEBI's then chairman, G.V. Ramakrishna, was firm about his decision and refused to budge. In the meantime, SEBI had also started introducing systemic reforms in the stock exchanges.

One of its first tasks was to end their clubby nature. SEBI had been in discussion with the exchanges to overhaul the functioning of their governing boards. While the exchange officials had initially seemed agreeable to the changes, they indicated their reluctance to accept the changes by delaying their implementation. SEBI then decided to take matters into its own hands. Under the powers conferred to it by the Securities Contracts (Regulation) Act, 1956, it directed the exchanges to amend their rules and articles of association so that governing boards would comprise an equal number of elected members and non-elected members, the latter of whom would be public representatives. In addition, capital adequacy norms for stockbroking member firms at the exchanges were introduced, comprising a base minimum capital and additional capital. The base capital was regardless of the size of the broking firm, and the additional capital was pegged to the volume of business transacted. Brokers were also asked to abandon their proprietorship or partnership structures and adopt a corporate structure, which would give the regulator a clear line of sight to their capital base.

Predictably, in keeping with the nature of India's political economy, as soon as GVR started cracking the whip and tightening the regulations, he was transferred out of SEBI in January 1994 to the Planning Commission in New Delhi. Former IDBI chairman, S.S. Nadkarni, took over as the new chair and, though his tenure was limited to only one year, he came up with an alternative to badla in March 1994, which could not be implemented due to the lack of agreement about it between the brokers and SEBI. Nadkarni was succeeded by career bureaucrat D.R. Mehta on 21 February 1995.

The BSE brokers and their colleagues from the other exchanges had not relented in their demand for the re-introduction of badla. The lobbying had continued incessantly, under the argument that market liquidity had suffered in the absence of badla, even though this was not entirely true. At the end of 1992, after badla had been banned, the BSE 30-scrip Sensex closed at 2615.37 but at the end of 1994 on the eve of D.R. Mehta's assuming office, the Sensex was at 3927. This clearly showed that the ban on badla had not deterred true-blue investors from returning to the capital market.

SEBI had already started discussions on introducing futures and options as exchange-traded derivatives instead of badla, which as a forward contract is a bilateral deal and lacks transparency. But a groundswell of opposition was mounted by the market lobby to run down these derivatives. Their arguments included the use of national exceptionalism—that derivatives were unsuited for India, and badla best fit the country's market structures—as an excuse to adopt badla instead of market-traded derivatives such as futures and options.

The new SEBI chairman, D.R. Mehta, appointed a committee under the chairmanship of G.S. Patel, a former chairman of UTI, to review the system of carry-forward transactions. Mehta's choice of chairman for the committee seems to have stemmed from Patel's chairmanship of another key committee on reforming the capital markets in 1985, in which Mehta was a member. Interestingly, in a display of remarkable alacrity, the committee completed its report in a month and recommended the resumption of badla. It is not known what circumstances led to an easing of the regulatory environment, but the speed of reintroduction of badla and the circumstantial evidence do point to influence-peddling. The long chain linking ministers, bureaucrats, Parliamentarians, other politicians, SEBI officials, some G.S. Patel Committee members, stockbrokers and their lobbyists had many weak links where political pressure could be applied successfully. It must also be remembered that going into 1996, when another general election was due, P.V. Narasimha Rao's minority government was extremely vulnerable and subject to all manner of persuasion, from both within and without.

Consequently, badla was reintroduced in January 1996, albeit with some conditions that would help maintain the optics of regulatory continuity. It was even renamed as the Revised Carry Forward System (RCFS), with the difference being that this time there was SEBI insistence on screen-based trading and that brokers had to stump up daily margins, requiring them to deposit a certain percentage of the outstanding trade in cash with the exchange authorities. The percentage would go up every time the broker failed to square up and carried the transaction forward to the next settlement.

Among the conditions imposed by SEBI for re-allowing badla, two stood out: exchanges had to switch to screen-based trading, and transactions could not be carried forward beyond ninety days.

However, the brokers managed to dilute some of the RCFS provisions. They managed to convince SEBI to replace the telescopic margin system—where the money deposited with the exchanges would increase every time the same transaction was carried forward within the prescribed ninety days—with a capital adequacy norm of 3 per cent for individual members and 6 per cent for corporate members, and a flat 10 per cent daily margin.

RCFS was subsequently subjected to scrutiny by another committee and renamed the Modified Carry Forward Scheme (MCFS).

In May 1997, SEBI also introduced a securities borrowing and lending scheme, under which all market participants (barring foreign investors) could borrow and lend securities, but only through an authorized intermediary. Investors with idle securities could lend them to the intermediary—which happened to be the clearing corporation or clearing house—and earn a return on them.

The NSE, which had been quietly watching from the sidelines and had refused to introduce carry-forward products, decided to join in by launching a deferral product called Automated Lending and Borrowing Mechanism. This would allow buyers to carry forward their trades which, when combined with the Stock Lending and Borrowing Scheme, spelt out a return of badla in a new avatar. The BSE, realizing the competitive imperative, also launched a similar product, called the Borrowing and Lending Security Scheme (BLESS).

Things started coming to a head around this time, post-1996. The political imperative to reform the capital markets on one side collided with the traditional political influence of the prominent brokers on the other. The government at the Centre had changed and India's political temperature had started throwing up fractured mandates, necessitating coalition governments, which were subject to the varied pulls and pressures exerted by the coalition members.

Even as the government and SEBI obliged the stock market lobby by reintroducing badla, albeit in mutated forms, pressure was simultaneously building up to bring the Indian capital markets up to international standards, especially from foreign investors. It is also worth considering that despite professing opposing political ideologies, the different governments in New Delhi kept to the reforms path, with varying degrees of intensity.

The impulse to reform the capital markets took the form of setting right the market micro-structure, with the specific objective of ending the long settlement periods. The appetite to reform the markets got a fillip when Ketan Parekh's elaborate pan-India operations tripped up in the east, with his associates unable to pay up and the resulting payments crisis at the Calcutta Stock Exchange setting off a chain reaction across all stock exchanges.

The crisis arose due to the gross misuse of badla through an unofficial system.

One outcome was the launch of rolling settlements. As a result, speculators no longer had the luxury of settling trades a week or two after they had cut the deals. The settlement cycle was cut, first to five days, and then in April 2002 to three days. The finance ministry's Economic Survey of 2000–01 mapped the shift:

> Rolling settlement is an important measure to enhance the efficiency and integrity of the securities market. The shift from the traditional account period settlement marks an important change in the market design and age old practices. In January 1998, SEBI had introduced rolling settlement on a voluntary basis on the stock exchanges for securities, which were eligible for dematerialized trading. However, as there was hardly any response to the voluntary scheme, SEBI introduced compulsory rolling settlement initially for 10 scrips in January 2000 and then increased the number of scrips in a phased manner to 163 by May 2000. The announcement made by the Finance Minister in March 2001 to introduce rolling settlement in 200 scrips, which were then eligible for trading under MCFS or ALBM, or BLESS, gave rolling settlement a further boost. SEBI thereafter announced a list of 251 scrips for compulsory rolling settlement from July 2, 2001, on all exchanges. With effect from December 31, 2001, rolling settlement was extended to the remaining scrips on all exchanges. In December 2001, SEBI announced that from April 1, 2002, the settlement cycle for all securities would be shortened to T+3 basis. With this the Indian market would be complying with the standard for clearing and settlement laid down by the Joint Committee of Clearing and Payment System of the Bank for International Settlements and the International Organisation of Securities Commissions.

SEBI, which was slow in accepting the view that badla or the deferral products which had metamorphosed out of badla over time were flawed financial products, finally saw merit in doing away with badla and its mutants after the CSE payments crisis. SEBI's reluctance to abolish badla completely is reflected in the time it took to allow exchange-traded derivatives. The L.C. Gupta Committee set up in November 1996 finally submitted its report in May 1998, recommending index futures. And SEBI finally gave permission to the NSE and the BSE to allow trading in index derivatives in 2000. SEBI's regulatory oversight of the deferral products, specifically ALBM, came in for sharp criticism from the Joint Parliamentary Committee set up to investigate the Ketan Parekh scam:

> Though SEBI discontinued ALBM and other deferral products w.e.f. 2.7.2001, SEBI did not initiate any investigation of ALBM after the crash. It was only at the instance of JPC that SEBI took up investigation of ALBM and came out with a detailed report after persistent and probing questioning by the JPC. The Committee would expect SEBI to be more alert in the performance of its functions. They would also expect SEBI to provide more checks and balances and exercise better regulations for all financing schemes relating to the stock market in future.

The Ketan Parekh scam forced SEBI to ban badla, including all manner of deferral products. On 21 June 2001, SEBI put out a terse circular, the opening lines of which read: 'All deferral products namely ALBM/BLESS/MCFS/CNS shall cease to be available for all scrips except for transitional measure . . .' This brought the curtains down on one of the most opaque products in the Indian financial system, one that left in its wake multiple scams, distorted markets and bankrupt institutions.

Even in its final moments, badla found some supporters within Parliament. Nitish Sengupta stood up in Parliament on 16 August 2001 to decry the ban on deferral products. The former bureaucrat, elected to the Lok Sabha on a Trinamool Congress ticket, was probably reacting to the payments crisis on the Calcutta Stock Exchange and its ripple effects, including bankruptcies and broker suicides:

> Sir, it is a serious situation caused in the capital market due to arbitrary and highhanded withdrawal of badla trading from the 2nd of July.
>
> Suddenly, like a midnight decree of the great Moghul, on the 2nd of July, SEBI introduced the following changes: ban on deferral products such as ALBM/BLESS; introduction of Options Trading; uniform settlements on all exchanges; rolling settlements in leading scripts; and reduction in bank finance to the securities industry.
>
> As a result, the brokers community has been much maligned, which perhaps has been more sinned against than they have sinned. They have been practically reduced to paupers. The annual market values have shrunk from around Rs.20 crore till about two or three months ago to about less than Rs.5 crore in the post-July period. Many of the Stock Exchanges are facing closure. Many of the broker houses are also facing closure. As a result of this ban, some have committed suicide. I think the remedy has been worse than the disease which the Ministry of Finance has tried to control. They have no care for what is called 'sentiment' which is the biggest factor in the capital market which has been killed. There has been no single public issue in the last one year. Apart from the closure of the primary market, even secondary market has been closed as a result of this. So remedial action should be taken. By this I do not mean that Badla trading should continue for all time to come but its abolition should be a process rather than an event. It should be phased out and along with the new changes, it should be allowed to continue for some time.

But both the government and SEBI had made up their mind this time, despite this heartfelt appeal from a coalition partner.

The new coalition government, styled as the National Democratic Alliance under the leadership of the BJP, with Atal Bihari Vajpayee as prime minister and Yashwant Sinha as finance minister, had taken office in October 1999. The year 2001 was particularly unkind for the alliance: it was greeted with the Ketan Parekh scam in March and the UTI's politically influenced misallocation of funds in June. The revelations from just these two scams were politically devastating, thereby informing the government's resolution that it was time to end the long chain of scams in the capital markets.

In transitioning the Indian capital market into a modern, efficient one, SEBI decided to introduce exchange-traded derivatives. Badla was a forward contract, a bilateral deal between two parties which by its very nature was not transparent. The badla could not be traded, and could potentially distort pricing. The derivatives being discussed were futures and options, standardized products which would be traded on the market between anonymous buyers and sellers at market prices visible to all market participants.

The L.C. Gupta Committee, which examined whether exchange-traded derivatives should be introduced in the Indian markets, strongly endorsed the idea:

> The Committee is strongly of the view that there is urgent need for introducing equity derivatives in India from the viewpoint of market development because the Indian market lacks hedging facility against market risks to which equity holders are exposed. The hedging facility has become necessary for institutional equity holders, such as mutual funds and other investment institutions, which have been accumulating equity portfolios. Futures trading through derivatives may be appropriately phased, starting with stock index futures. Apart from protecting financial institutions, the introduction of stock index futures will enhance the efficiency and liquidity of the

cash market equities through arbitrage transactions. It will also create pressures for reforming the cash market.

The apprehensions and misgivings over introducing derivatives were understandable. In 1995, one of Britain's oldest and storied investment banks, Barings plc, collapsed after a lone trader in Singapore lost $1.4 billion in rogue trades. The bank had to be liquidated and was bought over by the Dutch institution ING for just 1 pound sterling. But that incident was due to a rogue trader who took advantage of the institution's lax internal regulations. It was not derivatives—which allow for speculation, hedging and proper price discovery in the markets—that were at fault.

Another similar incident in 1996 saw a rogue trader bet indiscriminately on copper futures at the London Metals Exchange, without the necessary authorization, eventually causing a $1.8-billion loss to his employer, Japanese conglomerate Sumitomo Corporation.

Derivatives trading in India had to wait for legislative clarity. The Securities Contracts (Regulation) Act had to be amended to recognize derivatives—namely, futures and options—as 'securities' to make them eligible for trading. Once the amendment came through in December 1999, the NSE and the BSE started off with index futures in June 2000, with SEBI subsequently allowing trading in index option contracts in June 2001 and trading in option contracts in individual stocks in July 2001. The NSE offers derivatives on its own indices, such as the Nifty, while the BSE offers derivatives on its own index, the Sensex. So far, so tepid.

The real action in derivatives began after SEBI banned all forms of badla on 21 June 2001, masquerading under whatever moniker. The markets and its operators, distraught with the banning of badla, had to try to do something to get it reinstated. Initially, they tried all modes of protests, which included marching to the SEBI headquarters, striking work or burning effigies of the SEBI chairman in other cities. The incongruity of free-market proponents using protest mechanisms to torpedo modernization or deregulation seemed to have escaped them. They even met the finance minister, Yashwant Sinha, but to no avail.

When they realized that the government was unwavering in its resolve to bury badla for good this time, they changed tactics. They used their political clout to get the derivatives policy tweaked. The regulator's momentous decision in November 2001 to allow exchanges to trade in individual stock futures had the broking community's fingerprints all over the decision.

The decision to introduce individual stock futures so soon in a market's development arc was unusual, and the policy had many detractors. In fact, the L.C. Gupta Committee's 1997 report on the introduction of derivatives trading in India had specifically recommended that individual stock futures not be introduced because the market was not ready for it. But SEBI seems to have rushed to allow individual stock futures in only six months after it banned badla. The haste has raised eyebrows; to many, it seems as if SEBI was caught between banning badla (a decision it could no longer afford to prolong) and offering the traditional brokers a substitute. The decision on individual stock futures seemed doubly odd, given that the L.C. Gupta Committee had found out through a survey that individual stock futures were lowest on the priority list of most market agents.

Writing in the 18 March 2006 edition of the *Economic and Political Weekly*, R.H. Patil, the driving force behind the establishment of the NSE, said:

> The world over, stock futures are not favoured in view of the risks they pose to the investors as also to the markets. Futures in individual stocks are considered to be highly risky primarily because they can be manipulated by unscrupulous speculators.

A group of large speculators can come together and manipulate the futures prices of an individual stock by acting in a concerted fashion. Since a trader in futures has to shell out only margin amounts and not the full price of the value of the contract, leveraging becomes easy. In other words, the amounts required to manipulate futures prices of an individual stock would not be very large if a group of speculators can act in concert to manipulate its market price.

The haste with which SEBI introduced individual stock futures left nobody in doubt that the move was to compensate brokers and provide them with a speculative financial product that could fill the void left behind by badla; stock futures were not quite like badla but had enough characteristics to meet what the speculators required. What further aroused suspicions was the mode of settlement for individual stock futures: cash and not physical settlement.

When an investor buys a stock future, he is committing to take delivery of a particular stock on a future date, at a price fixed today. But on the appointed day, if the price is different from what the futures contract bears, the difference is settled in cash. No shares are delivered. Physical settlement requires the exchange of the exact number of shares contracted as well as the exchange of money. SEBI's initial excuse for not introducing physical settlement was that exchanges did not have the requisite technology, market infrastructure or management capacity to deal with it. The regulator promised to introduce physical settlement as soon as its capacities were enhanced. But, and there are no prizes for guessing this, the regulator continued with a cash settlement for trading in individual stock futures, which soon overtook all other derivatives trading, both in volume and value terms.

The irony is that various expert committees and internal panels, including the L.C. Gupta Committee, had been recommending physical settlement over cash settlement. And while the regulatory wheels turned slowly, the cash settlement process worked better for speculators rather than for genuine hedgers or arbitrageurs.

Post the Gupta Committee, even SEBI's advisory committee on derivatives suggested in 2002 a broad framework for physical settlement. Many other bodies also kept repeating the same suggestion at frequent intervals. It was only in 2018 that SEBI finally relented, seventeen years after the introduction of individual stock futures. What is ironic is that SEBI took such a long time to get its technology, infrastructure and capacity in place. It is also worth noting that the regulator's logic for finally pushing the button on physical settlements was excessive speculation in the futures market. It is also quite likely that SEBI's belated adoption of physical settlements in 2018 could have been prompted by the general elections scheduled for the summer of 2019; another payments crisis or scam arising out of excessive speculation would have been politically unacceptable. It therefore seems that SEBI moved in to head off an impending crisis that was developing in the equity markets, unlike in the past when it would react to a crisis only after the event. In reality, the futures trading platform had become a virtual casino, allowing untrammelled intra-day manipulation of prices through excessive speculation. The market also lent itself to tax-shopping, under which simultaneous sham buy-sell transactions would allow the transfer of profits and losses from one party to another, one showing losses and another showing profits.

A bit of history about the efforts to dampen speculation in the derivatives market might be necessary. After the government led by Atal Bihari Vajpayee allowed the simultaneous introduction of individual stock futures in 2001, which in itself was a departure from global practices, transaction volumes in the derivatives market surged immediately. The value of single stock futures shot up from Rs 2,27,207 crore during calendar 2002 to Rs 14,98,892 crore in 2004, a jump of about 560 per cent in just two years.

A change of government in 2004 witnessed policy attempts to dampen speculative fervour in derivatives trading. In 2004, the United Progressive Alliance government, under Prime Minister Manmohan Singh, introduced a 'securities transaction tax (STT)' in its first budget, presented by former finance minister P. Chidambaram. This levy was a variation on the famous Tobin tax, named after economist and Nobel laureate James Tobin, which in its original form sought to impose a small transaction tax on currency trade to deter speculators; since then, this deterrent levy has been used to curb all manner of speculative trades and has come to be known as 'throwing sand in the wheels' of business or commerce. An STT of 0.01 per cent was made applicable on all futures and options transactions. The STT rate was increased every year, first to 0.0133 per cent in 2005 and then to 0.017 per cent the next year. These rate increases seemed more focused on reining in speculative impulses in the capital markets rather than increasing tax revenue collection.

The STT rate for stock futures stayed untouched for the next seven years, till Finance Minister P. Chidambaram reduced it to 0.01 per cent in 2013. Timing is important here: the next year was a general election and the second term of the UPA had come under severe criticism for corruption and poor governance.

But, in the interim, the STT rate for stock options had witnessed some structural changes. In 2008, when markets worldwide had turned volatile on the eve of the financial crisis in the US, P. Chidambaram imposed a lower levy (0.017 per cent) for buying an option but not exercising it, and a higher rate (0.125 per cent) on the settlement price after exercising the option. He, however, left the taxes for stock futures untouched. Coincidentally, the next year—2009—was a general election in which the UPA returned for a second term.

Stock options are a category of financial derivatives that give an investor the right (but not the compulsion) to buy or sell a stock at an agreed price and date. Investors have to pay a small premium to acquire that right, regardless of whether they eventually exercise the option to buy or sell the stock. And so the STT structure levied a smaller levy on the premium but a higher rate on the total value of the transaction if the investor exercised her right to buy or sell the stock. In essence, this rate structure seemed designed to deter speculators from converting their bets, thereby affecting the cash market and the stock indices on the eve of a general election. This structure was reversed by the late Arun Jaitley when, as finance minister in 2016, he imposed a higher levy of 0.05 per cent on the premium if the option is not exercised. This continued till the budget of 2023, when Finance Minister Nirmala Sitharaman increased the STT rate for both stock futures and stock options by 25 per cent: 0.0125 per cent and 0.0625 per cent, respectively.

The twists and turns in STT, between its introduction in 2004 and the latest rate increase in 2023, reflect its use as an instrument to influence the mood of speculators in the derivatives markets. The government's tweaking of STT rates over time might have, apart from attempting risk containment, also incorporated some elements designed to favour a particular category of speculators. For example, the split taxation structure introduced in 2008 encouraged higher speculation in stock options.

SEBI's actions, on the other hand, were motivated to some degree by the incipient crises developing in the derivatives markets. The total turnover in the equity derivatives market during 2017–18 increased by close to 75 per cent over the turnover recorded in the previous year[11], 2016–17, reflecting the heightened speculative activities in the market. Here is another data point to indicate the rising tide of risks in the equity derivatives market: turnover in the equity derivatives markets during 2017–18 was 20 times that of the cash market, compared with 15.5 times in 2016–17. The trend was visible even earlier, but by 2017–18, it accelerated, raising apprehensions of a payments crisis and a breakdown in market stability.

Derivatives Turnover vs Cash Market Turnover (in Rs lakh crore)

|          | Cash Market | Total Derivatives Segment | Derivatives to Cash |
|----------|-------------|---------------------------|---------------------|
| 2013–14  | 33          | 474                       | 14.37               |
| 2014–15  | 52          | 760                       | 14.61               |
| 2015–16  | 50          | 693                       | 13.86               |
| 2016–17  | 61          | 944                       | 15.47               |
| 2017–18  | 83          | 1650                      | 19.87               |

Source: NSE and BSE

Something else was threatening to blow up into another crisis. Many brokers had been misusing the client–broker contracts under which clients give their brokers a 'power of attorney', effectively a right to deal with their shares to use as margins or to trade in them. Many brokers had misused this trust, using their clients' stocks to speculate on their own account and then defaulting; or, used clients' stock as collateral for obtaining loans from banks and other financial institutions to either speculate in the capital markets or to invest in real estate. This had been going on for a while and, despite a few large collapses, SEBI had refused to make systemic changes. The biggest default was committed by Karvy Stock Broking Ltd, which had borrowed over Rs 2000 crore from various financial institutions, against the collateral of client shares, without taking the consent of their clients.

The accelerated speculative activity in the derivatives market forced SEBI in April 2018 to finally resurrect the L.C. Gupta report, dust off the cobwebs and make physical settlement compulsory for equity derivatives, seventeen years after the original recommendations were made. SEBI then brought into play its other regulatory weapon—margins. It has been a steep learning curve for SEBI in managing its arsenal of margins and using it against the continuing onslaught by speculators. The first lesson came during the first decade of derivatives trading: SEBI's mandate to brokers to provide margins to clearing corporations for client positions was ambiguous and did not specify that brokers had to collect the money from clients; brokers took advantage of this loophole and started paying the margin on behalf of clients, since the financing cost worked out to be lower than the brokerage revenue, leading to excessive leveraging and speculation. As a result, in 2011, SEBI made course corrections by introducing daily reporting of client margins and penalties for shortfalls. SEBI continued tweaking these but reserved its sledgehammer for 2020 when it introduced intra-day peak margin penalties. This sought to close another loophole: brokers would allow clients excessive leveraged trading during the day but close or minimize open positions at the end of the day because all margins were calculated only on end-of-day open positions. SEBI decided to close this loophole from September 2021 by ascertaining the customer's position five times during the day, at random intervals, and charging an intraday peak margin penalty if the client did not have sufficient margin to hold any of the positions.

It is evident from the above examples that once the futures and options genie was let out of the bottle, primarily to provide some succour to badla traders, authorities have been hard put to keep speculative forces from spiralling out of control. It is also clear that the various regulatory measures—whether through taxation or imposition of margins—have neither been adequate nor managed to dampen the speculator lobby's ingenuity. It is also in keeping with the broader template of the financial sector reforms that these regulatory measures were initiated only when excessive speculative activity threatened to either upset market equilibrium or pose an immediate threat to political stability. It is perhaps the enduring legacy of the Indian capital markets that reforms occur only when there is a crisis, when matters reach a point of no return and when not reforming is not only not an option but runs the serious risk of blotting the reforms report card of the government.

# Chapter 5

## Home Trade and Cooperative Banks

Large, gleaming billboards had sprung up all across town, bringing some hope and balm to despairing souls. The city's favourite talismans graced these hoardings put up at important spots in the city, tempting passing commuters to steal a second look at them and draw some anticipation of good times ahead. Cricketing legend Sachin Tendulkar, and Bollywood stars Shah Rukh Khan and Hrithik Roshan, smiled down at the city's teeming millions from their lofty perch, promising people a glowing future with a new Internet-based finance company called Home Trade.

It was 2002 and the world was recovering from two shocks delivered in quick succession. The first was the collapse of the dot-com boom in which hundreds of Internet companies had gone under, leaving behind the debris of broken hopes and disrupted careers. The next came in September 2001, when trained operatives commandeered hijacked aircraft into vital buildings in the US, killing thousands and sending shock waves through the global economy.

India, which had tentatively started engaging with the global economy in 1991, was now fully tethered to it through trade and financial flows. The bearish global sentiment also reached India's shores, specifically Mumbai, where all the key financial markets were located. Even locally, Ketan Mehta's derring-do had forced punitive action from SEBI, which included the banning of badla and other forms of deferral products. The cold wave, which had originally started offshore, froze capital markets and sent shivers across the domestic economy. These billboards were like a spot of sunshine for a city desperately in need of some good news.

But there was a problem. Those luminous, beaming visages staring down from on high had no clue as to what they were representing. Home Trade had spent upwards of Rs 20 crore—a largish sum in those days—plastering the city with these billboards, promising endless good times. Initially, people were mystified—the advertisements were ambiguous about the end product. It later emerged that the company was promoting stock trading through the Internet.

The person behind this elaborate scheme, Sanjay Aggarwal, had made one cardinal error in his calculations: what man proposes, the markets tend to dispose of. The bearish sentiment in the market was barely the right environment for retail investors. Aggarwal, in his mid-thirties at the time, had already spent some time as chief executive of Lloyd's Securities, a brokerage firm launched by the medium-scale Lloyds Group, which had diversified from metals into financial services. Aggarwal's stint with Lloyds Securities had run into heavy weather when SEBI investigations discovered that the firm had been active in price manipulation. But, presciently, Aggarwal managed to dodge the bullet by helping the Lloyds Group promoters sell off a 75 per cent stake in Lloyd's Securities to a Mauritian firm. It was this company that went through various name changes, a reshuffling of owners and eventually emerged as Home Trade with, mysteriously, Sanjay Aggarwal as the main shareholder.

When Aggarwal realized that ordinary retail investors were not yet ready to bite the e-broking bait, he managed a crucial pivot, one that got him lots of free float but also spelt his downfall. He moved to selling government securities, especially to cooperative banks and small pension funds, promising them a yield kick of 2–3 per cent over the coupon. This was a period (1999–2002) when the RBI was working hard to bring system interest rates down, and Aggarwal used this opportunity to breach the thinly manned treasury desks of these institutions. The RBI's push to bring down interest rates had made government bonds attractive, resulting in increased bond trading. Prices of bonds rise when interest rates go down, the two being linked in an inverse relationship.

Most of these organizations that Aggarwal was servicing had no expertise in bond trading and they bought whatever snake oil was on sale. They paid cash upfront to Aggarwal, agreeing to buy government securities in the hope that they could sell them for a profit later whenever the promised price appreciation happened. Except, when the price appreciation did come about, they did not have the securities on hand to take advantage of the capital gains. It was then that the Nagpur District Central Cooperative Bank filed a complaint, saying it had failed to get the securities even after handing over money for them to Aggarwal. One by one, many other cooperative banks came forward with the same complaint. This was when the mask shifted and the grime behind the glitter and glamour of Aggarwal's company became visible.

There was, naturally, a hue and cry. The system had just recovered from the Ketan Parekh scam and this was another example of blatant misuse of the system. Sanjay Aggarwal went on the lam and was subsequently arrested. So was the director of NDCCB, Sunil Kedar. But the money was nowhere to be found, having possibly been diverted to stock market trades and untraceable real estate transactions.

On 13 May 2002, BJP member of Parliament from Mumbai, Kirit Somaiya, raised the issue in the Lok Sabha:

More than Rs. 600 crore have been lost in the Cooperative Bank Scam in Mumbai and rest of Maharashtra for the last few days. Mr. Sanjay Aggarwal of the 'Home Trade' was not arrested by the Maharashtra Government for 14 days. Not only this, Director of the Reserve Bank and the Director of State co-operative Ministry had issued notices to various banks including the District Co-operative Bank and Osmanabad Co-operative Bank that these Boards may be dissolved and then the Board and its officers asked about the rule in this regard . . . 14 separate agencies are conducting enquiry in this regard. These are Reserve Bank of India, NABARD, SEBI, Provident Fund Commissioner, Labour Ministry, Economic Offences of Gujarat Government, Economic Offences of Maharashtra Government, Gujarat Government, Mumbai Stock Exchange, Pune Stock Exchange etc. But no investigation is going on. I urge upon the Government that CBI should be entrusted with the enquiry. The Reserve Bank of India has Technical Expert knowledge and therefore it should co-ordinate the investigation . . . so far the names of 19 banks have come to light but there are hundreds of such co-operative societies in Maharashtra which have made investments in Government securities. No enquiry has so far been conducted to that effect. Today we have come to know that a Public Sector Bank has also deposited its money through the Home Trade. The Provident Fund Commissioner has informed that Rs. 92 crore are lost in the Home Trade Scam.

Replying to all related questions in the Lok Sabha on 17 May 2002, Union Minister of State for Finance Gingee N. Ramachandran made the following statement:

The amounts were paid by the banks to the brokers purportedly for acquiring government securities but no such securities were acquired or delivered. As these securities have not been received in physical or scripless form and the money involved has also not been recovered, the banks face the prospect of loss of the entire amount . . . In view of the manifest fraudulent transactions in violation of its guidelines, RBI has sought supersession of the Board of Directors of Nagpur, Osmanabad and Wardha DCCBs and Sadguru Jangli Maharaj UCB. Amravati Peoples Co-operative UCB, Swarnayug UCB and Raghuvanshi UCB under Section 110A(iii) of the Maharashtra Co-operative Societies Act, 1960. The Board of Directors of all these banks have since been superceded. RBI has also asked the Registrar of Cooperative Societies of Maharashtra to conduct special audit of investment transactions of co-operative banks. Meanwhile, Government of Maharashtra has filed criminal complaints against the brokers/Chairmen of these five banks.

The minister also provided a rough estimate of the money lost by these cooperative banks. Many other complainants would come forward later:

|    | Name of bank | Amount involved (Rs crore) |
|----|--------------|----------------------------|
| 1. | Nagpur DCCB | 153.04 |
| 2. | Wardha DCCB | 25.00 |
| 3. | Osmanabad DCCB | 29.99 |
| 4. | Sadguru JangU Maharaj UCB | 40 |
| 5. | Amravati Peoples Cooperative UCB | 9.50 |
| 6. | Swamayug UCB | 5.79 |
| 7. | Raghuvanshi UCB | 5.40 |
|    | **TOTAL** | **268.72** |

DCCB = District Central Co-operative Bank; UCB = Urban Co-operative Bank

Faced with persistent questions in Parliament, Minister Ramachandran also made the following reply on 17 May 2002:

Reserve Bank of India (RBI) has reported that it has advised all scheduled urban cooperative banks in April, 2002 to cause a special audit of the securities transactions undertaken by them by a Chartered Accountant and to place the report of the special audit before the Audit Committee of the Board, or before the Board of Directors of the bank, in case the bank has not constituted any Audit Committee, together with a certificate to the effect that the bank has strictly adhered to the instructions issued by the RBI for transactions in Government securities. This has been done to ensure that all the extant instructions issued by RBI in this regard have been complied with.

When asked how the RBI proposed to stop future occurrence of such scams, Ramachandran replied:

Based on the findings of the rapid scrutiny of the books of the urban cooperative banks, RBI has taken several steps. These include restricting the role of the broker to bringing the two banks together with the settlement of the transaction being undertaken directly between the banks, calling of explanations from banks which have exceeded the 5% norm for dealing through an individual broker to show cause as to why penal action should not be taken against them, causing a special audit of securities transactions by a Chartered Accountant, requesting the Registrar of Cooperative Societies of some States to cause a special audit of the securities transactions undertaken by the Urban Cooperative Banks (UCBs) and to take appropriate action in this regard, etc.

And so began an RBI exercise to bring in some reforms and, with it, operating discipline in the cooperative banks. Unfortunately, this scam visited India close on the heels of Ketan Parekh's defrauding of Madhavpura Mercantile Cooperative Bank, which had led to a run on the bank in Ahmedabad and imperilled the deposits of millions of customers. The 2002 JPC had estimated that Parekh owed the cooperative bank close to

Rs 890 crore. The Madhavpura scam, perpetrated by Ketan Parekh and his cohort, had also provoked an earlier round of regulatory tightening for cooperative banks.

The cooperative sector in the banking industry has habitually been in the eye of multiple storms, and the RBI's attempts to regulate the sector have been stymied by this sector's mishmash ownership structure, with dual control exercised by the state governments and the RBI. In the case of Madhavpura Mercantile Cooperative Bank, the JPC report on the Ketan Parekh scam observed the following (section in italics provided by author):

> The Committee's investigation has revealed that the activities of some Urban Co-operative Banks (UCBs) were manipulated by virtue of their nexus with broker-entities; *and in the absence of careful regulation,* such broker-entities used large funds provided by UCBs to manipulate the stock market. The acquisition of substantial funds from the Madhavpura Mercantile Cooperative Bank leading to defaults in payment, led to the arrest of Ketan Parekh by the CBI. This significant act led to a run on the bank which, in turn, had a negative impact on the stock market. (Para5.2)

In the aftermath of the scam, the RBI introduced some additional regulatory measures for urban cooperative banks, announcing them in its monetary statement of April 2001. Some of them were the following:

1. UCBs were barred from lending against shares or debentures, etc. They were advised to unwind their existing exposure to the capital markets by a certain date. They were also prohibited from granting advances for the financing of IPOs.
2. UCB's excessive reliance on the call money market was curtailed, with borrowings on any day limited to a maximum

of 2 per cent of their aggregate deposits as at the end of previous financial year.

3. UCBs were prohibited from parking their funds with other UCBs in term deposits; the interlocking of UCB deposits was found to pose a systemic risk.

4. UCBs were directed to hold a larger portion of their SLR investments in government securities.

The JPC took note of these changes and observed wryly: 'The Committee commend these constructive steps and only regret that they were not taken earlier. The Committee recommend that the RBI should constantly review the feasibility of implementing these guidelines.'

But barely had the central bank recovered from the Madhavpura mishap when the Home Trade scam emerged, revealing that unscrupulous brokers had been siphoning out cash from cooperative banks on the pretext of false promises, with or without the active connivance of the bank executives.

In its annual report for 2001–02, the RBI took note of the incident without, in its usual detached style, naming any of the perpetrators or victims:

Following the detection in November 2001 by the Reserve Bank of unusually high transactions between broker entities and some banks in the co-operative sector in SGL transactions, a scrutiny of co-operative banks as also inspection by NABARD brought out gross violations of the Reserve Bank's guidelines as well as manifestly fraudulent transactions in a few cases. The broad nature of the violations relating to investment transactions was the use of broker in the settlement process, disproportionate transactions through one or few brokers, undertaking large value transactions in the physical mode, delivery of securities without funds being received, issue of power of attorney to brokerage firm for mobilisation of funds and for deployment of resources and absence of the management oversight, internal controls and audit. UCBs were advised to strictly follow the extant guidelines relating to investment portfolio, empanelment of brokers and other matters relating to investment transactions. Scheduled UCBs were advised to conduct a special audit of the securities transactions by a Chartered Accountant and to place a report before the Board.

Stung by the Home Trade scandal, the RBI issued a circular on 7 July 2002 on securities investments by cooperative banks— 'In the light of recent fraudulent transactions in the guise of Government securities transactions in physical format by a few co-operative banks with the help of some broker entities . . . '— and leading the list of dos and don'ts was an exhortation to the banks to abjure trading in physical securities: 'All purchase/sale transactions in Government securities by the primary (urban) co-operative banks should necessarily be through SGL account (with RBI) or constituent SGL account (with a scheduled commercial bank/State Co-operative Bank/Primary Dealer/Stock Holding Corporation of India) or in a dematerialized account with depositories (NSDL/CDSL/NSCCL), with immediate effect.'

But the RBI's intervention went only this far and no further. Even later interventions by the central bank had little impact. In its annual report for 2021–22, the central bank listed the number of times RBI-regulated entities in the financial sector were penalized. Out of the total of 189 penalties levied on regulated entities during 2021–22, cooperative banks accounted for 145, or close to 77 per cent, indicating that they continued to remain the centrepiece of financial-sector scams, defying all attempts to regulate or discipline them. There is a reason why cooperative banks remain unaffected by the RBI's remit or regulatory gaze. Cooperative banks have a strange, hybrid structure, with multiple masters breeding multiple regulatory pathways, allowing them the comfort of following rules selectively.

Replying to another question in the Lok Sabha on 17 May 2002, Minister Ramachandran had conceded:

> Presently, the co-operative banks, which are registered as co-operative societies under the respective State Cooperative Acts, are under the dual control of Reserve Bank of India (RBI) and the respective State Governments (or Central Government in case of Multi-State urban cooperative banks). This causes constant irritants and ambiguity in regulation and supervision of these banks. This issue has been examined in detail by various committees in consultation with State Governments and it is felt that to remove this duality of control, banking functions should be fully brought under RBI. Effort is being made to evolve a consensus in this regard in consultation with the State Governments.

Multiple committees have examined this tangle, and some of the influential ones have unequivocally suggested that the RBI should be the regulator of last resort. State and Central governments, however, have been reluctant to cede control over cooperative banks, given the political patronage that can be extracted from ownership of these institutions. What further queers the pitch for them is the appointment of key political personnel to the boards and key management positions of these cooperative banks.

It must be mentioned here that the NDCCB chairman, Sunil Kedar, who was found guilty of having handed over Rs 100 crore to Sanjay Aggarwal of Home Trade without receiving government bonds in return, is a member of the Congress party and was appointed minister for animal husbandry, dairy development, sports and youth welfare in the Maha Vikas Aghadi coalition government in Maharashtra. His prosecution in the Home Trade case continues to drag on in the courts. A division bench of the Bombay High Court observed in 2019:[1]

It stands almost at the same stage at which it stood in 2002. Definitely, the justice administration system owes an explanation to the society for such inordinate delay, especially when public money to the tune of Rs 150 crore and interests of unsuspecting victims, largely poor agriculturists and depositors are at stake.

But this was not an isolated case or limited to only one side of the political divide. In August 2022, the BJP appointed Pravin Darekar as chairman of the Mumbai District Central Cooperative Bank after the party regained power in Maharashtra in coalition with a breakaway faction of the Shiv Sena. Darekar had been forced to resign as director of the same cooperative bank earlier, in January 2022, after it emerged that he had sought election to the board of the bank as a labour representative even though he had declared himself a businessmen in his affidavit for the legislative council elections. But as soon as the BJP-Sena government was established in Maharashtra in mid-2022, Darekar was re-appointed as chairman of the board of the bank.

The cooperative sector has a convoluted structure. It was designed primarily to deliver credit to rural areas, especially the agricultural sector, at a time when the formal banking network was still growing. The rural cooperative credit institutions are of two categories: short-term credit cooperatives and long-term institutions. The short-term cooperative credit structure operates through a three-tier system—the primary agricultural credit societies (PACS) at the village level, the district central cooperative banks (DCCBs) at the district level, and the state cooperative banks (StCBs) at the state level. The long-term rural cooperative credit institutions are the State Cooperative Agriculture and Rural Development Banks (SCARDB) and the affiliated Primary Cooperative Agriculture and Rural Development Banks (PCARDB). There are cooperative credit institutions in the urban areas too, called urban cooperative banks (UCBs), to service the credit needs of the financially excluded in urban and semi-urban areas. Their operations can be limited to a single state when they are registered under the State Cooperative Societies Act; and they can operate across multiple states when they are registered under the Multi State Cooperative Societies Act, 2002.

In terms of the regulatory structure, the RBI does not regulate PACs as they are not covered by the Banking Regulation Act and are also not in the category of long-term rural cooperative institutions. This leaves the central bank responsible for the supervision and regulation of DCCBs, StCBs and UCBs. Currently, the RBI directly oversees the regulation of urban cooperative banks but regulates the rest—RCBs, StCBs and DCCBs—indirectly through the government-owned National Bank for Agriculture and Rural Development (NABARD).

The government's extension of the RBI's regulatory gaze over the cooperative banks has been glacial, with each additional legislative enabler taking time to come into force, often after a large scam. The Banking Regulation Act of 1949—to consolidate and amend laws related to banking—was first extended to cooperative banks in 1966 through an amendment. This particular amendment was extended to StCBs and DCCBs only in April 2021.

This extension was also provoked by an incident, the collapse of another UCB in Mumbai—Punjab and Maharashtra Cooperative Bank—as a consequence of indiscriminate lending, bordering on corruption. The multi-state UCB was founded in 1984 and boasted of 137 branches across seven states. As per the investigation report, the bank management colluded with Mumbai-based real estate developers HDIL Ltd and extended loans close to Rs 6500 crore to the company, which amounted to over 70 per cent of the bank's total loan book. The problems began when the borrower stopped servicing the loan, forcing the RBI to step in and stop the bank from either accepting fresh deposits or advancing new loans. The UCB had to be forcibly merged with Unity Small Finance Bank.

On the amendment, NABARD's annual report for 2021–22 noted:

> The amendments aim to improve the management and regulation of cooperative banks, thus protecting the interests of the depositors by increasing professionalism, enabling access to capital, improving governance, and ensuring sound banking. It also enables the RBI to formulate a scheme to achieve this aim. The provisions of the amended Act have overriding effect over other laws.

It is also worth noting that the amendment to the Banking Regulation Act was first brought in through an ordinance in July 2020, in the midst of the first wave of the coronavirus pandemic. When the Lok Sabha reconvened, the Bill was put up for discussion in September 2020. While the amendment sailed through both the lower and upper houses, many Opposition members expressed apprehensions about it, suspecting that it was the Centre's way of wresting control over cooperative institutions from the states. They discerned in this move a larger design of weakening India's federal structure and a greater centralization of power. Member of Parliament from the Congress Manish Tiwari was even explicit about this in his intervention: 'State Governments are more than competent to discharge their functions and in a federal polity, this Ordinance, and the Bill which seeks to replace it, is a frontal assault on the federal structure of the Constitution and this will have long-term implications on the democratic polity of India.'

These apprehensions were further inflamed in 2021, when a ministry of cooperation was created through a gazette notification, transferring all cooperation and cooperative businesses to it from the Ministry of Agriculture.

The RBI is trying to further improve the regulatory structure for cooperative banks. It has facilitated the establishment of a non-banking finance company, called National Cooperative Financial and Development Company Limited, which will be capitalized by the National Federation of Urban Cooperative Banks and Credit Societies Limited and certain UCBs. The new umbrella organization has been in the works since 2006 and it is likely to get off the ground sometime soon. It is expected to provide some common services—such as information technology-related services—that many small UCBs may not be able to afford. Over time, the plan is to make the umbrella organization into some kind of a self-regulatory body. And yet, some misgivings refuse to go away, such as the suspicion as to whether a self-regulatory organization will have persuasive powers over the many different political parties and state governments that have eluded the RBI so far.

The long arc of crafting regulation for cooperative banks is still a work in progress, bending only when a scandal breaks out or a scam surfaces. This is in keeping with the broader leitmotif of reforms in the financial sector, which is invoked only upon provocation. Consequently, the desire to reform is quickly forgotten, somewhat similar to the blinding speed at which the Shah Rukh Khan, Sachin Tendulkar and Hrithik Roshan billboards were pulled down all across Mumbai city.

# Chapter 6

## Controlling NBFCs

During the final months of 1996 and the beginning of 1997, several staff members of an up-and-coming finance company were severely pressured to subscribe to the company's fixed deposits and non-convertible debentures. This was an official edict, and it applied equally to the seniors and the trainees, and to decline was not an option, even if the staff member's salary did not leave much disposable or investible income for such an investment. There were other signs of trouble. Senior members of the research team were increasingly being asked to sign off and endorse research reports on specific companies that they were seeing for the first time, presumably authored by external researchers, without being afforded time for a closer look at the reports or an opportunity to dissent.

As anybody familiar with the death throes of an organization will testify, these were the visible signs of the management's last-ditch but futile efforts to salvage the company. Things invariably collapsed soon thereafter, leaving an army of investors bereft of their savings and without any access to them. Many even lost their entire life savings. This collapse was to become a turning point in the history of finance companies—or non-banking finance companies (NBFCs), as they're more familiarly known in the financial literature.

The public outcry and the systemic impact of the company's bankruptcy was another crisis that prompted the RBI to recognize that it needed a regulatory framework for NBFCs, somewhat similar to the one it had for the banking sector. RBI regulations for NBFCs until that point had been focused solely on their deposit-taking activity and nothing else. Even that was the outcome of an earlier crisis, which we will deal with later in this chapter.

The company on the verge of collapse was CRB Capital Markets. It had started life as a nondescript company with an amorphous identity and business plan. The man behind it was C.R. Bhansali, a Kolkata-based chartered accountant and jute trader who moved to Mumbai (then Bombay) in the early 1990s in search of money and fame and decided to try his deft hand at finance. In the interim, he had managed to befriend many political leaders and religious gurus, which lent him some modicum of credibility while raising money from the public.

He spawned in record time a sprawling web of companies and subsidiaries, all raising money from the market in various forms. For example, CRB Capital had raised close to Rs 180 crore from the public by January 1995. Another company, CRB Corporation, raised Rs 84 crore through three public issues in a short span of thirty months; CRB Share Custodial raised close to Rs 100 crore in 1985; CRB Mutual Fund was launched in August 1994, and it raised close to Rs 230 crore from investors. All this was over and above the debenture sales and fixed deposit issues that totalled about Rs 200 crore. Market apocrypha claims Bhansali raised anywhere between Rs 900 crore and Rs 1000 crore between 1992 and 1995.

The money was used for a variety of nefarious purposes. Some of it was routed through various shell companies to pump up CRB Capital's share prices, the appreciated share value providing another springboard for a renewed bout of money-raising. Multiple bets were initiated in the equity and real estate markets. Then, all it took was the 1995 bearish phase in both markets to catch Bhansali on the wrong foot. Overextended, but brimming with ambition, Bhansali continued to use sleight of hand to borrow money from a variety of sources, which included overdrawing from a current account with SBI to try and pay off his debts and recoup his market mojo. Unfortunately, the desires of men and the moods of the market are often not aligned, and Bhansali was caught short. In April 1997, deluged with complaints from multiple institutions and investors, the RBI finally barred CRB from raising deposits or disposing of his assets. This order sent a surge of panic among retail investors. Many of them even stationed themselves outside the RBI headquarters in central Mumbai to see if their presence could persuade the central bank to coax Bhansali into returning their deposits.

Like always, public outrage this time too caught the attention of numerous politicians. Answering questions about the CRB scam in Parliament in July 1997, then Minister of State for Finance, Satpal Maharaj, told legislators:

> The main activities of CRB Capital Markets Ltd. (CRBCML) were hire purchase, leasing finance and merchant banking. A complaint was received in December, 1996 by Reserve Bank of India (RBI) from Tourism Finance Corporation of India Ltd. regarding default of repayment of deposits by CRB Capital Markets Ltd. Global Trust Bank Ltd. has also reported to RBI in March, 1997 about development of Letter of Credit opened by a group Company. Further, CRBCML fraudulently overdrew its accounts with the State Bank of India, Mumbai Main Branch (MMB) for payment of interest warrants, deposit refunds and brokerage warrants by an amount of over Rs. 58 crores. Keeping in view the findings of the Inspection carried out by RBI between November, 1996 to January, 1997 and the subsequent developments, especially relating to the SBI, the RBI issued prohibitory orders in April, 1997 under section

45MB(1) & (2) directing the company not to accept any
further deposits and not to alienate any assets without prior
permission of RBI. RBI filed a winding up petition in the Delhi
High Court under section 45 MC of the RBI Act on 21.5.1997.
A provisional Liquidator has been appointed by Delhi High
Court. The Liquidator has initiated action to crystallize the
assets and liabilities of the company.

What left everybody astounded were the subsequent revelations
about CRB and Bhansali's modus operandi. But what really took
the cake was the information that the RBI had granted CRB Capital
Markets a letter of intent for promoting a private bank which, if
Bhansali had not overplayed his hand, might have been converted
into a licence at a subsequent stage. There were no explanations or
justifications for how CRB was granted such a letter of intent, but
to many, it seemed to indicate that Bhansali had used his political
contacts to wangle it, though the episode did not reflect well on the
RBI or its capacity for due diligence. Worse, it confirmed long-held
suspicions about the many unequal planes in the RBI-government
relationship space. Also, the regulatory slip-up or oversight did
not end with the RBI; even SEBI came in for its share of flak for
having allowed CRB to launch a mutual fund, raise money from
the public and then invest those funds in various CRB companies.
Ironically, the CRB episode also showed up the yawning rift between
regulators. The collapse of CRB led to an unexpected blame game
between the RBI and SEBI, with the RBI hinting darkly that its
decision to grant the banking letter of intent was predicated on
SEBI allowing CRB to launch a mutual fund. In the final analysis, it
might be fair to treat the episode as a growing-up moment for both
regulators as they adjusted to a deregulated market with completely
new dynamics and emerging con artists.

As all the preceding chapters have shown, there is no better
impetus for change (and opportunity to salvage one's reputation)

than a good crisis. The CRB blowout provided the RBI with just the leverage it needed to introduce wholesale changes in the regulatory structure for NBFCs.

The thing with NBFCs is that they are in many ways like a bank: they raise money from the public and then lend it to various economic agents—industry, retail, agriculture, services. Given their smaller size and nimbler disposition, they often provide the last-mile connection between credit suppliers and those with credit demand. The only features that distinguish them from a bank is that they cannot issue chequebooks to their depositors, and the deposits they accept from the public are not insured. In addition, NBFCs cannot accept demand deposits like banks—better known as savings accounts or current accounts, which depositors can withdraw at will, at any time—but offer only deposit schemes of fixed maturity periods.

The first sliver of RBI regulation for NBFCs came in 1964, springing up even at that time from a crisis. There were concerns about the growing chasm between the currency in circulation and how only a small fraction of that ended up as bank deposits, prompting then finance minister T.T. Krishnamachari to mention in Parliament the menace of unaccounted money circulating in the economy, hinting that one of the conduits for that could be the deposit schemes of finance companies which were, in all likelihood, funnelling these funds into various speculative ventures.

Moving the Bill to amend the RBI Act in Parliament on 16 December 1963, Minister of Planning B.R. Bhagat told Parliament:

> The objectives of the Bill can be divided into three broad categories. Firstly, the deposits which are now received and handled outside the banking system, should be controlled, not only in the interests of the depositors themselves, but also in the general and wider public interest. We also intend that the activities of loan, investment and hire-purchase companies or

firms, or other financial institutions, which grant loans and
advances for a variety of purposes, or purchase securities or
shares, and thereby influence or affect the money and capital
markets, should be controlled by the central bank of the
country, so far as these activities are concerned . . . It is not
appropriate, for example, that we should allow institutions,
which are not themselves banks and which are not, therefore,
bound by the inter-bank agreements regarding deposit and
lending rates, to compete with one another and also with the
banks for deposits, by pushing up interest rates, or in some
odd cases by resorting even to unfair practices, which may
be harmful to the interests of the depositors concerned . . .
Among non-banking institutions, financial corporations and
loan and investment companies or firms are obviously in a
special category. The terms on which advances are granted by
them, their investment policies and their transactions in the
securities market generally are of direct interest and concern
to the Reserve Bank. But unfortunately, and very largely as a
result of historical accidents, the Reserve Bank is not able to
exercise any control over these transactions or operations.

This led to the introduction of a completely new chapter
in the RBI Act, Chapter IIIB, titled 'Provisions Related to
Non-Banking Institutions Receiving Deposits and Financial
Institutions'. The issue of NBFCs offering higher interest rates
than commercial banks on deposits and intensifying their deposit-
collection efforts, despite NBFC deposits being an insignificant
fraction of bank deposits, would exercise policymakers and
became the central theme of an RBI committee in 1969, which in
its 1972 report advocated tighter regulation for deposit-accepting
NBFCs. The concern was that while NBFCs' reliance on public
deposits was growing, their liquidity in relation to the deposits
accepted was declining. This set off fresh concerns about
whether NBFCs would be able to repay depositors in the event

of a crisis. Tighter controls in the form of empowering the RBI to levy penalties were introduced through an amendment to the RBI Act, introducing a completely new chapter (Chapter V). The regulatory space for NBFCs would witness ongoing tinkering. For example, in 1974 the RBI Act was again amended by introducing Chapter IIIC, which prohibited unincorporated bodies from soliciting deposits from the public. But all these changes still left the RBI with constricted powers, limited mostly to NBFCs' deposit-taking activity.

In 1991, the Narasimham-I Committee (henceforth Narasimham-I) had examined the role of NBFCs in the financial system and was firmly convinced that these financial entities needed to be brought under the central bank's regulatory framework. The committee felt that NBFCs were an essential cog in the financial system and that they should be provided support for growth with a concomitant buttressing of the regulatory and supervisory framework.

Narasimham-I was essentially echoing what many financial-sector academics and professionals had been saying for a long time. NBFCs were, in almost all respects, like banks. But they had been spared the regulatory rigours that had been imposed on banks—mandatory reserves, capital adequacy norms, provisioning requirements, and priority sector credit, among others. This skewed the competitive field and was seen as handicapping the banks while opening up the Indian financial sector to competition.

Subsequently, spurred by the Narasimham-I recommendations, the RBI appointed a committee in 1992 under the chairmanship of A.C. Shah, then chairman and managing director of Bank of Baroda, to suggest regulatory measures for the NBFC sector. There were exigent reasons for the policymakers to start taking a fresh look at the NBFC sector. The number of NBFCs had jumped from 7063 in 1981 to 24,009 by 1990, a rise of about 240 per cent in less than ten years. Deposits with NBFCs had jumped almost ten-fold during this period: from Rs 1475.7 crore to Rs 14,775.8 crore.

The next jolt from NBFCs to the regulatory regime came during 1990–92, when the securities scam was being perpetrated by various market intermediaries. The JPC appointed to look into the 1992 scam focused on the activities of the bank-sponsored NBFCs, most of which were in the public sector. These public-sector NBFCs—SBI Capital Markets, Canbank Financial Services Ltd, Andhra Bank Financial Services Ltd, and Allbank Finance Ltd, among others—were all complicit in the execution and perpetuation of the securities scam. In addition, many of these NBFCs had attracted large deposit funds but, unlike their parent banks, did not have to maintain either the mandatory reserves (CRR, SLR) or even comply with the priority-sector lending norms for these deposits. This invested the subsidiaries with some hubris, a sort of mistaken belief that they were exempt from all regulations, emboldening them to push the envelope.

The JPC also expressed astonishment that the RBI had completely overlooked these subsidiaries when conducting inspections at the parent banks. In short, the JPC felt the NBFCs had enjoyed a free run during the 1980s till 1992, dodging regulation, bending the rules and playing fast and loose with other people's money. The JPC was also forced to observe that two separate departments within the RBI were entrusted with exercising supervision over banks and NBFCs—the Department of Banking Operations and Development, and the Department of Finance Companies, respectively—but there was a lack of clarity and coordination over who would supervise the NBFC subsidiaries of public-sector commercial banks. 'This resulted in loss of control, absence of monitoring of the activities of these subsidiaries and insufficient adherence to such regulations as were meant to inculcate prudence in monetary activities.'

The JPC felt the securities scam had conveyed the urgency for amending the RBI Act to increase the central bank's regulatory jurisdiction over NBFCs:

> The Committee conclude that some non-banking financial companies played a dubious role in the scam. In this connection they note that the powers of the Reserve Bank of India to supervise and monitor the working of nonbanking financial companies are derived from chapter IIIB of the Reserve Bank of India Act. However, the control exercised by RBI in terms of the said provisions is not adequate being confined only to deposit taking activities. It is astonishing that no authority, either in the Government of India or in the Reserve Bank of India, appears to have taken stock of the possible role of non-banking financial companies in securities and banking transactions nor of the limitations in the Reserve Bank of India Act to deal with such contingencies. Over a period of several years, an entirely new sector of financial activity was allowed to grow and flourish without giving any thought to the deleterious consequences of the activities of this new sector. In the light of the role of the NBFCs in the current scam the Committee are of the considered view that there is an imperative need to ensure that the financial companies follow prudent practices for inculcating healthy financial discipline and, therefore, their overall functioning, particularly the deployment of funds has to be brought within the purview of some guidelines. The Committee, therefore, recommend that Government should examine whether the provisions in Chapter IIIB of the Reserve Bank of India Act are sufficiently wide to cover the necessary regulation. If not, the question of reinforcing the existing legislation or to enact a separate legislation for the non-banking financial companies be examined so as to ensure proper functioning of NBFCs and also to protect the interest of the depositors.

The problem of dual supervision was not limited to the RBI's internal contradictions but existed on another plane as well. While the RBI had some regulatory responsibilities, especially related to the acceptance of deposits, the Department of Company Affairs (DCA) also had some responsibilities charted out for it, since it was the body charged with administering all entities registered under the Companies Act, which included most NBFCs (the exceptions were the NBFCs or financial institutions created under special Acts of Parliament).

The DCA had an interesting backstory. Its life as a department saw it being shuffled around various ministries— those of law, finance and commerce. It was finally converted into a full-fledged ministry in 2004 and is now called the Ministry of Corporate Affairs.

The JPC, which submitted its report in December 1993, may have had the benefit of perusing the A.C. Shah Committee report, which had been released in September 1992. Change, which had so far been glacial, now seemed possible. The consequences of the scam, the unavoidable need to do something remedial (or the pressing need to be *seen* as doing something), and fortified with inputs from the A.C. Shah and JPC reports, armed the RBI with the overwhelming impetus to finally begin tightening its grip on the NBFC sector. This book's central protagonist—the financial sector crisis—had again provided the tipping point.

In April 1993, the RBI made it mandatory for all NBFCs with net-owned funds (NOF, sum of paid-up capital and free reserves) of Rs 50 lakh and above to register with the central bank. Then, in June 1994, some more prudential norms were introduced for all registered NBFCs. Deposits accepted by NBFCs had to be for a minimum tenure of twelve months and a maximum of eighty-four. Some NBFC categories had been offering ten-year deposit schemes, and those schemes now had to be pared down to seven years. Liquidity norms were also set down: hire-purchase finance and equipment-leasing companies were required to maintain liquid assets at 10 per cent of deposits, while loan and investment companies were required to maintain liquid assets at 5 per cent of deposits, of which half had to mandatorily be invested in government bonds.

In addition, registered NBFCs with NOF of Rs 50 lakh and above were required to achieve a minimum capital adequacy ratio of 6 per cent by March 1995, and 8 per cent by March 1996. NBFCs were also advised to get themselves rated by a credit rating agency.

This was also a time when the RBI was seeking to introduce some regulatory sameness to the unregulated sprawl of multiple NBFC categories: residuary non-banking finance companies (RNBCs, residuary because they did not fit into any of the other existing categories), chit funds, blade companies, *nidhis*, and so on.

Of particular interest was the RBI's progressive tightening of regulations for RNBCs, some of which were challenged all the way to the Supreme Court but eventually went in the RBI's favour. In the end, only two RNBCs mattered—Peerless in Calcutta and Sahara in Lucknow. Over time, their ability to raise deposits has been diminishing, largely due to the RBI's investment norms, which have got more stringent every time the RNBCs decided to stray outside the framework of rules. One example is the misuse of the RBI's liberal investment policy, which gave RNBCs the discretion to invest 20 per cent of their deposits in any project of their choice, with the balance 80 per cent mandatorily invested in government securities and other 'safe' investment avenues. The RBI's logic was that the higher returns on the 20 per cent would make up for the low returns on government bonds, giving depositors some competitive returns. However, the RNBCs invested this 20 per cent in airlines, hotels, television channels, retail trade and other similar vanity projects which did not yield the desired returns for depositors.

Ironically, in the absence of the required statutory or legal powers for the RBI over NBFCs, these norms became more like guidelines and were not made mandatory.

The RBI decided to implement the Shah Committee recommendations in 1994 by instituting prudential norms for NBFCs on asset classification, provisioning, income recognition and capital-adequacy requirements. Initially, the RBI was a bit wary of going ahead with the regulatory changes without any legislative amendment to the RBI Act—specifically to the provisions of Chapter III-B of the Act—fearing that the norms could face some legal challenges. The official *RBI History* mentions that there was a detailed exchange of views with the finance ministry officials to impress upon the administration how the introduction of these prudential measures would improve transparency in NBFC operations which, as various committees and the JPC had found, were shrouded in non-standard and non-uniform disclosures. A draft legislation was also prepared. The discussions dragged on interminably, with an Ordinance finally getting promulgated in January 1997, three years after the start of discussions. The Ordinance was replaced by an amended RBI Act in March 1997.

While the exchange of views between RBI and finance ministry officials is not available to the public, the prolonged discussion should perhaps be seen through the lens of the prevalent bureaucratic ethos which resented any intrusion into the DCA's jurisdiction. The notion of turf was strongly embedded in the iron framework.

The amended Act began with a compromise. The RBI wanted to maintain the earlier entry barrier of Rs 50 lakh NOF, and even the Ordinance stipulated that. But between the promulgation of the Ordinance and the new amended Act coming into force, this entry barrier was lowered to Rs 25 lakh. The Act also included provisions for mandatory registration for new NBFCs, compulsory maintenance by all NBFCs of liquid assets (preferably government bonds) ranging from 5 per cent to 25 per cent of deposits, and creation of reserves by them by transfer of at least 20 per cent of the profits every year. It gave the RBI authority to issue directions on prudential norms and capital adequacy. It even gave the RBI the powers to issue prohibitory orders and file winding-up petitions for non-compliance with its directions or the provisions of the Act. The amended Act gave the RBI the muscle that it had so far lacked.

Until this point, the RBI's directions to the NBFC sector were in the nature of guidelines, undergirded by the moral authority of the financial sector regulator but lacking legislative or prosecutorial teeth. The directions tended to be relatively tame, compared with the regulatory framework for commercial banks. For example, while the RBI could shut down a private bank and replace its board of directors overnight, its hands were tied when it came to disciplining errant NBFCs.

CRB and 1997 changed much of that. The funny thing is that some of the changes could have been introduced between the A.C. Shah report of September 1992 and the CRB denouement of 1997, but the desired regulatory changes required an amendment to the RBI Act. And systemic inertia seemed to prefer the status quo over rapid change. Till, of course, there was a crisis.

Nothing invigorates like a good crisis, especially when there is public money involved. A policymaker's worst nightmare is when stories of defrauded middle-class families who lose their savings to institutions under the regulator's gimlet gaze start dominating the news. In March 1997, Chapters IIIB, IIIC and V of the RBI Act were all amended. Starting in April 1997, and then all through the year going on to 1998, the RBI issued a series of circulars relating to prudential norms, guidelines for NBFC auditors and making credit rating mandatory for NBFCs wanting to raise deposits from the public, among other regulations.

In January 1997, NBFCs were classified into three categories to facilitate regulation:

i.  Those accepting public deposits
ii. Those not accepting public deposits but engaging in financial business
iii. Core investment companies which held at least 90 per cent of their assets as investments in shares of other companies in the same group

The stringency of the regulations was calibrated based on the extent of public money involved: the whole range of regulations was applicable if the NBFC was accepting deposits, and some regulatory leniency was afforded in the case of NBFCs not accepting deposits. More importantly, the minimum NOF for new NBFCs seeking registration with the RBI after April 1999 was raised to Rs 2 crore.

One of the peculiarities of the NBFC sector that remained untouched and unaffected by the waves of crises was the denial of insurance to depositors, unlike in the case of the banking sector. Even the Narasimham-II Committee (henceforth Narasimham-II) advised against providing any insurance for deposits with NBFCs. The committee's logic was that extending the insurance facility would blur the distinction between bank deposits (which are more closely regulated) and NBFC deposits in terms of the safety mechanisms in the respective institutions. The committee was worried that the provision of deposit insurance would create a serious moral-hazard problem for NBFCs, which could even encourage adverse portfolio selection and a build-up of risk. Assurances that depositors would get their money back, even when an NBFC is on the verge of going bust, would embolden many of them to make risky credit choices and introduce complacency into board-level governance (and, perhaps, regulatory supervision).

Interestingly, despite these new powers being vested with the RBI, the government still wanted to retain some of its earlier powers over NBFCs. The amended RBI Act of 1997 contained a funny provision. The RBI could act against any NBFC which did not comply with the Act's provisions; it could lodge a criminal complaint against an NBFC for non-compliance, cancel its registration certificate and, in extreme cases, even order the winding-up of the company. But, strangely, it could not order the NBFC to repay depositors their money, because that power was reserved for the government's Company Law Board (which was dissolved in 2016 after the formation of the National Company Law Tribunal). Among all the changes that were forged through the amendment, it is difficult to overlook the embedded rent-seeking opportunity in the choice of power that the government chose to arrogate to itself—forcing an NBFC to repay depositors.

This set the ground for a series of interactions between the RBI and NBFC representatives. The NBFCs lobbied hard to get the credit rating provision diluted or removed. Eventually, in December 1998, the RBI relented, withdrawing its earlier norms of compulsory credit rating for NBFCs accepting public deposits of Rs 10 crore or up to 1.5 times their NOF, whichever was lower. But the RBI left one small proviso in: the relaxation would apply to companies which had a capital adequacy ratio of 15 per cent or higher. In later years, the RBI would perform another climb-down by reducing this threshold.

The battle for power and supremacy among the authorities continued in different forms, especially between the central bank and the political class.

One particular letter of 15 September 1999—forming part of the appendices of Volume V of *RBI History*—written by former RBI deputy governor S.P. Talwar to E.A.S. Sharma, former

Secretary at the Department of Economic Affairs in the finance ministry, makes for interesting reading. Talwar writes:

> There are a number of other deposit taking entities which are not governed under the extensive regulatory framework of RBI. While deposit acceptance activities of nidhis are only within the jurisdiction of RBI, their operational and other activities are within the purview of Department of Company Affairs (DCA). DCA has not prescribed comprehensive prudential norms to the Nidhi companies and they are also not reported to have put in place a mechanism to ensure compliance with various norms. Likewise, chit fund companies are functionally regulated under the provisions of the Chit Funds Act, 1992, by the State Governments. RBI directions permit these companies to accept public deposits to the extent of 25 per cent of their NOF to meet their short-term funding requirements. Further, non-banking non-finance companies, like manufacturing, trading companies etc. although coming within the jurisdiction of DCA, are not subject to any prudential norms although they are accepting public deposits.

The subject matter of the letter was: 'Need for extension of prudential requirements to all non-banks'.

Nidhis are closed-loop companies based on the principle of mutual benefit and accepting deposits from and lending money to only its members. Most of the nidhi companies are based in southern India, with Tamil Nadu reportedly hosting almost 80 per cent of the nidhis in the country. The rules require a nidhi company to be a public company with a minimum equity capital of Rs 0.05 crore. Within a year of incorporation, the nidhi must have at least 100 members and a minimum NOF of Rs 0.10 crore. It is allowed to accept deposits of up to twenty times its NOF. Nidhis, as mentioned in Talwar's letter, were regulated by the DCA, which has now morphed into the MCA. In April 2022, the MCA, through a gazette notification, changed the eligibility criteria for nidhis to a minimum NOF of Rs 0.20 crore and a minimum of 200 members.

Chit funds are also non-banking organizations but have a completely different business model. A chit fund is basically an arrangement between a group of people who contribute a predetermined sum of money at predetermined intervals into a common pool. Chit funds are unique because the money is to be contributed to the pool for as many months as there are members. So, for example, if there are ten members in the chit fund, they will need to contribute the predetermined sum each month for ten months. The payout terms are also predetermined.

Both nidhis and chit funds were difficult to regulate and had enough local political support. Talwar, realizing that the government would be unwilling to cede control over both nidhis and chit funds, asked for an alternative arrangement:

> Although it would be desirable that all these organisations/institutions accepting public deposits are brought under one regulator/supervisor for the purpose of protection of depositors interest and uniformity of law applicable to each one of them, it may, perhaps, be very difficult for one single regulatory authority to supervise such a vast system and in any case RBI cannot accept responsibility in case of State level institutions which are governed under different Acts. It may, therefore, be both necessary and desirable that the concerned regulatory authorities like DCA, SEBI and State Governments are advised to bring these institutions/organisations accepting public deposits under some prudential regulation by prescribing prudential norms, viz. income recognition, asset classification, provisioning, capital adequacy, credit exposure norms, etc. They should also put in place a comprehensive supervisory mechanism to ensure compliance and safeguard depositors' interest.

Earlier, Narasimham-II had expressed a view to the contrary:

The large number of NBFCs operating in the country makes the
supervision of NBFCs a difficult task. As a result, the inspection
and audit of NBFCs have been delegated to external auditors and
Chartered Accountancy firms while the RBI has set up a separate
department to oversee NBFC sector under the guidance of BFS.
While appreciating the practical considerations that have led to
this decision, the Committee, nonetheless, has some reservations
on the decision to rely entirely on the assessment of the financial
position of the NBFC and linking the quantum which it can raise
as deposits to the rating given by credit rating agencies. This
we believe is an essential regulatory function to be performed
by the body entrusted with financial supervision. The recent
developments have led to the need for an integrated approach
to supervision. The blurring of distinction between banks and
DFIs on the one hand and banks and NBFCs on the other as
also the multiplicity of activities undertaken by them necessitates
such an integrated approach.

In its Action Taken Report on the Narasimham-II
recommendations, the government preferred to kick this can
down the road:

BFS (Board for Financial Supervision) needs to be strengthened
before regulatory functions are vested with it. It was, therefore,
felt that while the Committee's recommendations to set up an
agency named Board for Financial Regulation and Supervision
(BFRS) to provide an integrated system of regulation and
supervision over banks, FIs and NBFCs could be a long-
term objective. For the time being, BFS may continue with its
present mandate.

In 2000, the RBI informed the government that it was
drafting a new legislation for NBFCs, somewhat on the lines of

the Banking Regulation Act, to better regulate NBFCs through a comprehensive legal framework. The government helped the RBI in drafting the Bill, which was then bumped up to a standing committee of Parliament. The draft Bill bore the imprimatur of then finance minister Yashwant Sinha. The forty-five-member standing committee's July 2003 report expressed many reservations about the draft Bill, even though the members frequently voiced their concerns regarding the safety of depositors' funds. In short, the committee felt the RBI should focus on regulating only the deposit-accepting NBFCs registered with it and exclude the non-deposit-accepting NBFCs, investment companies and special purpose vehicles from the Bill's purview. A final shape to the Bill never materialized, and it lapsed when the thirteenth Lok Sabha was dissolved in 2004.

This would later prove to be costly. The regulatory response, in the meantime, continued to be influenced by critical events, of which two stand out.

The RBI was blindsided in October 2010 by a legislation introduced by the Andhra Pradesh government (the state was subsequently split into two in 2014: Andhra Pradesh and Telangana) seeking to control microfinance institutions (MFIs). The state government's legislation was a response to complaints about MFI operations in Andhra Pradesh, specifically allegations of adopting aggressive lending and coercive recovery practices which, apparently, had led to more than sixty suicides. There were also concerns over multiple loans to the same beneficiaries, resulting in heightened indebtedness. The Andhra government's legislation sought to regulate the sector by mandating MFIs to register with district authorities and disclose the interest rate charged, among many other restrictive clauses.

Andhra Pradesh's evolution as a crucible for enhanced microfinance activity (the state accounted for 30 per cent of all MFI loans in the country in 2010) can be traced back to its remarkable financial inclusion policies of the 1980s, which had created a fertile ecosystem for MFIs. However, the lack of policy and regulatory clarity for MFIs, specifically their inability to raise deposits, had forced many MFIs to rely on equity capital from private sources (including private equity firms) and borrowings from commercial banks to expand their lending programme. This had a direct impact on the cost of funds and the interest rates charged to borrowers, which on an average ranged between 25 and 30 per cent per annum, and occasionally was higher than that. It might be worth mentioning here that another peculiarity continues to bedevil the microfinance universe: microfinance by definition encompasses micro-savings, micro-pensions and micro-insurance, but the MFI activity in Andhra Pradesh restricted itself to only micro-lending.

The new Andhra Pradesh microfinance law brought all MFI activity to a sudden halt, imperilling ongoing loan recovery and putting the health of hundreds of institutions into jeopardy. The RBI's conversations with bank representatives in December 2010 revealed that MFI collections in Andhra Pradesh had deteriorated considerably and there were initial signs of the contagion spreading to other states. There were demands from banks that the RBI allow them to restructure loans to MFIs; but there was one snag: the central bank's rules then did not allow for restructuring of unsecured loans, which applied to almost all bank lending to MFIs. In January 2011, heeding the requests, the RBI relaxed its loan restructuring rules to allow for a temporary reprieve to banks.

The RBI, which was already in the process of developing a variegated regulatory framework for specialized NBFCs (such as factoring, microfinance), reacted to the Andhra Pradesh development in its November 2010 monetary policy:

Considering the more recent developments in the MFI space, a Sub-Committee of the Central Board of the Reserve Bank (Chairman: Shri Y.H. Malegam) has been constituted to examine the various issues relating to micro-finance extended by non-banking financial companies (NBFCs) . . . The Sub-Committee will make recommendations, among others, relating to regulation of micro-finance activities of NBFCs, especially with regard to issues impinging on borrowers' interests. The Sub-Committee is expected to submit its report by end-January 2011.

The Malegam Committee's report[1] of January 2011 recognized that MFIs, given their funding patterns and unique borrower profile, needed to be treated as a special category—NBFCs-MFIs. In addition, the committee also specified the conditions necessary for lenders to be defined as NBFC-MFIs, mandated transparency in interest rates charged, as well as a margin cap and interest rate cap on individual loans, apart from a host of other regulations for MFIs. It is worth noting here that till then, the RBI had not created a special category of NBFCs operating in the microfinance sector. The RBI, in its monetary policy statement of April 2011, announced that it had accepted the Malegam Committee's recommendations, and specified that bank loans to MFIs would be considered priority sector loans subject to certain conditions, including MFIs adhering to a 12 per cent margin cap and 26 per cent interest rate cap. The RBI later, in August 2012,[2] relaxed the rules to afford some flexibility to MFIs.

But one problem refused to go away: the Andhra Pradesh legislation was still on the table and NBFC-MFIs now had to abide by two sets of regulations. In addition, many states had also resurrected their old anti-usury or anti-moneylender laws and were demanding that NBFC-MFIs adhere to them. Some individual MFIs, as well as the microfinance industry lobby, MicroFinance Industry Network, had moved the court in 2010–11 against the dual regulatory structure emerging in almost all states. The Telangana High Court finally passed a verdict in February 2023 in which it ordered that NBFC-MFIs can only be regulated by the RBI. Earlier, in May 2022, the Supreme Court had also held[3] that the moneylending Acts of Kerala and Gujarat would not apply to NBFCs registered with the RBI and regulated by the central bank, thereby providing a conclusive judicial stamp of approval to the RBI's regulatory authority over NBFCs.

The second incident that forced the RBI to revisit its NBFC regulatory framework occurred in June 2018 when IL&FS Ltd (formerly known as Infrastructure Leasing and Financial Services Ltd, an infrastructure financing NBFC promoted in 1987 with shareholding from public sector financial institutions and Housing Development Finance Corporation Ltd) defaulted on commercial paper repayment obligations. This non-payment was followed by a series of defaults across IL&FS and its subsidiaries, exposing the group's indebtedness of around Rs 1,00,000 crore.

The problem with contemporary financial systems is that an adverse episode does not affect only one player; the sector's innate characteristic of inter-connectedness—through an intricate and interdependent web of investments, borrowings and lending—means that one negative event can have a rapid cascading effect across the sector, with the weak and vulnerable players usually bearing the brunt. The IL&FS debacle also sent a ripple across the entire NBFC sector: Reliance Home Finance, Reliance Commercial Finance and Altico Capital were some of the NBFCs that had to be either shut down or sold off. All NBFCs became untouchables overnight and the entire sector's sources of financing dried up. The credit famine in the NBFC sector had a ripple effect across the financial sector.

The vulnerability in the industry had been building up since the end of demonetization, around February 2017, when banks realized that they were flush with deposits but with limited credit demand. Banks became excessively eager to lend and NBFCs, taking advantage of this vulnerability, borrowed beyond their capacity to on-lend or repay. Also, miscalculating how long the system would tolerate excess liquidity, NBFCs kept borrowing short-term money for lending to long-term projects, in the hope that repayments could be funded through repeated borrowing from the market. The asset–liability mismatch was ripe for an upset and it came on 6 June 2018, in the form of an interest rate hike from the RBI. As the system started collapsing, the RBI's first instinct was to enhance NBFC access to credit, to avoid monetary pipelines in the entire financial system gumming up, by encouraging banks to lend more to NBFCs. The second significant step was to harmonize the categorization of NBFCs to reduce the number of categories. The RBI kept offering all kinds of relaxations to the sector as the onset of the coronavirus pandemic in March 2020 further aggravated stress in the sector.

In October 2021, the RBI finally introduced a new paradigm for regulating NBFCs, called scale-based regulation. The new framework seeks to align regulation with the sector's evolution over time in terms of its size, complexity and interconnectedness with the rest of the financial sector. Under the new dispensation, four layers have been created—base, middle, upper and top— to house NBFCs based on their size, activity and perceived riskiness. A detailed notification[4] spelt out how the four layers will be populated. This is the current regulatory framework for all NBFCs and all regulatory actions for NBFCs are predicated on this template.

# Chapter 7

## Banking Reforms

It did not take long for the self-congratulatory, smug smile to turn into a frown. The chief executive of this middling public-sector bank was addressing a press conference to announce its annual results. Headlining his presentation was the proud claim of a handsome rise in deposits, followed by the successful meeting of priority-sector targets. An irrepressible and impatient young journalist piped up and asked, 'What was the profit?' The chief executive's face darkened visibly.

The banker can be forgiven for momentarily losing his cool. It had been dinned into him that profit was not the endgame in his business. This was in the mid-eighties, and public-sector banks were viewed largely as instruments for achieving the country's social justice and redistributive objectives rather than as economic agents entrusted with the specific task of collecting deposits and using these funds to allocate credit efficiently for asset growth and productivity improvement, which would eventually lead to economic growth and deepening of financial inclusion. One of the social objectives of the nation was to expand its banking sector footprint to enable formal deposit collection, a large chunk of which would then be mandatorily pre-empted by the government for meeting its social welfare expenditure.

But, even as the absurdity of deposit primacy over profit growth continued to dominate the prevalent banking model, many Indian administrators, planners and regulators were seized with concern during the mid-1980s over the serious crisis building up in the Indian banking industry. Commentary on the sector had been warning about the ticking time bomb and the disastrous effects it could have on the economic system as a whole.

Former RBI governor C. Rangarajan writes in his book, *Forks in the Road*:

> The banking system, since the nationalisation of major banks in 1969, had made tremendous progress in terms of extension of banking into rural areas and wider reach to agriculturalists and small borrowers. However, this massive expansion led to low profitability and poor management of the loan portfolio. In the context of changes that were happening in the banking system in the rest of the world and the changes that were happening in the real sector in India, fundamental reforms in the banking sector became urgent.

Rangarajan's book was published in 2022. But even in 1991, he had expressed similar concerns. Addressing the annual Bank Economists' Conference as the RBI's deputy governor in January 1991, Rangarajan had painted[1] a dismal picture of what confronted India's banking industry:

> In India, bank profitability has been under severe strain for some time now. Given the nature of banking as a business which has inherent risks, it is essential that banks earn enough to build reserves and enhance their owned resources . . . Bank profitability is affected considerably by policy actions—what we may term the 'external environment' that banks face. But profitability also depends on the internal efficiency of operations. Banks in India have had to operate under several

constraints dictated by socioeconomic objectives, which have had a bearing on their profitability. These relate primarily to the rapid and vast expansion of banking facilities with its associated costs, the allocation of credit for priority needs and the element of cross subsidisation to assist preferred sectors. Banks have also been subjected to a large pre-emption of funds by way of the Cash Reserve Ratio (CRR) and the Statutory Liquidity Ratio (SLR), which have also imposed constraints on their profitability.

It took the 1991 BoP crisis, the Harshad Mehta scam, the threat of bad loans hollowing out the industry and other subsequent financial perturbations to force the government's hand in reforming the banking industry. The RBI's dominant narrative, across its various publications, has stressed that reforms in the banking sector were not occasioned by any banking crisis. But that is a fallacious argument. As this chapter will show, even though the banking sector was racked internally by a long-standing crisis that threatened to implode the industry, all those responsible for the sector—shareholders and regulators alike—were either in denial or had become prisoners of an outdated model. It took an economic crisis, perhaps not a banking crisis specifically, to make reforms palatable and sellable to all the stakeholders.

## Beginnings of a Journey

The Indian banking industry's journey has been tumultuous, with many twists and turns. The source of banking troubles in India, it seems, emanated from excessive government ownership and control. However, the Indian banking sector was not always under government ownership. Indian bankers had been around in history for centuries, financing wars and lending money to potentates against future revenues. Many of them were influential and were sought out by the powers-that-be of their times. Seth Manik

Chand Sahu and his progeny, Oswal Jains who had migrated from
Rajasthan to Murshidabad in eastern India during the fifteenth
or sixteenth century, were conferred the title of Jagat Seths (or
bankers to the world) for their financial muscle and banking
prowess. In fact, apocrypha describes their wealth in bullion as
sufficient to dam the river Ganga which flows past Murshidabad
town. The Jagat Seths' disaffection towards the ruling nawab,
Siraj ud Doula, and their financing of Robert Clive's marauding
army are considered to have been pivotal in the establishment of
the East India Company's control over the Indian Subcontinent
(Clive defeated Siraj ud Doula in Plassey in 1757 and became the
ruler of Bengal, then India's richest province, before extending
his sway over the rest of the subcontinent).

First under the East India Company and then, post-1857,
under the British Crown, banking became a little more formal and
corporatized. The banking system in India began to be owned
by the largest private business groups in the country. The first
European-style bank in India, Bank of Hindostan, was set up in
Calcutta in 1770 by managing agents Alexander and Company.
This was followed closely by Commercial Bank, established by
McKintosh and Company. In 1809, the East India Company and
the Crown jointly set up the first state-backed bank, the Bank of
Bengal. In the subsequent years, many banks were formed, many
merged and many had to be shut down. It was not until 1894,
amidst a resurgent spirit of nationalism, that Punjab National
Bank was established as the first significant Indian-owned bank
styled on European institutions. In 1921, the Crown merged the
three Presidency banks of Madras, Bombay and Bengal to form
the Imperial Bank of India.

Business historian Dwijendra Tripathi writes in his magisterial
book, *The Oxford History of Indian Business*:[2]

> The conditions thus were hardly conducive for the modern
> institutions to make a dent on the age-old sources of credit

in India. The Indian industrialists' dependence on funds from these sources inevitably impacted on their strategies which understandably were marked by relatively low investment, short gestation period, and quick returns. Their dependence on the traditional sources of business finance also provided continued reinforcement to the management structure of their industrial concerns. If family dominance remained a salient feature of the management of industrial enterprises, even though the enterprises themselves were organised as joint stocks, it was at least partly because the community and family linkages continued to remain the principal source of industrial finance.

The nationalistic spirit and the difficulties faced by Indian entrepreneurs in sourcing loans from European institutions impelled many business houses to start their own banks, mainly as joint stock companies. The system continued unchanged after Independence too. The Tatas, Birlas, Thapars and some of the other large industrial groups owned banks in post-Independence India. This pattern underwent a change when most of the banks in the country were nationalized in two waves by the Congress government of Indira Gandhi, first in 1969 (fourteen banks) and then in 1980 (six banks). Earlier, in 1953, the Indian government had taken over the storied Imperial Bank of India, which was closely associated with colonial rule, and renamed it the State Bank of India. The government also acquired banks owned by some of the erstwhile princely states—Travancore, Bikaner, Hyderabad, Patiala, Jaipur, Indore, Mysore and Saurashtra—and brought them under the State Bank family. These banks came to be known as associate banks of the State Bank of India, such as the State Bank of Indore or the State Bank of Travancore.

The close and inextricable links between Indian banking and the country's political economy became set in stone during the late 1960s. Indira Gandhi as prime minister was facing stiff opposition from Congress party seniors—nicknamed the 'Syndicate'—who wanted to exercise greater control over the government's economic and social policies. Indira Gandhi split the party, received support from other parties and continued as the prime minister. Her subsequent move to nationalize fourteen banks, the selection criterion being deposits over Rs 50 crore, coupled with her populist anti-poverty slogans, saw her return to power in the 1971 general elections with a landslide victory. There were, of course, other valid structural and emotive reasons too. More than 350 banks had failed since Independence, wiping out depositor money. In addition, most of these banks had not only become in-house piggy banks for the promoting business groups but also indulged in suspect lending practices. Credit flows were focused towards the corporate sector, and the stagnation in the rural-agri sector, starved for credit, became a continuing source of anxiety, especially since it supported close to 80 per cent of the national population at the time. Indira Gandhi was astutely able to tap into this festering sense of injustice in society.

The election results seemed to signal to Indira Gandhi the future, and acceptable, path for economic policy. The initial experience with nationalization was also rewarding, as these fourteen banks were able to meet the rising credit demand in the wake of the Green Revolution—finance for farm equipment, fertilizers and rural transport vehicles. There was demand from some other sectors too. RBI data[3] shows that bank credit in India moved from Rs 3599 crore in 1969–70 to Rs 22,068 crore by 1979–80, a six-fold increase in just ten years. Deposits in the banking industry during the same period rose from Rs 4646 crore to Rs 33,377 crore, a seven-fold increase. There was a massive expansion in bank branch networks as well, with the emphasis being on increasing the rural footprint.

The experience of nationalization brought about two huge changes in Indian banking that persist to date. The nationalization of banks was fuelled by a distrust of industrialists, or industry groups, owning and managing banks. That misgiving exists even today with the regulator reluctant to allow industrialists, or industrial groups, to gain management control of banks. The pre-nationalization scars of funds misappropriation and diversion at banks continue to haunt financial regulators today, even after more than half a century. Contemporary bank shareholding rules have been designed to discourage cross-holding between industry groups and the banking sector.

The second was the evolution and concretization of something called priority-sector lending, under which banks had to compulsorily lend a certain percentage of their loans to agriculture, the rural sector and small-scale industry at concessional rates of interest. The need for such a policy design had been on the table even pre-nationalization, when the concentration of credit to large industries had become all too obvious. But lack of policy coherence and diffused choice of agency to implement the agenda failed to get it off the ground. Finally, in 1972, the agenda was defined as 'priority sector credit' and was made operational by 1974. The scheme initially demanded that banks lend 33 per cent of their total credit to agriculture and small-scale units by 1979. This scheme in many ways symbolized the government's push to turn banking into an instrument of social change.

For the priority sector, banks were asked to undertake a special scheme—the differential rate of interest (DRI) scheme—for financing the weakest sections of society, through a grant of small loans at a highly concessional rate of 4 per cent. The rule required banks to advance at least 1 per cent of their total loans as DRI loans. The priority-sector quota also got raised over the years to 40 per cent, and the list of segments eligible for priority-sector credit also grew over the years, converting the real motive behind the policy thrust into a pro forma exercise for banks.

Encouraged by the record of the banking sector post-nationalization and emboldened by the Congress winning 353 seats in the 1980 elections despite the grim memory of the

Emergency (1975–77) of only a few years ago, Indira Gandhi nationalized another six banks in April 1980. This time, the criterion for candidate selection was banks with deposits over Rs 200 crore. The second phase of nationalization, when completed, brought a total of 91 per cent of bank deposits into the public sector fold.

This is important, because the growing branch network of the nationalized banks, complemented by their enormous market share in deposits, became the springboard for the government's rapid escalation of social-sector schemes and redistribution of credit through priority-sector rules. The story of Indian banking post-nationalization became one long tale of government appropriation of depositor funds, a radical rewiring of the banking sector to sub-serve the state's cause— and, by extension, the government's political ambitions—at the expense of the sector's overall financial health. The government used the banking sector to dip into the growing savings pool of Indian households and re-route these savings into its burgeoning development programmes. The government was able to achieve this by making branch expansion and deposit mobilization—even at the cost of bank profitability—an economic priority, which was then bolstered by myriads of rules, regulations and laws which left banks with little independent agency. The banker mentioned in the opening paragraphs of this chapter had been hardwired to deliver this framework of outcomes and not profits.

It must be remembered here that the signals emanating from the political economy, especially Indira Gandhi's decisive electoral victories in 1971 and 1980, seemed to endorse this economic model. Bolstered by populist political slogans—the most famous one being *garibi hatao*, or abolish poverty, which was used to great effect in the 1971 elections—the government's messaging that the country's resources, both natural and financial, had to be shared in an egalitarian manner had instant emotive appeal.

In agrarian states such as Maharashtra, Bihar or Uttar Pradesh, Indira Gandhi's party, Congress (R), won handsomely.

There is a flip side which merits mention. It can be assumed with some degree of certainty, and causality, that the focused expansion in the branch network of banks did help in improving India's savings rate. The formal banking network was now able to reach a larger proportion of the country's population and re-route household savings away from physical assets—such as gold, jewellery, landholdings or even cash—into financial assets, especially bank deposits, which had the largest share among all categories of financial assets. There was only one mutual fund—Unit Trust of India—and most Indians were wary of investing directly in the equity markets. Gross domestic savings as a percentage of GDP moved up from 11.9 in 1968–69, the year before nationalization phase I, to 20.3 in 1978–79, on the eve of bank nationalization phase II. Drilling down to a disaggregated basis, household savings went up from 8.2 per cent of GDP to 14.6 per cent during this period.

While there appears to be a causal link between growth in bank branch networks and deposits, the association between domestic savings and investment rates (gross capital formation went up from 14.1 per cent of GDP to 22.9 per cent during the same period) is tenuous and provides an insight into the reasons behind the build-up to the balance-of-payments crisis by 1989–90. The positive difference between the investment rate and the gross domestic savings rate implied that the gap was being met by net capital inflows, mostly in the form of foreign exchange loans. Given the public-sector nature of the banking industry and the large-scale appropriation of its lendable resources, capacity formation by industry or infrastructure building had to depend on foreign currency borrowings.

The Indian government was forced to approach the IMF in 1981 when the country's balance of payments came under stress

as a result of rising oil prices. Montek Singh Ahluwalia writes in
*Backstage*:

> Our executive director in the World Bank, M Narasimham,
> advised that we should approach the IMF for a loan under the
> Extended Fund Facility (EFF), which had been established in
> 1974 in response to demands from India and other developing
> countries . . . The EFF loan was the largest IMF loan ever
> until then, and gave India access to a total of SDR 5 billion
> over a three-year period from 1981 to 1984. The arrangement
> was unusual because the corrective policies included increased
> public investment in key sectors such as petroleum, cement and
> steel to help expand domestic production and save on imports.

M. Narasimham, who was appointed RBI governor for a brief
period of six and a half months in 1977 (2 May to 30 November
1977), also had a key role to play in banking sector reforms. This
is discussed later in this chapter.

While it is incontrovertible that the huge bank branch
expansion made possible the impressive increase in the savings
rate, it would, however, be politically naïve to assume that the
purpose behind branch expansion was to solely increase the
rate of domestic savings and earn a macro-economic badge of
honour. It was certainly one of the reasons, but not by any stretch
of imagination the only one. The regulations of the day forced
banks to invest 38.5 per cent of their deposits in government
securities, under a scheme called the statutory liquidity ratio (SLR),
with the interest rates being predetermined by the government
and the RBI. Typically, the coupons—the interest rate offered
to investors—on these government bonds was kept artificially
low. Another 15 per cent of the deposits had to be compulsorily
kept with the central bank as a deposit, called the cash reserve
ratio (CRR), also at an extremely low rate of return. In fact,
many studies have shown that returns from these investments

were even lower than the banks' cost of funds. The RBI used these deposits-turned-reserves to absorb the growing volumes of government debt, partially obviating its need to absorb the full amount of government bonds, which would have required the central bank to print money, which would then impact the economy's inflation rate.

Now assume, as a simplistic exercise, that a bank gets Rs 100 in deposits. Right away, as soon as the money enters the portals of the bank, 53.5 per cent of it is pre-empted by the government system—through SLR and CRR—at a rate over which the banks had no control. Of the remaining Rs 46.5, another 40 per cent had to be compulsorily lent to priority sectors—which includes agriculture and the small-scale sector—at concessional rates. This took away another Rs 18.6, leaving the banks with only Rs 27.9 to lend commercially.

On top of this, the RBI decided the interest rates for all deposits and all categories of loans. This pre-determined rate structure left banks with little or no agency in calibrating lending interest rates on the Rs 27.9 of commercial borrowing to match the borrowers' risk profile. Such an abnormal structure engendered another distortion: interest rates for commercial lending were inordinately high, structured to cross-subsidize the bank's losses from the forced pre-emption and concessional lending.

Apart from setting and supervising each and every category of loan and deposit rate minutely, the RBI also oversaw a programme called the Credit Authorization Scheme, which rationed out credit to the corporate sector. The RBI had detailed rules for this, instructing banks on the ways in which to calculate 'maximum permissible bank finance' for eligible borrowers, a euphemism for rationing out credit to industry, based on certain balance-sheet parameters. This code, called the Tandon-Chore Committee norms and developed by the RBI in-house, became the gospel for all bank officers.

Consequently, as is usually the case with most combinations of shortage and rationing, commercial lending became an island of rent-seeking, influence-peddling and loan defaults (some of them committed wilfully, arising from funds siphoning). Combined with the cross-subsidization model that was in vogue, bad loans and losses kept mounting in bank after bank, threatening to wipe out the net worth of many institutions. Opaque reporting laws ensured that the bad news was always kept under wraps. Yet there were enough indications of the approaching storm.

The Indian banking system was also unfamiliar with competition. There were only a few old private banks that had managed to dodge nationalization, and the government had stopped giving licenses to new private banks. Nothing in either of the operative legislations—the RBI Act or the Banking Regulation Act—precluded the central bank from handing out new banking licences to private-sector operators. However, the overwhelming prevalence of the developmental banking model, combined with a lingering suspicion of private sector motives from the 1960s, created a forbidding barrier for any new entrant.

New foreign banks, desirous of conducting business in India, were granted licences only selectively, and the choice was often dictated by India's strategic geo-political and geo-economic priorities. Even the existing foreign banks in the country had to jump through multiple hoops to open new branches, and the RBI's branch-licensing policy appeared to be designed to ensure that public-sector banks got the best access to household deposits. The banking sector was also assured of corporate business through restrictions imposed on companies wishing to tap alternative channels for finance. For example, a company could only borrow 10 per cent of its net worth directly from shareholders and another 25 per cent from the public as deposits (the rates on these deposits were also fixed by the government), forcing many of them to rely, willy-nilly, on bank finance.

As the banking industry navigated the choppy economic and political waters of the 1980s, the sector's internal crisis was visibly worsening. At the start of the 1990s, Indian banking was characterized by the large presence of public-sector banks, some old private-sector banks and a token presence of foreign banks. The public-sector catastrophe was threatening to sink even the private and foreign banks. The malaise in the public-sector banks was taking its toll on the health of the industry as a whole.

The loan portfolios of most banks were contaminated with non-performing assets, or NPAs, banking argot for loans that have gone bad with no hope of being repaid. Bank officers had no incentive to follow best practices, which included proper credit appraisal while advancing loans to borrowers. Most bank officers concentrated mainly on achieving the loan targets for each sub-sector of society that were mandated by government fiat. There were no mandates on the quality of loans advanced or the amount of loans recovered. As a result, credit appraisal norms or follow-up for recovering loans were tardy. And, to make matters worse, banks were extremely sluggish in recognizing bad loans. They would continue to account for interest income in their books long after borrowers had stopped paying interest, show paper profits but pay out real dividends to the government from their operating cash flows. This was a disaster in the making, but nobody objected as long as everybody felt that this treacherous treadmill would continue to function till kingdom come, or till the rules changed.

Promotions and senior appointments were political instruments, leaving incumbents with very little incentive to pursue proper banking practices. Governance at the board level was an alien concept and many board directors were political appointees, a practice that continues to this day. There was also political interference in the extension of individual loans, not to mention the spate of loan *mela*s, or fairs, organized by politicians as a platform for mass distribution of loans using bank funds during the late 1980s to keep voters happy.

Even regulation was sub-par. Given the RBI's preoccupation with credit rationing, fixing interest rates, monitoring compliance with the multi-layered administered interest-rate regime and ensuring that banks not only fulfilled their mandated loan targets but also met their quota of government-bond investments, the central bank was left with limited capacity for fulfilling its role as a supervisor, or for tracking market intelligence. The other problem was to do with data: the time that would lapse between the RBI requesting individual banks for performance trackers, the banks responding with the relevant numbers, the RBI officers analysing them and the central bank then initiating corrective action would be at least two years. Much of the ground conditions would have changed by then, forcing the central bank to always play catch-up. Consequently, the system suffered. The reporting system, auditing and normal banking prudential norms were the immediate casualties, and this ultimately impacted the health of the banking system.

The regulator was most apprehensive of revealing the true extent of bad loans on banks' balance sheets. The RBI's internal committee on finalizing bank accounts, chaired by former deputy governor A. Ghosh said in its 1985 report:

> The Committee is of the view that in Indian conditions the time is not yet opportune for practising full disclosure in respect of secret reserves and loan loss provisioning. The issue, however, may be reviewed in due course. It is, however, of the opinion that correct income should be reported in the profit and loss account and the amount transferred to contingencies may, therefore, be shown along with various other provisions for depreciation on investments, income tax, specific provisions for bad debts, etc as a 'conglomerate' item on the expenditure side. This would reveal the true trend of income and at the

same time the procedure would not reveal the amount of secret
reserves and loan loss provisions held by banks.

The first whiff of deregulation in the banking sector came in
the form of the Sukhamoy Chakravarty Committee report of 1985.
The committee was set up to look at India's monetary system and
recommend reforms. The report pointed fingers at the ballooning
RBI credit to the government leading to rising money supply and
inflation. The RBI was using credit growth as its monetary policy
target for inflation control, under the assumption that turning off
the credit tap or slowing down credit growth at the right moment,
could help moderate price levels. However, the Chakravarty
Committee instead saw monetary targeting—based on anticipated
growth in GDP, the inflation rate and the income elasticity of
demand for money—as a more meaningful means of inflation
control. The committee also afforded the new framework with
some flexibility by calling it 'monetary targeting with feedback'—
which meant the RBI had the latitude to keep shifting the target
range during the year depending on developments in the real
sector. Once the committee's recommendations were accepted,
money supply effectively became an intermediate target, to be
calibrated for achieving higher growth with price stability.

The committee also raised many questions about the
complex system of administered interest rates, the quantitative
credit controls in vogue, and the viability problems of projects
funded with concessional credit, among other matters. However,
it stopped short of recommending the free determination of
interest rates and instead felt that the RBI should determine a
simpler matrix of administered interest rates in consultation
with the government, using the inflation rate as the benchmark
for fixing the relevant interest rates. The committee, which had
expressed its views about monetization of deficit leading to
rising money supply and inflation, also made observations about

the drawbacks arising from state ownership of banks and the concomitant adverse impact on their competitive spirit, efficiency and profitability.

*RBI History* observes that the Chakravarty Committee report, 'transformed the policy paradigm concerning the objectives of monetary policy, regulation over money and credit, interest rate policies and coordination of monetary and fiscal policies'.

The Sukhamoy Chakravarty Committee's recommendations led to a relook at the existing structure of interest rates and the introduction of measures for changing interest rates as well as rationalizing and reducing the number of administered interest rates. One immediate fallout of the recommendations was the withdrawal of the 10 per cent ceiling on the inter-bank call money rate (the rate at which banks lent to each other) which, apart from being artificial and absurd, was often observed in the breach and highlighted the irrationality of the interest rate framework. Selective credit controls also came under the guillotine.

The committee's report came in for some criticism too. Economist Bhabatosh Datta, for example, felt the committee did not go the full distance. He felt the committee missed the chance to make a clear separation between SLR as a reserve requirement and its default role as a financier of government expenditure. He also asked, rather presciently, whether it was not time for some body or organization, or a committee, to lay bare the provisions of the RBI Act and address the subordinate nature of the RBI to the government of the day, or highlight the insecurities of its governor's position and that of its board. It is interesting that forty years on, the same unaddressed concerns continue to bedevil the RBI.

But, beyond the Chakravarty Committee's recommendations, two other developments allowed the RBI to substantially dampen the deleterious effects of fiscal policy on monetary policy.

One was the acceptance of the recommendations made by a working group on the money market, chaired by N. Vaghul, former chairman of the development financial institution Industrial Credit and Investment Corporation of India, which was later converted into the commercial bank ICICI Ltd. The working group based its work on the Chakravarty Committee report suggestion that a proper, functioning money market would be a critical component of monetary regulation. The group's recommendations of 1987 led to the introduction of a number of market-based instruments over the next few years, such as certificates of deposit (CD) in 1989 and commercial paper (CP) in 1990.

The second development was to allow three state-owned banks—State Bank of India, Canara Bank and Bank of Baroda—to launch their own mutual funds in 1987. Banks were also allowed to diversify into leasing, housing finance, venture capital and merchant banking. This would give them an alternative source of income which was not subject to government caprices and allow them to repair some of the damage to their balance sheets.

But that was not enough. As Part A of Volume IV of *RBI History* notes: 'The early reform measures were, however, sporadic and ad hoc and lacked a coherent approach. These did not culminate in the promotion of competition and efficiency.'

In short, despite the banking system remaining a heartbeat away from disaster, the linkages of political rent-seeking in this segment of the financial sector were so strong and so deeply embedded that any change or reform seemed improbable. Many reports kept pointing out the impending disaster the banking sector was headed towards. The IMF's staff report on India for the annual Article IV[4] consultation in May 1990 drew attention to the state of the banking industry: 'During the 1980s structural reforms were successful in improving efficiency and raising growth. Nevertheless, the need for further structural reform is great . . . a large number of non-performing loans and complex government regulations weaken the health and efficiency of the banking system . . .'

The summing-up report on the Article IV consultations in June 1990 pretty much endorsed the staff opinion:

> Directors welcomed the recent liberalization of financial markets, in particular the short-term money market. They noted, however, that the banking system continued to operate in a heavily-regulated environment. They urged the authorities to reduce, in particular, the burden imposed on banks by priority lending, and increase the role of market forces in determining deposit rates. Several Directors also advocated greater reliance on market-based instruments of monetary control, including use of open market operations.

Even the RBI's 2008 special compilation, 'Reports on Currency and Finance', acknowledged the problem:

> A major issue faced by the banking sector in the early 1990s was its fragile health, low profitability and weak capital base. A related issue was also to assess the true health of the banking sector as the health code system being followed then was based on subjective considerations and lacked consistency.

The situation in the banking industry was, admittedly, precarious and just one step short of a cataclysm. The final spark emanated from a series of shocks—the balance-of-payments crisis, the securities scam and a number of other setbacks. These shocks to the system forced the government and the RBI to overhaul the creaking banking system, but only to the extent of fixing the immediate problems. Each episode merited initiation of only a limited reforms process . . . and then the status quo would continue till the next systemic shock forced another round of reforms.

## The Reforms Process: Phase-I

The balance-of-payments crisis that burst upon the Indian economy not only held up a mirror to the unstable state of India's foreign exchange reserves but also provided a snapshot of all that was wrong with the command-and-control economic philosophy relating to industry and financial institutions. Delivering his maiden budget address on 24 July 1992, Manmohan Singh said:

> The widening and deepening of our financial system have helped the spread of institutional finance over a vast area and have contributed significantly to the augmentation of our savings rate, particularly financial savings. This has been a most commendable achievement, but our financial system has developed certain rigidities and some weaknesses which we must address now. The objective of reform in the financial sector would be to preserve its basic role as an essential adjunct to economic growth and competitive efficiency, while improving the health of its institutions. In this task, it is essential to ensure capital adequacy, introduce prudential norms and improve profitability of our commercial banks and financial institutions. There are no magic solutions. These are complex issues which need careful consideration. Therefore, **I propose to appoint a high-level committee to consider all relevant aspects of structure, organisation, functions and procedures of the financial system.** This committee would advise the Government on appropriate measures that would be needed to enhance the viability and health of our financial sector so that it can better serve the needs of the economy without any sacrifice of the canons and principles of a sound financial system.

The committee was set up under the chairmanship of M. Narasimham, whom we met earlier in this chapter when discussing India's IMF loan in 1981. A brief profile of Narasimham might help us understand the man and his mission. Narasimham, a graduate of St John's College, University of Cambridge, was a career central banker, joining the RBI as a research officer in the economics department in 1950. He also spent some time in the government, as an additional secretary in the finance ministry's Department of Economic Affairs before being appointed RBI governor in May 1977 for a short stint of seven months. He was subsequently India's director in the World Bank and later in the IMF.

As an insider and as somebody who had seen the industry up close, Narasimham was well acquainted with the problems plaguing Indian banking and seemed to know exactly what kind of medication was required to nurse it back to health. Appointed on 14 August 1991, the committee was able to submit its full report in just three months, on 6 November 1991. Narasimham's report on the broad sweep of hard reforms required in the Indian banking industry, and the broad political acceptance of the committee's recommendations, led to a deep cleaning of the Indian banking industry. The extent of changes that Narasimham suggested and implemented earned him the sobriquet 'Father of Banking Reforms', as well as the responsibility of chairing a subsequent committee in 1998 to recommend a second phase of reforms for the banking industry.

The first phase, which roughly spans 1992–97, saw some drastic changes in the banking industry. In the introduction to the report, Narasimham laid down its broad tenor and direction:

> Institutions should operate in an environment where their decisions are not influenced by extraneous pressures but are based on their own commercial judgment and their professional

appraisal of loan proposals under competitive conditions. This calls for development of professional skills while, at the same time, complying with essential prudential norms and safeguards to govern their operations so that depositor and investor confidence in the system is sustained. Such prudential norms should cover aspects such as liquidity, asset portfolio quality, capital adequacy and transparency in accounts. The aim of regulation would thus be to promote the healthy growth of the system and not to interfere with its operations. Rule based regulation rather than discretionary controls should inform the functioning of the financial sector and provide for the needed measure of discipline without stifling the spirit of innovation and calculated risk taking which is the characteristic of a dynamic financial sector.

Four terms are important to note in the above quotation from the report: liquidity, asset portfolio quality, capital adequacy and transparency in accounts. The reforms process for the banking industry initially focused on these four elements, which held the key to recovery and better health for Indian banks. But these were mostly reforms of an endogenous nature, requiring banks to change how they worked, including changes within the RBI's regulatory framework. They did not mean major changes in the systems configuration.

It must also be remembered that the government's acceptance and implementation of the Narasimham Committee's recommendations preceded another important trigger for change: the Harshad Mehta scam, which became public only in April 1992, almost five months after the Narasimham Committee had submitted its report. This is one reason why the Narasimham report did not focus so much on the externalities affecting the banking sector but chose to concentrate on overhauling the nitty-gritty of banking operations. Its advice was to also allow banks a degree of autonomy and freedom from government interference, but without necessarily altering the super-structure of the industry. In keeping with all previous committee reports, Narasimham also did not want his report to upset the public-sector orientation of the banking industry but instead suggested that the government and the RBI allow the entry of new private banks to infuse the sector with the competitive spirit.

But the overhaul suggested was indeed radical. For example, the committee echoed Bhabatosh Datta's views that SLR should not be deployed as an instrument for financing the government's public expenditure and recommended that it should be brought down to 25 per cent by 1996–97. The committee also felt that banks should be remunerated market-linked interest rates for their SLR investments, which meant that the government had to pay market interest rates on the money it borrowed through bonds. Even CRR was put on the block for a sizeable reduction.

The government and the RBI decided in April 1992 to implement the Narasimham Committee's recommendations in a phased manner but with certain modifications.

It may be fair to state that the Narasimham Committee's recommendations provided a critical pivot for the Indian banking industry's journey to a higher plane of efficiency and stability. It may also be instructive to pause here for a moment and re-assess the conditions leading up to the changes proposed, as well as the changes themselves. Former RBI governor Y.V. Reddy has postulated[5] that the policy framework for financial sector reforms had a grand design. First, the financial sector reforms were undertaken early in the reform cycle. Second, the reforms process—entirely home-grown—had not been triggered by any banking crisis but was occasioned by the structural adjustment packages supported by the IMF and the World Bank. Third, international best practices became the bedrock for the reforms design. Fourth, the reforms for both instruments and objectives were carefully sequenced. Consequently, the first to be introduced in the reforms cycle were prudential norms and supervisory strengthening measures, followed by a gradual deregulation of interest rates and a lowering of statutory pre-emptions. The more complex aspects of legal and accounting measures were introduced later, after the basic tenets of reforms were already in place.

While this brief snapshot does provide an inkling of the thinking behind the reforms framework, it also raises an important question. Even though the banking reforms process had not been induced by any specific banking crisis, it did take a balance-of-payments crisis to kick off the process. This becomes moot, especially when one considers the fact that the banking sector had been deep in crisis for more than a decade and yet nothing had been done. It did not require a specific, episodic banking crisis to justify reforms; all it needed was a mix of political and regulatory determination. However, the political will to reform the structural flaws in the banking industry was roused only when there was an adverse event. In other words, as has been repeated elsewhere in this book, there is nothing like a good crisis to validate reforms.

From the broad panoply of recommendations made by the Narasimham Committee, let us initially look at what was accepted and implemented. After that, we can turn our attention to what was left, because that is equally if not more important. First, two very important, and sacrosanct, banking areas came under the reforms momentum.

## The Rate Race

The priority was to focus on deregulating the structure of interest rates, which were administered and, despite some token reforms in the past, still looked like a complex latticework of rates. The RBI, over time, collapsed the multiplicity of interest rates for both deposits as well as loans into a few rates. In 1992, the RBI started the change by prescribing only one ceiling rate, against the multiple rates prescribed earlier. Over time, banks were given the freedom to determine what interest rates to offer on their deposits. They were also given the freedom in 1998 to decide on the penalty for premature withdrawal of deposits, as well as the kind of differential rates to offer for bulk deposits.

A few constraints still remained. For example, the interest rate offered on savings bank deposit accounts continued to be fixed administratively at 3.5 per cent but was finally deregulated in October 2011. This category of deposits—CASA, comprising current accounts and savings accounts—constitutes the cheapest source of liabilities for banks. Post the freeing-up, competition to corner relatively cheaper savings deposits sent the average rate offered by banks to 4 per cent. There were a couple of private banks which even ventured to offer 6 per cent in a bid to shore up their CASA deposits.

However, banks were perpetually playing catch-up with the rates offered on post office deposits and other categories of small savings. These rates were fixed by the government and were sticky in their downward movement. Montek Singh Ahluwalia speculates that since states get a share of these savings, state governments are likely to have resisted reduction in the rates for these deposits. Consequently, in the initial years after the deregulation of interest rates, the competition with small savings schemes for deposits saw commercial banks displaying amazing alacrity in raising their deposit rates when the RBI increased its benchmark rates, but failing to act with equal gusto in reducing deposit rates when the opposite happened. This invariably imparted a stickiness to their lending rates, which too were comparatively sluggish on their downward journey. Over time, as the legacy deposit pool was run down and new deposits were contracted at the deregulated rates, banks have become nimble in dropping deposit rates but slow in raising them. The opposite behaviour prevails in the case of lending rates: banks are swift in raising lending rates but unhurried in dropping them.

The RBI also turned the deregulation lenses on lending rates, but the going was not smooth. Inured by years of having the RBI think on their behalf, only a handful of Indian bankers knew how to price risk and balance it with the desired return. And, then, when you throw corruption in the mix and stir it with political interference in lending decisions, bankers had very little incentive to use initiative. And so, the effort to shake banks out of their torpor has been a long slog, consuming close to three decades.

In addition, the RBI kept a constant vigil on the rates being charged by banks and the methodology they used to determine those rates. Many critics found the RBI's involvement heavy-handed, saying that part of the reforms spirit required the central bank to invest banks with greater freedom to decide the sticker prices for their deposits and loans. But, on the flip side, the RBI's reason for maintaining a hawk eye over the rate structure stemmed from the system's imperfections in allowing for frictionless monetary transmission. As the central bank was moving away from instruments of direct control to indirect control, it wanted its rate actions to be transmitted to the real economy through the instruments of deposit and credit interest rates. Any distortions in the pipeline risked sending jumbled messages to all economic agents.

The earlier system of lending rates (effective 2 March 1981) had no general minimum lending rate but a broad framework of interest rates, with fixed rates on certain types of advances and a ceiling rate on other types of advances. On the eve of the banking sector reforms (effective 22 September 1990), a new structure of lending rates for commercial banks was introduced, which linked interest rates to loan size (for loans over Rs 2,00,000). Post the Narasimham Committee report, the six slabs for credit size were reduced to four with effect from 22 April 1992. A year later, this came down to three. Subsequently, in 1994, the RBI granted banks the freedom to fix their prime lending rate (PLR) for advances of over Rs 2,00,000. By 1998, the maximum rates banks were allowed to charge for loans below Rs 2,00,000 was the PLR. Banks also had to announce the spread they were charging over their PLR for other loans.

In reality, very few banks were actually able to fix their PLR independently, apart from some new private and foreign banks. Most of the public-sector banks waited for a signal from the country's largest commercial bank, the State Bank of India, before fixing their own PLR. This was symptomatic of not only the public-sector capacity deficit but also of a habit that seemed to have been carried forward from years of mandated banking.

As the RBI loosened its control and the economy started growing, the industry-banking nexus started gaming the PLR system. Initially, given the first taste of freedom and handicapped by the high cost of old deposits (which had been contracted pre-reforms), banks started charging lending rates that were far higher than their PLR on a significant percentage of their total bank credit. Then the RBI, in October 1996, made it mandatory for banks to also announce the maximum spread over the PLR while announcing their PLR for all loans except consumer credit. In time, though, the banks liaised with the RBI and got the central bank to agree to two PLR rates, one for short-term loans and the other for long-term loans. Another category was added—different PLRs for different loan maturities. What was supposed to be a simplistic feature soon turned into a complex, multi-layered structure. Predictably, system abuse also set in soon, with the RBI finding out that a large number of loans were being priced exorbitantly. In effect, the PLR—which technically means the rate offered to the best customer, or 'prime' borrower with the best credit rating, with the lowest probability of defaulting on the loan repayment schedule—became a floor rate or a minimum benchmark rate.

In 2003, then RBI governor Bimal Jalan expressed his dissatisfaction with the way banks had been using the PLR mechanism, especially their lack of transparency in fixing interest rates, and openly stated that the practice of multiple PLRs did not 'look compelling'. He felt that despite deposit rates falling and the cost of funds reducing, the range of PLRs offered by public-sector banks remained rigid. Therefore, a new system was required—not only to fill the transparency gap in banks' lending rates but to also reduce the complexity involved in the pricing of loans.

In his mid-term monetary and credit policy (the RBI used to announce only two policies every year at that time) of November 2003, Bimal Jalan's policy statement changed the PLR system to a new paradigm called the Benchmark Prime Lending Rate, or BPLR, which would be calculated on the basis of:

   (i) actual cost of funds,
  (ii) operating expenses, and
 (iii) a minimum margin to cover the regulatory requirements of provisioning and capital charge, and profit margin

The RBI also stated that banks could determine the lending rates for working capital and term loans with reference to the BPLR by taking into account term premia (or different premia for different loan tenures), with the premium over BPLR varying with the tenure of the loan, and/or risk premia (premium rising with the loan duration and/or the perceived riskiness of the borrower). The responsibility for implementing the BPLR throughout the banking system was handed over to the Indian Banks' Association (IBA), the industry's self-regulatory organization. By April 2004, almost all the banks in the country had implemented the BPLR mechanism for pricing loans.

The RBI also refrained from issuing detailed, computational guidelines on the pricing of BPLR. But banks, on the other hand, wanted the RBI to come out with a standardized methodology

for calculating BPLR; banks also sought the comfort of past
practices by demanding that the RBI allow for different BPLRs
for pricing loans for different sectors, such as housing finance.
This provided some early indications of how the BPLR was also
headed the PLR way.

The RBI, under Governor D. Subbarao, set up a working
group in 2009 to review the BPLR system and suggest a new
methodology that was more transparent in pricing credit. In its
introduction, the working group explained why the BPLR had
fallen short:

> . . . the BPLR system has fallen short of its original objective
> of bringing transparency to lending rates. Competition has
> forced the pricing of a significant proportion of loans far out
> of alignment with BPLRs and in a non-transparent manner,
> undermining the role of the BPLR as a reference rate. There
> was also widespread public perception that the BPLR system
> has led to cross-subsidisation in terms of under-pricing of credit
> for corporates and overpricing of loans to agriculture and small
> and medium enterprises. The Annual Policy Statement 2009–
> 10 noted that since the bulk of bank loans were lent at sub-
> BPLR rates, the system of BPLR evolved in such a manner that
> it had lost its relevance as a meaningful reference rate. The lack
> of transparency in the BPLR system also caused impediment to
> the effective transmission of monetary policy signals.

In October 2009, the working group suggested the Base Rate
as an alternative mode of pricing credit, and the calculations
for the Base Rate included costs that were not considered in
the BPLR mechanism earlier, such as the losses from money
deployed towards SLR and CRR, or certain overhead costs. But,
much like its predecessors, the PLR and the BPLR, individual
Base Rates too began to be distorted by banks as part of their
aggressive marketing outreach. In addition, many banks did not

fully understand the spirit and essence of the illustrative model that the RBI provided with its report on the Base Rate and tried copying it in toto, which, obviously, did not end well. The stickiness of bank lending rates to changes in the benchmark rates by the RBI—lending rates went up significantly faster when rates went up and came down much slower when rates were cut—made the central bank's execution of monetary policy somewhat incomplete and only partially efficient. On the downward interest journey, when the RBI wanted to signal lower interest rates to the system, banks were tardy in intermediating that message to the economy, thereby scrambling up all the monetary policy signals. In addition, the diffused and varied mechanisms used by banks rendered the process of determining the Base Rate rather opaque, making the RBI's job of assessing monetary transmission that much more difficult.

In 2015, then RBI governor Raghuram Rajan noted in the April monetary policy that banks were following different methodologies in computing their Base Rate—on the basis of the average cost of funds, the marginal cost of funds or the blended cost of funds (liabilities). An RBI internal study found that banks using the marginal-cost-of-funding mechanism for finalizing their Base Rate were more sensitive to RBI's rate changes. Rajan thus directed banks to move to a new methodology of determining the Base Rate, based on the marginal cost of funds, as a way to improve monetary transmission. Predictably, even that turned out to be disappointing, with the RBI discovering that banks were reluctant to lower their lending rates under the marginal costs of funds-based lending (MCLR) system for retail or small and medium enterprises even during an easy monetary cycle when benchmark rates were low and there was surplus liquidity in the system.

An internal study group set up in 2017 under Governor Urjit Patel to figure out a new, improved system, tested thirteen

variables and concluded that banks should base their lending rates
on three external benchmarks: the RBI's repo rate (or the rate
at which the RBI lends overnight money to banks), the rate at
which banks raise bulk money from the market through flotation
of certificates of deposit, and the 91-day T-bill rate. In September
2019, by which time Governor Shaktikanta Das had taken over
the corner office on Mint Street, the RBI decided, after extensive
discussions internally and with external stakeholders, to reference
all new floating retail and SME loans to external benchmarks
which were different from the original set: the RBI's repo rate, the
government's three-month treasury bill yield and the government's
six-month treasury bill yield. By end-December 2022, the share
of loans advanced at interest rates based on external benchmarks
was 48.3 per cent of the total outstanding floating rate rupee
loans, while that of MCLR-linked loans was 46.1 per cent.

However, the dual nature of the rate structure has given rise
to a small crinkle which unwittingly favours larger corporates over
retail or SME borrowers. The rates on loans to retail and SME
borrowers—based on external benchmarks—have to be reset
every three months but the reset period for loans under MCLR is
much longer (going up to even once a year). This makes rates on
loans to individuals or small units go up comparatively faster than
loans to medium-sized and large companies.

The long journey from administered rates to the current
state of dualism, in which rates based on external benchmarks
and the MCLR system both coexist, encapsulates in many
ways the long and tortuous arc of bank deregulation in India.
The process was explained by RBI Deputy Governor Michael
Debabrata Patra in a December 2021 address at the Indian
Institute of Management, Ahmedabad:

> In India, the growing involvement of people in the monetary
> policy process has led to more democratic approaches to

interest rate setting. The RBI moved away from regulating interest rates during the 1990s. This was followed by guideline-based loan pricing norms – prime lending rates; base rates; marginal cost of funds-based lending rates. The goal is transparency, customer protection and awareness, and being as market-based as feasible, all of which are intended to foster inclusiveness. Across these regimes, transmission of policy rate changes to both deposit and lending rates has improved. The process has come full circle with the external benchmark-based lending rates – applied first to retail loans and credit to micro and small units – under which transmission is even fuller. Clearly, sustaining the thrust on financial inclusion will leave the RBI better off in achieving monetary policy transmission.

It is quite possible that the three-decade-long evolution of interest rate benchmarks may have been influenced by other exogenous developments, over and above the central bank's manifest concerns about rates not allowing for smoother transmission of monetary policy signals. This speculation gains wings in view of the repeated failure of experiments introducing interest rate hedging, especially exchange-traded interest rate futures, which many banks may have deemed necessary to imbue their interest rate structures with flexibility. Banks, in short, were being asked to adopt a free-market framework with control-era tools. But, beyond that proximate reason, it is worth asking whether the interest changes were a by-product of other shocks that were occurring in the financial system.

## Prudentially Speaking

The second area of deep reforms entailed the improvement of the internal health of the banking sector by taking a broom to multiple cobwebs. The banking sector of the pre-1991 reforms was not acquainted with uniform accounting rules, especially those concerning income recognition (norms which determined when income had to be recognized as received and fit for inclusion in the accounting books), classification of assets (into performing and non-performing, which would then determine whether interest income from these assets could be recognized in the books), provisioning norms for deciding how much money was to be set aside for which class of assets, realistic valuation of investments and introduction of uniform capital adequacy requirements (amount of capital based on the bank's risk-weighted assets).

For close to two decades, banks in India had been steadily hollowed out from the years of heavy expenditure incurred in expanding their branch networks, loss of income from being arm-twisted into investing a large chunk of their deposits in low-yielding government bonds, the books reflecting the bonds at inflated values, the rising number of loans—both commercial credit and concessional loans—going bad but being shown as normal and income-yielding long after they had dried up, and deep capital erosion without any signs of recapitalization. The system had remained stubbornly oblivious to the crying need for change. The Narasimham Committee took urgent note of the problems:

> There has been a deterioration in the quality of the loan portfolio which in turn has come in the way of banks' income generation and enhancement of their capital funds. Inadequacy of capital has been accompanied by inadequacy of loan loss provisions. The accounting and disclosure practices also do not always reflect the true state of affairs of the banks and financial institutions. The erosion of profitability of banks has also emanated from the side of expenditures as a result of fast and massive expansion of branches, many of which are unremunerative especially in the rural areas, a considerable degree of overmanning especially in urban and metropolitan centres and inadequate progress in updating work technology.

The RBI's acceptance and implementation of the Narasimham recommendations followed a certain train of logic.

Asset classification became the first area of focus. The RBI had earlier devised a health code system with eight categories to rank the health of a loan asset. The bottom four of these categories indicated non-performance. But, given the lack of proper accounting norms or data-based qualification rules, the specifics for each category were quite fuzzy. The decision on which loan fitted into which category was thus left to the subjective choice and discretion of bank officers. Once the RBI accepted the Narasimham Committee recommendations, the categories were crunched down to four: standard, sub-standard, doubtful and loss-making.

Under the new rules, a loan would be considered a 'non-performing asset' if interest remained unpaid for four quarters. This rule was in force till 31 March 1993, when it was brought down to three quarters, which applied up to 31 March 1994. Eventually, it was brought down to two quarters, as is the international norm, from the next year onwards.

Income recognition was next on the list. Pre-reforms, banks booked income from loans which had gone sour, despite that income not actually accruing to the bank. During that period, of the eight health code categories in force, banks could not recognize income accrued from loans that fell in the four NPA categories. But in reality, bank officers relied on personal discretion and leavened it with some arbitrariness, wary of how a higher percentage of bad loans would reflect on their performance; as a result, creativity triumphed over transparency in the reporting of numbers. Consequently, many banks continued to book income on loans that had long gone bad. Abiding by the Narasimham Committee's imprimatur, the RBI stopped the habit of banks booking interest income on loan assets on which interest was due for two quarters, or 180 days. This, to some extent, improved the disclosure norms, and the bank books started reflecting a comparatively truer state of affairs. One uses the word 'comparatively' advisedly here because the industry-banking nexus soon devised ingenious ways to game this too.

Once the revised norms were introduced, a true picture of the banking loan book emerged in the public view. The RBI's special five-volume compendium of Reports on Currency and Finance (2003–08) states:[6]

> Aggregate domestic non-performing advances of all public sector banks, which constituted 14.5% of total outstanding advances at March-end 1992 based on the old health code system, worked out to 23.2% as on March 31, 1993, based on the revised classification. This implied that about one-fourth of banks' advances were locked in unproductive assets. This not only adversely affected banks' profitability but also prevented recycling of funds, thereby constraining the growth of their balance sheets.

Proper loan loss provisioning standards were also introduced. Banks usually set aside a small portion of the expected loan repayments from all loans to cover for the eventuality of some loans going bad, either completely or partially; the entire profits are not distributed to the shareholders so that some can be kept back to top up the depleted capital. In short, provisioning this way allows the bank to use the money set aside to make good any probable impairments to the balance sheet by a loss asset.

As with everything else earlier, banks also had a lot of discretion as to whether to provide, or how much to provide, for loans going sour. Once the reforms process was initiated, this was corrected because the earlier episodes of non-provisioning had weakened the banks' balance sheets. Structural reforms meant removing the protective barrier around a wide swathe of industries, banking included, and their survival in a competitive future would require strong balance sheets. The provisioning norms have been progressively tightened by the RBI over the years, with the RBI now requiring banks to provision—even if in minuscule amounts—for loans that fall in the standard category too. The financial crisis of 2008 has accelerated the introduction of additional provisioning norms, with global regulatory institutions advocating counter-cyclical risk mitigation measures.

The RBI took many other measures as well to beef up the balance sheets of banks. The investment valuation norms were aligned with market reality, which was a big change from the earlier practice of banks valuing investments at the cost value, without accounting for any value attenuation. In addition, capital adequacy norms were formalized, requiring banks to corral capital in line with the riskiness of the assets they held.

The idea of capital adequacy had germinated in the Bank for International Settlements during the second half of the 1980s when many US and European commercial banks had to either write down or write off loans to many nations in South America, as part of a debt restructuring plan devised by then US Secretary of State James Baker. Given the resulting large-scale impairment to the balance sheets of multiple banks, BIS—the central banker for all central banks—had floated the idea of linking capital with the quantum of risk assets. Even the RBI started preparing the ground for capital adequacy sometime in 1988, though the final implementation would eventually occur in 1992.

Instituting the idea of capital adequacy meant that the government had to provide funds for the recapitalization of banks, given the larger number of weak public-sector banks than weak private-sector banks in the system. Until March 2002, the government had pumped in Rs 22,250 crore as additional funds to recapitalize weak public-sector banks.

The Reserve Bank of India undertook many other measures to bring Indian banks up to speed to face a new, competitive world. Transparency norms were stepped up by improving audit and disclosure rules so that bank balance sheets reflected the true state of affairs. The RBI is improving the standards even today. It has also made banks more aware of the multifarious risks in the system and has goaded them to proactively manage those risks. The RBI has impressed upon banks the need to actively manage a variety of other risks—apart from credit risk, which banks have to deal with daily—such as foreign exchange risk, operating risk, treasury risks and asset-liability mismatch risks, among others.

Many of the other relics of the control regime, such as credit rationing, have also been completely abolished. The RBI not only used to tell banks how much to lend to whom, but it also laid down the rules for banks on how to calculate eligible bank financing for a corporation, and on the correct level of receivables or inventory to qualify for financing. All that has now gone. From 1993, banks were given the freedom to assess their clients' loan requirements themselves.

One of the Narasimham Committee recommendations which the RBI readily accepted related to the pre-emption of funds via SLR and CRR. It is interesting to note that SLR has been successfully brought down to 18 per cent, a long drop from the pre-reforms level of 38.5 per cent. Initially, though, the rate was brought down to 25 per cent, as per the Narasimham Committee's prescription, and could not be dropped further because the Banking Regulation Act of yore had laid down a floor. This was subsequently removed through an amendment in 2007, allowing the SLR to drop to its current rate of 18 per cent. But, and this is ironic, the Act still retains the ceiling of 40 per cent, allowing the central bank to raise it all the way to the legislative limit should a need for it arise. This can be seen as indicative of either the central bank's residual apprehensions of risks to the banking system or a lingering desire to re-utilize SLR as a tool to raise resources for public expenditure.

It is also ironic to note that over the past couple of decades, even as the RBI has progressively reduced the mandated SLR requirement, many banks continue to hold government securities in excess of the minimum requirement. For example, the RBI's six-monthly Monetary Policy Report of April 2023 says the banking system's SLR level is over 26 per cent, against the stipulated 18 per cent. The case is extreme in the case of foreign banks, where the average SLR holding is over 50 per cent. This is telling, because it could be seen as a reflection of the banking industry's eroding faith in the system's creditworthiness. This demonstration of extreme risk-averse behaviour by banks, opting to invest in safe government securities even at the cost of earning lower interest incomes instead of indulging in the core activity of advancing loans, makes for a disconcerting commentary. A spectacular rise in credit demand may eventually lead to a drawdown of the excessive SLR positions, but anything below the current minimum of 18 per cent will also require the government to reduce its fiscal deficit.

The RBI has also been consistently reducing the rate of CRR (as a percentage of a bank's net time and demand liabilities) since 1992, except for brief periods intermittently, when it has been increased for a variety of reasons—such as to suck out excessive liquidity from the system or to prevent speculation and volatility in the currency market, among other things. For example, in 1994, the RBI raised the CRR rate to pump out some of the liquidity from the market to deter speculators from borrowing cheap money from the system to speculate in the currency market. But on occasion, the RBI has also acted in the other direction, such as in the early stages of the coronavirus pandemic in 2020. During that period, the RBI did not hesitate to reduce the CRR rate to 3 per cent to ensure that the system had enough liquidity to prevent any credit defaults and that there was adequate money to feed the demand for credit.

In fact, the CRR cuts have been substantial if one considers that not so long ago—in August 1998—the CRR was still 11 per cent.

But it must also be remembered that the CRR reduction had to be calibrated with the movements in the fiscal deficit, as well as the financing of the deficit. Pre-1991, the RBI needed to maintain large cash balances to directly subscribe to government bond issues, which led to a direct monetization of the deficit and, consequently, high inflation rates. The reduction could be implemented once the RBI moved to indirect instruments of monetary management, such as open-market operations.

Former RBI deputy governor, the late S.S. Tarapore, explained it lucidly in an article[7] he contributed to the book *India: A Financial Sector for the Twenty-First Century*:

> A high CRR is a heavy tax on the banking system and distorts the cost of funds as well as the deployment, and there is a strong case for refraining from a high CRR. It should be the endeavour of policy to ensure that the CRR is raised above 3% only for very short periods, and when monetary conditions stabilise the CRR should be very quickly brought down to 3% . . . Progressively, the medium-term objective should be to give up the CRR as an instrument of monetary control. Open market operations as an instrument of monetary control are substantially more efficient than a CRR-refinance regime as the former pick up the liquidity where it is in surfeit and provide liquidity where it is required whereas the CRR-refinance system is a blunt instrument.

There was another balancing act required when reducing the CRR. Any rapid CRR reduction had the potential of flooding the monetary system with excess liquidity, which could have disastrous consequences in the absence of credit demand. An overhang of excess liquidity does impact price levels as well as interest rates. The ripple effects also have the potential of spilling over to the foreign exchange market, imbuing currency rates with volatility.

The one measure that was implemented with great seriousness was the throwing open of banking to new private banks, though links to corporate groups were largely discouraged. Ten new private banks were set up (nine with new licences and one which was converted from an urban cooperative bank into a private-sector universal bank) in January 1993, though the RBI's choices raised eyebrows when the names of the new licence holders were disclosed, raising suspicions of political influence in the granting of licences. These reservations were further amplified when the central bank issued 'in-principle' approval to CRB Bank Ltd and Cox and Kings Bank Ltd in 1996. Fortunately, these 'in-principle' approvals were never converted into banking licences. It is also a matter of irony that from the original list of nine new private banks, only four have survived: HDFC Bank, ICICI Bank, Axis Bank (which started out life as UTI Bank but underwent a name change later) and IDBI Bank, which is in such a precarious financial state that the government's attempts to sell it have found no takers so far. The next phase of licensing saw the introduction of only two new private banks in 2001: Kotak Bank and Yes Bank. Another thirteen years would go by before another two banks would acquire private bank licences: IDFC Bank and Bandhan Bank in 2014.

In the meantime, under governor Raghuram Rajan, the RBI tried to experiment with differentiated banking licences in November 2014 with two new categories: payments banks[8] and small finance banks (SFBs)[9]. The former category allowed for limited entry of private sector business groups, such as companies engaged in mobile telephony. SFBs, on the other hand, were designed as small-scale universal banks with the mandate to lend 75 per cent of credit to designated priority sector areas. Interestingly, while the RBI guidelines included a proviso allowing SFBs to graduate into universal banks, the payments bank category was designed as a closed loop, allowing no opportunities for upgrade or advancement.

Subsequently, the RBI has moved away from episodic granting of licences to a system of on-tap licensing, under which applications for new banking licences can be filed with the RBI at any time during the year.

As is evident, the 1991 balance-of-payments crisis presented the government and the RBI with an opportunity to clean up the Augean stables of Indian banking. This reforms process could well have been initiated at any time prior to the crisis, but it took an emergency to push through meaningful reforms. The next set of reforms was again prompted by another crisis, which came close on the heels of M. Narasimham submitting his committee report to Finance Minister Manmohan Singh in November 1991.

## The Next Phase of Reforms

In April 1992, all hell broke loose upon the news that stock market speculator Harshad Mehta had left behind large, unfunded holes in the treasury operations of leading Indian banks. The Joint Parliamentary Committee (JPC) formed to investigate the contours of the scam found many loopholes in the functioning of the RBI, especially in relation to the discharge of its core duty of regulating banks. When upbraided by the JPC members, the RBI scrambled to fix the lacunae in its regulatory framework.

C. Rangarajan admits in his book *Forks in the Road* that the scam had some nudge-like qualities: 'In one sense, the securities scam accelerated the process of reforms.'

*RBI History* (Volume IV) acknowledges that the securities scam, among other factors, played a role in the financial sector's transformation: 'The period 1992–1997 witnessed a sea-change in the financial system in general and in the banking system in particular. There was a transformation in the outlook, and the need to foster a sound and healthy banking structure took root, especially in the Government's philosophy and the Reserve Bank's approach.'

At the government's prodding, the RBI set up an internal committee, chaired, ironically, by Deputy Governor R. Janakiraman, who had been in charge of the public debt office, one of the nerve centres from where the scam was perpetrated by the nexus of brokers and bankers. The JPC was forced to state:

> . . . two important departments of the RBI headed by two Deputy Governors Shri R. Janakiraman and Shri Amitava Ghosh principally concerned with SGL displayed insufficient concern in the matter contributing greatly to subsequent damage to the system. It is this gross dereliction of duty in PDO and DBOD which greatly contributed to the scam.

PDO is the public debt office and DBOD is the department for banking operations and development.

As mentioned earlier, the Janakiraman Committee, which included five other members, submitted a total of six reports between May 1992 and April 1993. In its first report, the committee made a number of recommendations, which were accepted by the RBI. These were more in the nature of the RBI scrambling to seal the gaps in the banking system through which resources had leaked out to numerous individual brokers and eventually to the stock market. Some of the remedial measures in the RBI's first-responder list were the following:

(i) Banks were permitted to enter ready-forward and double ready-forward deals with other banks for only government securities, and not other securities (such as PSU bonds, units and shares).

(ii) Ban on ready-forward and double ready-forward deals under portfolio management schemes.

(iii) Banks had to strictly adhere to the RBI's prohibition on entering buy-back deals with non-bank clients.

(iv) Banks had to formulate internal exposure limits for transactions, as well as limits for individual brokers.

(v) Banks had to strictly comply with the prohibition on issue of cheques drawn on their account with the RBI for third-party transactions.

(vi) A separate custodian was to be created for banks to route all their transactions in PSU bonds, units and similar securities through; this was to obviate any future need to issue BRs.

(vii) The RBI would speed up its work in the SGL section of the PDO and in furnishing information to banks.

(viii) The RBI would widen the scope of its bank inspections, including on-site inspections, with greater emphasis on treasury transactions.

(ix) The capacity of bank internal audit departments were reviewed by the RBI.

(x) Bank statutory auditors were compelled to conduct separate audits of banks' portfolio management operations.

The governor C. Rangarajan (who had taken charge in December 1992) and former deputy governor of RBI Amitava Ghosh deposed before the JPC. The JPC did not mince words when pointing out the RBI's evidently lackadaisical attitude to inspections and supervisions. Citing examples, the JPC observed how a mid-level RBI officer had, way back in 1986, found irregularities of the kind that had precipitated the securities scam—such as irregular transactions by use of bank receipts in Andhra Bank and Syndicate Bank. However, these inspection reports by junior or mid-level RBI officers would often take a long time to wind their way to someone in a senior position where some action could be taken. Usually, it was too late by then. For example, the JPC during its hearings discovered multiple delays on the RBI's part in finalizing inspection reports, forwarding them to the relevant banking institution and pursuing the reports with the bank management for compliance. The committee specifically provided the example of SBI, where the inspection report of 1986 was finalized and forwarded to the bank management eighteen months later, and final compliance discussions were held on the same report after thirty-six months. Planet Earth had made three trips around the sun by then, the ground realities in India's financial sector had perceptibly shifted, and the 1986 inspection report was only marginally relevant to SBI by then.

It can be argued in the RBI's defence that the central bank was too preoccupied with managing the fallout from the Centre's expenditure bill, over and above the onerous tasks of monitoring the subordinate banking system's delivery on multiple mandates—expansion of branch networks, meeting of annual deposit collection targets, maintaining of the requisite reserves, ensuring credit flow to the priority sectors and ensuring full subscription for all government bond issues—while trying to build a coherent picture from the complex and disjointed jigsaw puzzle of interest rates. Its skewed hierarchy of priorities left the RBI with little time to act as a supervisor or classic regulator of the banking sector. *RBI History* (Volume IV) also provides the same justification for the RBI's tardiness, but admits to the central bank's laxity in the whole process:

The Reserve Bank emphasised the issues involved and stated that while such irregularities could not be condoned, these irregularities occurred in the context of very large pre-emptions of banks' resources through CRR and SLR and regulations on interest rates. There were, however, undoubtedly certain lacunae in the monitoring system and market information collection mechanism.

The JPC members in 1992–93 had also noted, with some sense of amazement, that the PDO was finally computerized by July 1992, after a delay of six years, catalysed by the revelation of the scam in April 1992.

In 1997, a crisis broke out in East Asia. Major currencies across Thailand, Indonesia, Malaysia and South Korea fell catastrophically. The ripples began in Thailand when foreign investors started pulling out of Thai baht assets after the revelation of over-leveraged bank balance sheets, and soon became a tsunami across the region, battering one currency after another. The crisis found the IMF bailing out many of the region's economies, imposing severe economic austerities on them.

India remained relatively unscathed from the turmoil. Many policymakers were prompt to attribute this to the Indian economy's sound policies, though many critics felt that it was India's relatively closed economy that had, by default, shielded it from the roiling currency-market volatility. Whatever the reason, policymakers realized that one of the reasons for the crisis lay in the skewed bank balance sheets in the region. Given that the Indian economy was now fully committed to opening up to foreign investors, this was a wake-up call for many policymakers and regulators.

This inspired prompt implementation of the Narasimham-II recommendations in the second phase of banking reforms which, commencing from 1998, focused on strengthening the prudential norms introduced in 1993, specifically those related to income recognition, asset classification and provisioning. There was an added emphasis on improving the banking sector's asset-liability management norms, which had been one of the key tripwires in the case of the East Asian banks. This was to ensure that, first, banks must be aware of any asset-liability imbalance in their books and, second, implement measures to reduce the risks arising from such imbalances. Other measures—such as sprucing up corporate governance norms, improving credit delivery, enhancing customer service, and, further fortifying capital adequacy norms—were also added to the long menu of reforms.

## What Got Left Out

The Narasimham-I report in 1991 represents a watershed moment for the Indian financial system, a true inflexion point that changed the fortunes of the banking industry. But what is equally instructive is what got left out.

A large number of the Narasimham Committee-I recommendations were accepted immediately by the government and the RBI. In fact, many of these issues had already been debated and discussed in the past and raised by various RBI governors in different forms on different platforms. A closer examination of the proposals accepted and rejected also seems to convey the impression that the reforms process was limited to what was immediately expedient, or was permissible by the political economy at that point in time. Some of the proposals were indeed radical and would require a complete reworking of the political economy, which seemed somewhat unfeasible then.

The Narasimham-II report of 1998 made this wry observation about the reforms implementation track record:

> These have been very major and significant changes but it would be observed that while the 'arithmeticals' of the CFS recommendations in relation to various ratios, rates and accounting have been accepted and put through, the same measure of progress has not been made with regard to structural and systemic aspects of the reform agenda outlined by the CFS. Even with regard to 'arithmeticals', an important

recommendation relating to directed credit has not been accepted. In some cases, as for instance, in respect of the ways to handle the problem of non-performing assets (NPAs), while the problem has been recognised the approach adopted has differed [*from what was recommended in Narasimham-I*].

Here are examples of two interesting recommendations from Narasimham-I that were conveniently shoved under the carpet.

**Separate Supervision Body**: Public-sector banks were, and continue to be, regulated by both the RBI and their principal shareholder, the Indian government. The Narasimham Committee felt this dual structure should instead be replaced with one where the RBI becomes the primary regulator. In fact, the committee also felt that supervisory responsibility over banks should be vested with an independent body that can be hived off from the RBI. The proposal envisaged a quasi-autonomous body working under the RBI but devoid of all the usual central banking functions.

The proposal was heeded only partially: a separate organization was indeed set up, but it was not completely independent of the RBI, as had been suggested by the committee, nor was it headed by a full-time chief executive or managed by external independent directors in the manner prescribed by the committee. In November 1994, the RBI created a separate Board for Financial Supervision (BFS), which comprised four members drawn from the RBI's board of directors and was chaired by the governor of the day. The deputy governors are ex-officio members, but one deputy governor—usually the one in charge of supervision—is designated the BFS vice chairman. *RBI History*, Vol IV, says a separate organization with statutory supervisory powers over the banking system, outside the RBI, could not be pursued because that proposal would have necessitated legislating a new Act of Parliament.

In its current incarnation, the BFS, created from the RBI board of directors, houses as members RBI Governor Shaktikanta

Das as governor, Deputy Governor M.K. Jain as vice chairman, two other deputy governors (Michael Debabrata Patra and T. Rabi Sankar) and two external directors (Satish Kashinath Marathe and Sachin Chaturvedi). It is moot as to whether this format was found convenient also because it has so far precluded the BFS from publicly communicating the outcome of its meetings, important developments, or any of its concerns over supervision or the methodological changes required to the current regulatory framework in the face of the rapid technological transformation currently underway in the financial sector.

Unfortunately, duality of control still exists over banking, with the government continuing to exercise its rights as a shareholder as vigorously and robustly as in the past. The RBI, which vets almost all senior management appointments and director nominations at private and foreign banks, has either no say or very little say in the appointments process in public-sector banks. Political functionaries and party officials still get board nominations in the state-owned banks. A story in the *Times of India* dated 30 April 2023 noted: 'The government has approved the appointment of new chief executive officers to Bank of Baroda and Bank of India. The notifications came after the approval of the Appointments Committee of the Cabinet, headed by Prime Minister Narendra Modi.'

**Political Economy vs Reforms**: Two suggestions of the Narasimham Committee-I were sacrificed at the altar of realpolitik and expediency. One was the recommendation that the government reduce its involvement in public-sector banks, including in the recruitment of senior management personnel and board directors. Successive governments, even those with outspoken commitments to reforms, have demurred on this issue. What is, however, left unsaid is that control over banks as distribution hubs and patronage networks has been deemed to have become necessary for all regimes, regardless of their political ideology. This is also perhaps the reason why the committee's proposition that the priority-sector credit requirement be reduced from 40 per cent to 10 per cent has found no resonance across party lines.

When entrusted with drawing up the second phase of banking reforms, the Narasimham Committee in 1998 admitted that there could be valid reasons for not bringing down the mandatory limit of priority-sector loans to 10 per cent: 'The Committee recognizes that the small and marginal farmers and the tiny sector of industry and small businesses have problems with regard to obtaining credit and some earmarking may be necessary for this sector.' The original stewards of the reforms process—the Congress-led coalition of P.V. Narasimha Rao—had lost the 1996 elections because of the combined reasons of elevated inflation and growing public disillusionment with Rao's shifting moral boundaries. The ragtag coalition that succeeded the Rao government seemed even more hesitant to meddle with a loan system that had overt political overtones, even though it seemed committed to continuing the reforms process.

Having climbed down from its original position, Narasimham-II however managed to wrest a promise that the largest chunk of priority-sector loans would be extended at non-concessional rates. The prevalent argument around that time, which had its genesis during Governor C. Rangarajan's tenure at the RBI,[10] was that borrowers accorded greater priority to timely credit access and availability than credit pricing. In short, the agricultural borrower or small-scale entrepreneur valued credit availability much more than the interest rate at which it was supplied, provided the rates were not usurious. The government in 1998 also bought into this argument, and the rules were re-aligned along the Narasimham-II recommendations in a grand bargain: while banks still had to keep aside 40 per cent of their credit for priority-sector categories, they were allowed to charge commercial rates on most of the categories to ensure there was no loss of interest income.

## The Reforms Continuum

In the decade following Narasimhan-II of 1998, banking sector reforms continued to progress at a speed largely being dictated by events. For example, the 2008 financial crisis, which germinated in the advanced Western nations and subsequently engulfed economies across the globe, inspired some policy reconfiguration in India as well. One immediate reaction—based on the learning from the US markets about the issue of interconnectedness and systemic risks—was to create a non-statutory body of regulators, called the Financial Stability and Development Council, a sort of coordinating body between the regulators to exchange information and views to get an idea of the system as a whole. The primary aim in doing this was to strengthen the existing institutional mechanism for financial stability by emphasizing macro-prudential regulation and regulatory coordination.

The RBI was, however, not very enthused by the idea and was openly critical of the body's effete, non-legal structure. Its annual report for 2009–10 included a small note of caution about it:

> While coordination councils comprising both government functionaries and regulators would serve the intended objectives, particularly through exchange of information and views, there has to be a clear recognition that committees cannot assume executive responsibility for financial stability, especially in a crisis situation where speed and surprise could be the key elements of response. Moreover, explicit demarcation of responsibilities can help in strengthening crisis prevention, through speedy and effective response in the demarcated areas. Clarity in responsibilities is critical for effective accountability.

Most of the other attempts to overhaul the banking system subsequently remained focused on improving the existing norms or on further strengthening the prudential norms, especially the capital adequacy rules or provisioning norms. Many other attempts to introduce structural reforms failed, in the absence of a proximate crisis. The government-appointed Financial Sector Legislative Reforms Commission (FSLRC), for example, attempted to introduce a comprehensive, omnibus legal framework to reform the overall financial regulatory architecture, but the draft Bill never made it to Parliament. However, some of the individual elements from the draft managed to make it through the policy pipeline, such as the merger of the Forwards Market Commission (the commodities trading regulator) with SEBI.

One view about the reasons behind the draft Bill's failure is that it unabashedly tried to whittle down the powers of the existing regulators and thus hit a bureaucratic wall. The other reason is that in the absence of a crisis, both the executive and the legislative lacked enough incentives to sell it to their respective constituencies.

This peculiarity is best exemplified by the failed attempts to introduce reforms in the bankruptcy and insolvency laws through legislation. This, of course, altered as soon as crises forced the government's hand, resulting in two crucial policy measures. The first was the enactment of the Indian Bankruptcy Code to deal with the insolvency of firms. The second was the creation of a legal framework for dealing with the resolution of failed financial firms. All that in the next chapter . . .

# Chapter 8

## NPAs: A Problem That Refuses to Go Away

There was general jubilation in the stock markets on 29 February 2016. Then finance minister Arun Jaitley had just finished reading his budget speech for 2016–17 in which he happened to announce a scheme to sort out the messy tangle of bad loans in the banking sector. The equity market's optimism surprised everybody because NPAs—or non-performing assets, as bad loans are technically referred to in India—have remained an intractable problem for close to three decades, impervious to a steady procession of schemes formulated by both the government and the RBI.

This is what Jaitley said that caused the markets to combust:

> A systemic vacuum exists with regard to bankruptcy situations in financial firms. A comprehensive Code on Resolution of Financial Firms will be introduced as a Bill in the Parliament during 2016–17. This Code will provide a specialised resolution mechanism to deal with bankruptcy situations in banks, insurance companies and financial sector entities. This Code, together with the Insolvency and Bankruptcy Code 2015, when enacted, will provide a comprehensive resolution mechanism for our economy.

Truth be told, those looking askance at the stock market buoyancy seemed justified; there was nothing in Jaitley's statement that was different from what his various predecessors had said on numerous occasions, especially when announcing yet another new scheme for tackling NPAs.

The story of NPAs, thus, needs to be told.

In 1991, the Narasimham Committee-I had recognized that rising NPAs on the balance sheets of Indian banks were a menace which, left unchecked, could engulf the entire banking sector in India, threatening financial stability and bringing the entire economy to a standstill. The committee members saw bulging NPAs tucked away deep in the balance sheets of banks, ominously lurking in the background as a permanent threat to the industry and economy. All and any reforms would be infructuous if bad loans continued to weigh on banks' balance sheets.

The danger can be understood from the basic business model of a bank: unlike any other business, a bank is a highly leveraged entity. In other words, a bank borrows in multiples of its capital, mostly through the instrument of deposits, making it much more vulnerable to shocks than any other commercial unit. Mounting NPAs in a bank is a source of severe stress, directly eroding the bank's capital and jeopardizing its existence. As the Indian economy entered the decade of the 1990s, it was clear to policymakers that the gnawing NPA problem could undo all the good work done over the decades.

It was a crisis by any other word. What is unfortunate is that the NPA problem existed at the time of the Narasimham Committee report, and it exists even now, waxing and waning with shifts in the economy. The suite of solutions to fix it has also swung from the absurd to the ineffective, with some half-way legal solutions working hard to wrest half-way solutions from within the politico-industry complex. As with the rest of the financial sector reforms, the sporadic attempts to provide solutions were felt necessary only when matters got out of hand. But whenever the law or rules proved antagonistic to its interests, industry wielded its superior collective bargaining powers, using the cracks in India's distorted campaign finance structure to press home its advantage and to ease the pressure.

It may therefore be instructive to look at all the attempts made to solve the problem of NPAs and all the solutions brought to the table to see which of those worked and which had to be junked.

There are two kinds of NPAs in India. One is the genuine bad loan, arising from external factors such as a war, a drought, an earthquake or a flood affecting business or farming operations. Often, it is also the result of inefficiency or mismanagement, a business strategy going wrong, or just plain simple business obsolescence. There are also instances of NPAs resulting from banks not conducting due diligence or from haphazard credit appraisals on their part.

The second kind is the wilful default, where the borrower does not repay the loan on purpose, either safe in the knowledge that political pressure would be brought upon the banks to write off the loan (such as farm loans on which there are mass waivers before an election) or that the long and winding legal process is typically structured to favour the borrower and not the lender.

The second category is usually monopolized by large- and medium-scale industries and, over time, started contributing to a larger share of the NPAs in the economy. The slow-burn liberalization of the economy in the 1980s, which saw a new breed of entrepreneurs testing the system, collided against what was still a capital-scarce economy in which even banks exercised severe funding restrictions. The RBI would decide which organizations deserved credit, and how much, based on some internal formula, and at a pre-determined high rate to cross-subsidize other concessional loans. This gave rise to what is known as gold-plating, a euphemism for entrepreneurs inflating their project costs, borrowing in excess of the project's requirements and siphoning off the excess. The money would usually come back in the form of the promoter's equity contribution to the project or would be diverted to finance another project. Sometimes the siphoning off also occurred to finance the entrepreneur's lifestyle. There are also well-known examples now of promoters siphoning off the entire loan amount and using illegal channels to transfer the funds overseas. The need for gold-plating seemed to increase after 1991, when the economic reforms programme allowed free competition and existing entrepreneurs realized they needed to inject additional capital into their companies to stay competitive.

It might be appropriate to note here that a study of NPAs by the RBI in its July 1999 monthly bulletin[1] titled 'Some Aspects and Issues Relating to NPAs in Commercial Banks', found diversion of funds by companies as the predominant reason for defaults. Here, companies would take loans for one project but divert them to other projects within their business group that would otherwise not have been found loan-worthy. The RBI study observed:

> 'Diversion of funds . . . mostly for expansion/diversification/ modernization, taking up new projects and for helping/ promoting associate concerns, is the single most prominent reason. Besides being so, this factor is also in a significant proportion of cases, combined with other factors like recessionary trends developing during the expansion/ diversification/promotion phase and failure to raise capital/ debt from public issue due to market turning lukewarm.'

Even former RBI governor Urjit Patel has mentioned in his book *Overdraft* that a nexus between the lender and borrower has stymied the speedy resolution of NPAs:

> The broad conclusion that has been universally accepted is that enterprises in India have over and over again received excessive credit during loan growth cycles, which is followed soon after with repayment problems. Rather than resolving

stressed credit problems swiftly, banks – either through loan-level fudges or refusal to recognize the true asset quality of the credits – have allowed promoters in charge of enterprises to have a soft landing; this has comprised of even more bank lending so as to keep the accounts artificially in full repayment on past dues, protracted control for promoters over failed assets, and effectively granting them the ability to divert cash and assets, often outside of our jurisdictional reach.

Attempts to find solutions to insolvency and bankruptcy have been made in India since pre-Independence. The Presidency Towns Insolvency Act, 1909, was introduced to cover the insolvency of individuals, partnerships and associations of individuals in the three erstwhile Presidency Towns of what are now known as Kolkata, Chennai and Mumbai. In 1920, the Provincial Insolvency Act was enacted as the insolvency law for individuals (including individuals as proprietors) in areas other than the Presidency towns.

Post-Independence, once the Companies Act was legislated and the government started building an industrial base for the nation, the associated problem of industrial sickness soon started rearing its head. There were attempts to tackle the rising incidence of sickness in industry, which was seen as a drain on the economy. Following up on the recommendations of a government-appointed committee, the government legislated the Sick Industrial Companies Act (SICA) in 1985 and later set up the Board for Industrial and Financial Reconstruction (BIFR) in 1987 as part of the Act for early detection of incipient sickness and its prevention. Companies experiencing an erosion of net worth due to losses were to report to BIFR, and the board would act as an operating agency and devise a revival strategy in consultation with all the lending agencies.

As policy instruments go, both SICA and BIFR turned out to be quite ineffective. BIFR's record in disposing of sick companies registered with it was patchy, the progress slowed down by conflicting interests between various parties (banks, companies, government organizations) and the fundamental flaws in SICA. For example, SICA recognized sickness in only manufacturing units and not in trading or service organizations. In addition, SICA recognized sickness only at an advanced stage, by which time it became difficult for BIFR to rehabilitate the unit. Rules that prohibited banks from taking legal action against companies referred to BIFR provided a safe haven for many indebted companies that registered willingly with BIFR to escape repayment, with the Board's prolonged quasi-judicial processes further helping companies defer repayment almost indefinitely.

Consequently, the failure rate of BIFR was as high as 40–50 per cent. Between 1982 and 1989, the outstanding credit to sick units rose by an average of over 30 per cent every year. By December 1989, 75 per cent of the outstanding credit owed by sick units was locked up in large- and medium-scale industrial units.

This was the turning point, in more ways than one. On the one hand, we see the beginning of some serious attempts to bring it all out in the open and seek a realistic, viable solution. On the other hand, we also detect parallel, but abortive, moves being made by the RBI and the government, which have been described in the following paragraphs.

The Narasimham Committee-I may not have been the first official body to train the arc lights on NPAs, but it forcefully drew attention to the ticking time bomb in the banking system. It made two recommendations for tackling the bad loans problem, of which one—a special tribunal—was implemented in 1993 after getting all the legal parameters in place. The other—the setting up of an asset reconstruction fund—was put on the back burner and implemented later.

One of the main problems confronting banks, once a loan went bad, pertained to enforcing the security collateral pledged by lenders. Not only did the winding-up legal process take a long time, thereby eroding the value of the collateral with the passage of time, but delays in court also meant rising legal expenditure for banks. As a way out, the Narasimham Committee-I recommended the establishment of a special tribunal, adding that financial sector reforms would be incomplete without a special legal body:

> The Committee is of the view that unless a proper judicial framework is established which could help banks and institutions in enforcing the claims against their clients speedily, the functioning of the financial system would continue to be beset with problems. We regard the setting up of the Special Tribunals as critical to the successful implementation of the financial sector reforms.

This recommendation was accepted. Consequently, in 1993, The Recovery of Debts Due to Banks and Financial Institutions Act (RDDBFI) was enacted; it envisaged the creation of a number of debt recovery tribunals as a way to speed up the legal recovery of bad loans. The first tribunal was set up in Calcutta (now Kolkata) in April 1994. By June 2022, there were thirty-nine debt recovery tribunals (DRTs) and five debt recovery appellate tribunals (DRATs) functioning across the country.

However, the process of getting the tribunals up and running sounded easier on paper than in reality, and it took over five years to get the tribunals operational. The first hurdle was erected in the form of a petition in the Delhi High Court, claiming that the tribunals were the executive's way of encroaching on areas demarcated for the judiciary. The Delhi Bar Association challenged the legal and constitutional validity of the RDDBFI Act in the Delhi High Court, which found the Act unconstitutional because it blurred the lines between the separate and independent jurisdictions of the judiciary and the executive. The Delhi High Court also pointed to some incongruities in the Act, especially the unavailability of provisions for borrowers to make counter-claims, which invested the Act with a bias in favour of the creditors. Basically, the court felt that borrowers who had defaulted on their loans should be allowed recourse to appeal against lenders selling off their collateral to recoup the money lent. The government duly challenged this in the Supreme Court which, in a March 1996 interim order, allowed the tribunals to function but requested the government to amend the Act. The amendment came about in 2000, investing defendants with the right to make counter-claims. The Supreme Court's final ruling, divining the amended Act as constitutional, was passed in March 2002, nine years after the original Act was legislated.

There were other reasons for the delays: inadequate staffing, shoddy infrastructure or budgetary constraints. Also, these tribunals came to replicate the protracted delays of the normal courts whose workload they were meant to alleviate. In addition, parties had the option of going in for an appeal if they were not satisfied with the tribunal's judgments. The process of recovery through the DRT route not only lengthened with time, but the percentage of recoveries has also been diminishing. Ironically, these tribunals were set up to provide speedy relief to the banking system because the pervasive delays in the civil courts made legal outcomes highly uncertain. But, in reality, these tribunals ended up looking like clones of the courts themselves.

In the final analysis, it would seem that the government lost interest in DRTs, what with the delays and mounting number of pending cases. By end-February 2022, there were 1,61,034 cases pending at the DRTs. The state of the tribunals had deteriorated,[2] with the government ostensibly losing interest, not even paying the bills. In addition, vacant presiding officer posts in many DRTs have seen pending cases pile up, eliciting some sharp comments[3] from the Bombay High Court in 2020.

Narasimham-I's second recommendations for sorting out the NPA tangle focused on setting up an assets reconstruction fund

(ARF), but it was rejected by the RBI outright. Setting up the tribunals called for a myriad of tasks—appointing them, finalizing their work procedures and equipping them with the necessary infrastructure to ensure smooth functioning. The committee felt that since the tribunals would take some time to get off the ground, the NPAs on the bank books would continue to weigh the institutions down and hobble their ability to expand credit, which defeated the idea of economic reforms. The committee members had studied similar models elsewhere in the world and felt that ARFs, which would buy out the bad loans from banks at a discount and pursue recovery from the primary borrowers, would relieve banks of the deadweight on their shoulders and help them get on with their core business of extending credit. The ARFs' capital would come from the government, the RBI, public-sector banks and financial institutions.

The committee had envisaged that banks would sell their assets to the ARFs at a discount, which would be determined on the basis of some guidelines. The ARFs, which would issue interest-bearing bonds to the banks as consideration for the loans acquired, would independently pursue recovery of the loans. There were some other procedural suggestions relating to ARFs too, and some that sought to reduce the capital stress for banks which would arise from the writing off of loans.

Why did the RBI not find this palatable?

The answer is found in its annual publication, 'Report on Trend and Progress of Banking in India, 1991–92'. The central bank expressed two concerns. One was over the volume of funding required for the proposed ARFs.

It is recognized that the introduction of an ARF combined with the prudential requirements will, as a consequence, require large amounts of funds. If these large capital requirements are to be met by the Government or the Reserve Bank, it may imply a large monetisation with obvious deleterious effects on the economy. Thus, the strategy for raising fresh capital by banks needs to be carefully worked out.

The second concern, expressed in the same report, was over a legitimate economic term called 'moral hazard'. There are many technical definitions of moral hazard, but the simplest one is perhaps the danger of repeated delinquent behaviour by an economic agent if he is secure in the knowledge of being bailed out in every default event. In the ARF context, the problem of moral hazard would imply that if banks knew that an external agent would eventually follow up on loan recovery, they were likely to exhibit laxity in both credit appraisal and the due process for recovery.

> An ARF poses the problem of moral hazard of lenders being distanced from the recovery process and this may not provide for the most efficient procedure for recovery; furthermore, such a fund could give rise to an erosion of accountability as a climate could get generated with expectations of a repetition of such waivers in the future.

But the RBI also threw a bone, suggesting that a 'limited' ARF could be conceived of, which would acquire the bad loans of only the smaller, weaker banks. But this was conditional on drastic changes in the management of these banks, sacrifices by the staff, control on the growth of assets and, above all, an increase in productivity, all of which had to be clearly spelt out in a Memorandum of Understanding. Interestingly, the next year's publication, 1992–93, also spelt out the same two concerns but dropped the idea of a halfway-house ARF. Tellingly, the following year, 1993–94, there was no mention of ARF at all, implying that the original recommendation had now been buried.

Strangely, in the midst of all this, the government set up another committee in April 1993, under the chairmanship of

Omkar Goswami, to review and examine the various aspects of industrial sickness and corporate restructuring. The committee submitted its report in July 1993 and its recommendations ranged from a change in the definition of sickness to converting BIFR into a fast-track facilitator. The committee's recommendations were taken into consideration in the drafting of a comprehensive new legislation to deal with sick industrial companies, and the government introduced a new Bill—the Sick Industrial Companies (Special Provisions) Bill, 1997—in Parliament on 16 May 1997. However, the Bill lapsed upon dissolution of the eleventh Lok Sabha in December 1997. Remember, this was during the term of the short-lived, third-front government which had two prime ministers—Deve Gowda and I.K. Gujral.

The NPA situation at banks, in the meantime, had definitely improved when compared with the state of affairs that had prevailed pre-reforms. Gross NPAs had come down from 23.2 per cent of gross advances in 1992–93 to 16 per cent by 1997–98. The prudential norms introduced as a consequence of the Narasimham-I report had started showing results, though the initial higher-disclosure norms had sent the gross NPA percentage spiking.

| Table I.4 : Gross and Net NPAs of Public Sector Banks - 1992-93 to 1997-98 | | | | | | |
| | | | | | (Amount in Rs. crore) | |
| End-March | Gross NPAs | % to Gross Adv. | % to Total Assets | Net NPAs | % to Net Adv. | % to Total Assets |
| --- | --- | --- | --- | --- | --- | --- |
| 1 | 2 | 3 | 4 | 5 | 6 | 7 |
| 1993 | 39,253 | 23.2 | 11.8 | | | |
| 1994 | 41,041 | 24.8 | 10.8 | | | |
| 1995 | 38,385 | 19.5 | 8.7 | 17,567 | 10.7 | 4.0 |
| 1996 | 41,661 | 18.0 | 8.2 | 18,297 | 8.9 | 3.6 |
| 1997 | 43,577 | 17.8 | 7.8 | 20,285 | 9.2 | 3.6 |
| 1998 (Provisional) | 45,653 | 16.0 | 7.0 | 21,232 | 8.2 | 3.3 |

Source: RBI's Report on Trend and Progress of Banking in India, 1997–98

But there was still a problem: even though the percentage of NPAs in gross advances was dropping, the absolute amount was rising. The percentage displayed an improvement only because gross advances had also gone up but at a faster rate. In absolute terms, gross NPAs in absolute numbers had shot up from Rs 39,253 crore in 1992–93 to Rs 45,653 crore in 1997–98. While this was an increase of only 16.3 per cent over five years, it still presented a potential danger. There would be pressure on banks to keep maintaining a high credit growth rate, even in lean years when credit demand tends to slacken a bit. In short, the NPA risk in the banking system had once again assumed a subterranean character, imbuing all policy frameworks with uncertainty and anxiety.

In the meantime, the government appointed the Narasimham-II Committee in December 1997, with M. Narasimham as chairman but with a completely different mix of members. The committee submitted its report in April 1998. One theme seemed to dominate: the malignant influence of NPAs that continued to pose a threat to the stability of the financial system and the inadequacy of all the remedial instruments that had been introduced to solve the problem.

A high level of NPAs represents a continuing potential threat to the viability of the system. The committee believed that the objective should be to reduce the average level of net NPAs for all banks to below 5 per cent of advances by the year 2000, and to 3 per cent by 2002. For those banks with an international presence, the minimum objective was to reduce gross NPAs to 5 per cent and 3 per cent by the years 2000 and 2002, respectively, and net NPAs to 3 per cent and 0 per cent by these dates. However, it was also true that achievement of these targets was well-nigh impossible in the absence of measures to first tackle the backlog of NPAs on a one-time basis and, second, the absence of strict prudential norms and management efficiency parameters which had to be implemented to prevent recurrence of this problem.

As the crisis mounted quietly, Finance Minister Yashwant Sinha accepted Narasimham-II's recommendation in the June 1998 budget and announced that asset reconstruction companies (ARCs, same as ARF) would be set up to take a shot at the backlog of NPAs that had been sitting on bank balance-sheets for many years, defying any resolution. The RBI also relented from its earlier stand and accepted the idea of ARCs. The government then drafted a Bill—the Securitization and Reconstruction of Financial Assets and Enforcement of Security Interest (SARFAESI) Bill, 2002— under which asset reconstruction companies (ARCs) would be set up and banks and creditors empowered to sell collateral, or security taken against any loan, without having to wait for courts to deliver a judgment. The ARCs would buy out loans from the banks at a discounted rate and pursue their recovery, which included selling assets pledged as security for the loans, leaving the banks with cleaner balance sheets and more cash to pursue fresh assets.

The RBI, which accepted the ARC proposal, had not been quiet in the meantime. It had been examining other methods for faster resolution of NPAs to save both money and management time for commercial banks. The central bank had started goading banks to use the Lok Adalats, which are alternative dispute redressal platforms. Lok Adalats, or people's courts, are deemed civil courts and have been conferred statutory status. These courts are forums for amicable settlement of or compromise of disputes or cases pending in the courts of law. An article, titled 'Some Aspects and Issues Relating to NPAs in Commercial Banks', in the July 1999 edition of the RBI's monthly bulletin said, 'For recovery of smaller loans the Lok Adalat have proved a very good agency for quick justice and settlement of dues.'

In August 2001, the central bank also introduced corporate debt restructuring (CDR), a mechanism for restructuring the debts of corporate entities that are intrinsically viable but whose loans may have soured because of some internal or external factors. This timely and transparent mechanism would lie outside the purview of the BIFR, DRT and other legal processes. Only loans over Rs 20 crore involving multiple lenders would be eligible for CDR.

However, it is the idea of ARCs that has endured, through multiple bumps and changes in the rules and procedures. As of March 2022, there were twenty-eight ARCs registered with the RBI, with the book value of the assets acquired at Rs 5,65,683 crore. Their fortunes have ebbed and flowed, depending on the regulatory landscape, betraying the promise of them becoming a silver bullet for fixing the NPA problem. Their performance has been uninspiring, whether in terms of recovering overdue loans or reviving the businesses behind the loans. According to RBI data, ARCs could recover only 14.3 per cent of the stressed assets acquired between 2003–04 and 2012–13. An RBI committee under the chairmanship of the bank's former executive director, Sudarshan Sen, was set up to review the working of ARCs. In its September 2021 report, it wrote:

> There are multiple factors behind the sub-optimal performance of the ARC Sector. These primarily include vintage NPAs being passed on to ARCs, lack of debt aggregation, non-availability of additional funding for stressed borrowers, difficulty in raising of funds by the ARCs on their balance sheet, etc. Also, ARCs have lacked focus on both recovery and acquiring necessary skill sets for holistic resolution of distressed borrowers.

In the interim, income tax raids on four ARCs in December 2021 blew the lid off suspected underhand dealings, apparently indulged in by a nexus of ARCs and borrowers, highlighting another reason why the ARC route had languished over time and reinforcing scepticism of any lasting solution for NPAs. The tax investigation alleged that the impugned ARCs were acquiring the assets from banks on behalf of the original borrowers. These original borrowers would allegedly route their purchase consideration through a maze of shell and dummy companies to the ARCs, thereby allowing the original borrowers to re-acquire the stressed asset from the bank at a fraction of what they (borrowers) would otherwise have to pay banks. In the end, it would seem that the ARC route, in its most simple form, was perhaps seen as a convenient way for habitual loan defaulters to retain possession of their secured assets without having to repay the full loan amount.

It is not that banks did not favour ARCs. This route offered them an opportunity to remove sticky assets from their books and focus on their core responsibility of lending without, and this is important, having to squander time, management energy and legal costs on various legal platforms. But the arrangement went off the rails for a variety of reasons—banks parting with only old NPAs which seemed beyond repair, ARCs lacking expertise for either loan recovery or business revival, disputes over the valuations at which ARCs would buy the impaired assets from banks, among others.

The real issue is that the NPA problem never went away permanently; it has risen and fallen, abated temporarily when new solutions were thrown at it, and then roared back again when there was either a new economic shock or the stakeholders got acquainted with the nuts and bolts of the new device and could finesse it once again.

The banking system's gross NPAs in 2001–02, just around the time when the SARFAESI Act was being drafted and the ground was being prepared for the launch of ARCs in India, was a worrying 10.4 per cent of gross advances. The golden economic period thereafter saw gross NPA numbers come down every year, reaching a low of 2.2 per cent of gross advances by 2007–08, just before the North Atlantic financial crisis broke out and sent tremors across the globe. The gross NPA numbers started climbing once again, after the government's adoption of fiscal measures and easy-money policies to ensure smooth economic recovery. Entering 2014–15, just around the time when a new government was taking charge in India, gross NPAs had clawed their way back to 4.3 per cent.

The period between 2011 and 2014 witnessed a palpable slowdown in the economy. The government had retrenched its fiscal stimulus programme launched in the aftermath of the 2008 financial crisis, and many companies suddenly woke up to the fact that they had borrowed way over their digestive limits. Some of the corporate borrowers had assumed that the accommodative policies would last forever; some had viewed the availability of cheap money as an opportunity to load up on debt and move the money out to other personal ventures. In the meantime, with an extended easy-money policy and persisting crimps in the supply chain and infrastructure, the rate of inflation had also started moving up, prompting the RBI to increase its benchmark rates by thirteen times on the trot between March 2010 and October 2011. In January 2014, before the general elections and before the new government could assume office, it was already evident to policymakers that a large number of Indian companies had borrowed way over their repayment capacity. The alarm bells had started going off.

Between 2014–15 and 2017–18, the banking system's gross NPAs shot up from 4.3 per cent of advances to 11.2 per cent. Fingers were being pointed at many different actors for the rising volume of bad loans, the identity of the accused varying with the accuser's political ideology. One side blamed the previous government of the Congress-led coalition for the loan binge, claiming that corruption and its lax regulatory frameworks had left a dent in the economy. The other side blamed the 2016 demonetization episode for the spike in bad loans: gross NPAs had gone up from 7.5 per cent in 2015–16 to 11.2 per cent in 2017–18. Regardless of which side made the accusation, there was concern.

This was once again another freshly-minted NPA crisis.

In the background, as NPAs started mounting, the central bank got busy announcing one scheme after another between 2013 and 2016, but many of them were bunched up and released in a single burst around the year 2014. Most of these involved restructuring, allowing banks enough latitude to try and restore their impaired accounts. This is how the Comptroller Auditor General of India has defined[4] loan restructuring:

A restructured loan account is one where the lender, for economic or legal reasons relating to the borrower's financial difficulties, grants concessions to the borrower that it would not have otherwise considered. Restructuring would normally involve modification of terms of the advances/ securities including alteration of repayment period/ repayable amount/ the amount of instalments/ rate of interest. Restructuring of loans also occurs due to the sanction of additional loan for meeting cost overruns due to cost escalations, delayed implementation of projects, increased scope of the project etc.

Key to the broad restructuring plan, initiated during the tenure of Raghuram Rajan as RBI governor, was a new asset classification system and a desire to catch the problem accounts before they turned bad. Here is a list of schemes that the RBI kept launching one after the other in the span of three years between 2013 and 2016.

**1. Central Repository of Information on Large Credit (CRILC):** Raghuram Rajan took charge as governor of the RBI on the afternoon of 4 September 1993. That same evening, without wasting much time, he issued a statement outlining his concerns and priorities. Sorting out the mounting NPAs in the financial system was obviously high on his agenda. In his statement, he also introduced[5] a new concept: 'RBI proposes to collect credit data and examine large common exposures across banks. This will enable the creation of a central repository on large credits, which we will share with the banks. This will enable banks themselves to be aware of building leverage and common exposures.' This proposed central repository of credit data for large borrowers (with outstandings of more than Rs 10 crore) was set up on 13 September. This database is available to all lenders and is aimed at reducing information asymmetry between banks, which has allowed tainted borrowers to go credit shopping.

**2. The Framework for Revitalizing Distressed Assets in the Economy**: The RBI, anxious about the rising NPA levels in 2012–13, released a discussion paper[6] in December 2013 to outline a corrective action plan, which essentially sought to 'incentivise early identification of problem cases, timely restructuring of accounts which are considered to be viable, and taking prompt steps by banks for recovery or sale of unviable accounts'. The final scheme[7] was launched in January 2014. The only hitch in this scheme was that it, naïvely perhaps, hinged on collective action by a bunch of disparate lenders, which included arriving at a common and time-bound agreement among different banks for a restructuring plan. Given how heterogeneous Indian banking had become, and the prevalence of perverse banker–industrialist ties in India, there was always one bank or the other that would invariably upset the collective action plan.

**3. Joint Lenders Forum (JLF) and Collective Action Plan (CAP)**: The discussion paper that had proposed a framework for revitalizing distressed assets through collective action also suggested that as soon as a loan account was reported to the

CRILC as principal- or interest-overdue for sixty-one to ninety days, banks were expected to immediately form a lenders' committee, to be called the Joint Lenders' Forum (JLF) under a convener and formulate a joint corrective action plan (CAP) for early resolution of the problems in the account.

**4. Flexible Structuring of Long-Term Project Loans**: More popularly known as the 5/25 scheme, this scheme[8] was introduced in July 2015 to allow banks to refinance infrastructure loans every five years. Essentially, banks could give loans of tenures of up to twenty-five years for an infrastructure project; after the expiry of five years of the loan, it had the option to either sell the loan or rewrite the terms of the loan.

**5. Strategic Debt Restructuring**: This was introduced[9] in June 2015 to ensure that promoters of companies also put in efforts, along with banks, to revive stressed accounts. Banks were given powers under this scheme to change the ownership of companies whose loans failed to meet certain conditions and milestones. Obviously, this hit a legal wall and banks did not display too much enthusiasm in executing this scheme.

**6. Scheme for Sustainable Structuring of Stressed Assets (S4A):** Introduced in June 2016,[10] this was an optional framework that banks could choose for the resolution of large stressed accounts. The scheme required banks to determine a borrower's sustainable debt levels and then divide the outstanding debt into sustainable debt and equity/quasi-equity instruments.

All these schemes, predictably, met with mixed success, one reason being that banks were not empowered legally to take over a company's reins, even in the event of a default. No legislation could deprive a promoter of his stake in a company. In addition, many banks were reluctant to go the distance because of apprehensions that it would also expose their flawed appraisal norms. The RBI's frustration at its own inability to discipline industry or to bring wilful defaulters to book was best expressed in a February 2017 speech[11] by former deputy governor Viral Acharya at an Indian Banks' Association Banking Technology Conference: 'Original promoters—who rarely put in any financing and primarily provide sweat equity—have had somewhat of a field day, facing limited dilution, if any, of their initial stakes nor much of a threat of being outright replaced.'

Where there was no danger of banks trying to acquire a defaulting company, many borrowers opted to get their loans restructured because it provided a breather of sorts to both banks and borrowers from loans getting tagged as NPAs.

But, more importantly, restructuring helped depress the actual stress in the banking system. At a banking summit organized by industry lobby Confederation of Indian Industry in February 2016, former RBI deputy governor S.S. Mundra made a presentation[12] on asset resolution and NPAs. He showed that while the year-end data for gross NPAs of 2014–15 was 4.6 per cent of advances, adding the restructured assets of 6.4 per cent and the written-off assets of 2.5 per cent took the total stress in the bank balance sheets to a scary 13.6 per cent of advances. This had climbed to 14.1 per cent by September 2015.

This is not to suggest that the RBI was masking the real numbers, but the scheme for restructured assets did provide a convenient shelter for impaired assets. When reporting on the banking sector's performance at the end of the financial year 2014–15, the ratio of 4.6 per cent certainly looked more comforting than 13.6 per cent. This artifice was further refined by mandating accelerated loan write-offs to show improved headline NPA numbers.

Replying to a question from DMK Member of Parliament Kanimozhi Karunanidhi in the Lok Sabha on 7 August 2023, minister of state in the finance ministry Bhagwat Karad revealed the loan amounts[13] that banks had been writing off every year. Two interesting points need to be mentioned. One, the pace of loan write-offs every year seems to have accelerated: from Rs 58,786 crore during 2014–15 to Rs 2,09,144 crore during 2022–23. The second interesting point to be noted is that the highest amount of annual write-off occurred in 2018–19: Rs 2,36,265 crore, which was almost 47 per cent higher than the previous year. This does raise doubts whether the general elections to the seventeenth Lok Sabha, scheduled to be conducted during April–May 2019, had any influence on the decision related to higher loan write-offs in the preceding period.

While the higher write-off could well be a coincidence, the RBI's silence on the policy regarding write-offs has been mystifying. It was only in June 2023 that the RBI announced, as part of its monetary policy, a policy framework[14] for technical write-offs. Banks are, of course, within their rights to write off bad loans that remain unrecoverable for prolonged periods. A loan write-off is a complicated accounting treatment and, in reality, the bank never fully obliterates the loan asset from its books. It is within its rights to pursue recovery from the borrowers even after the write-off. The government and the RBI have used this excuse—that loan write-offs help clean bank books without letting delinquent borrowers off the hook—to justify the rising loan write-offs. However, Karad's statement in Lok Sabha disproves this claim: out of Rs 14,56,226 crore loans written off in total between 2014–15 and 2022–23, only Rs 2,04,668 crore has been recovered, or a paltry 14 per cent.

Another interesting point merits mention here. Parliamentarian Kanimozhi Karunanidhi's exact question in Parliament was actually about the extent of corporate loans written off since 2014, the amounts recovered from these write-offs and details of the corporate entities that had availed the maximum loan write-offs. There have often been dark hints that the bulk of the loans written off by banks were owed by large, influential and politically connected corporate groups. Minister Bhagwat Karad replied that the RBI does not maintain information on corporate loans written off. But, making a fine distinction, Karad also told Parliament that large industries and services accounted for Rs 7,40,968 crore of the total Rs 14,56,226 crore loans written off. This one incident highlights the fog around data on the outstanding credit in the financial system and its overall health. Combined with the difficulty in accessing granular data from the RBI, along with the central bank's strategy of highlighting only headline NPA numbers (and maintaining a convenient silence on restructured assets or write-offs), this has successfully helped de-emphasize the turmoil that continues to eat away at the banking sector's resilience through different political regimes.

What has prevailed, though, is the belief in silver bullets to solve the intractable problem of NPAs.

In 2016, the government finally launched the Insolvency and Bankruptcy Code (IBC), which was legislated through an Act of Parliament. The code[15] was deemed necessary in light of the relentless build-up of NPAs and the growing delays in debt resolution, leading to problems in banking resilience, overall financial stability and economic growth.

The Insolvency and Bankruptcy Code (IBC) came into force after the repeal of the age-old Presidency Towns Insolvency Act, 1909 and the Provincial Insolvency Act, 1920. Enactment of the Code also necessitated amendments to eleven laws, including the Companies Act, 2013, the RDDBFI Act, 1993 and the SARFAESI Act, 2002. The Code also sought to consolidate the fragmented legislative framework, comprising multiple Acts, that had governed insolvency and restructuring and had led to delays and sub-optimal outcomes.

The promise of the IBC was that it provided for a resolution mechanism for corporations, partnership firms and individuals within a specified time frame, and the process could be initiated by either the lender or the borrower. Once a case is admitted to the National Company Law Tribunal (NCLT), which is the main adjudicating body for insolvency and bankruptcy cases, the insolvency process is to be completed in 180 days, with an extension of ninety days allowed with the consent of both the creditors and debtors.

The record, again, is mixed, with recoveries diminishing over time and the timelines getting progressively stretched over the years. The process had some interesting outcomes when it initially began, with the first resolution under the Code getting completed in 2017 within the mandated 180 days.

An April 2023 analysis by India Rating and Research, using data from the Insolvency and Bankruptcy Board of India (the organization responsible for creating the regulatory ecosystem necessary for implementing the IBC), calculated that each case that was closed during the first nine months of 2022–23 (ending 31 December 2022), either through a resolution process or liquidation, had taken an average of 588 days to complete, the highest in the IBC's short history. In contrast, the average number of days taken for cases that found closure during the full twelve months of 2021–22 was 531 days and for 2020–21 it was 463 days. The stretched timelines have an undesirable consequence: case admissions have outpaced case closures every year since FY18. The only exception was 2020–21, when pandemic restrictions played a role in dampening case admissions.

One of the problems that the IBC system faces is a lack of capacity in the NCLT infrastructure, with many vacancies on its various benches. There is an inescapable sense of déjà vu here: the DRTs too have been hobbled by a lack of enough professionals to man its various benches, leading to enormous delays. Negligence and lack of remedial intervention by the authorities, whether in DRTs or NCLTs, have been practised by administrations professing to political ideologies from both sides of the aisle, leading to the unavoidable conclusion that corporate-political connections, specifically campaign finance infirmities, will keep influencing outcomes.

The government conceived of another silver bullet to solve the NPA problem. Delivering the budget speech for 2021–22 on 1 February 2021, Finance Minister Nirmala Sitharaman announced[16] the setting up of a 'bad bank' to resolve the problem of bad loans: 'The high level of provisioning by public sector banks of their stressed assets calls for measures to clean up the bank books. An Asset Reconstruction Company Limited and Asset Management Company would be set up to consolidate and take over the existing stressed debt and then manage and dispose of the assets to Alternate Investment Funds and other potential investors for eventual value realization.'

A dual structure was incorporated in July 2021, with National Asset Reconstruction Company Ltd (NARCL) as the ARC responsible for the acquisition of bad loans from banks and financial institutions and India Debt Resolution Company Ltd (IDRCL) as the AMC for managing the stressed assets and providing resolution services to NARCL on an exclusive basis. The NARCL capital was contributed by public sector banks (51 per cent) and private banks (49 per cent), with Canara Bank as the sponsor bank. IDRCL's shareholding is a mirror image of NARCL's with private banks holding 51 per cent and public sector banks the balance 49 per cent.

NARCL was expected to acquire Rs 2,00,000 of stressed assets in two phases, with Rs 90,000 crore in the first phase ending in January 2022. Unfortunately, NARCL has failed to acquire the amount allocated for even Phase I. A written statement[17] submitted by Nirmala Sitharaman to the Lok Sabha on 24 July 2023, said that NARCL had been able to acquire only three assets worth Rs 21,349 crore by 17 July 2023. NARCL has failed to acquire assets because its offer prices have left the banks unimpressed; behind the banks' reluctance to part with assets at heavily discounted prices is also the fear of inviting probes by government investigative agencies.

Apart from undershooting acquisition targets, the dual bad bank structure has been facing a host of coordination problems internally. There is dissension within the organization, with pay disparity between employees of the two tiers being one of the reasons. The discontent intensified after NARCL chairman Karnam Sekar resigned on 19 August 2023, two years after the bad bank was set up.

It may well be that the government and the RBI will eventually sort out not only the teething problems in loan acquisition and resolution but also the rough edges in the relationship between the two tiers. But to hope that this will help solve the NPA problem might remain a fond wish.

The irony is that regulators and policymakers have kept thickening the alphabet soup of insolvency and bankruptcy schemes—DRT, CDR, RDDBFI, SARFAESI, CRILC, JLF, CAP, SDR, 5/25 scheme, ARC, S4A and, finally, IBC—every time a new NPA crisis burst upon the scene. The NPA crisis also seems to have some element of cyclicality built into it, and it may, therefore, not be too cynical to expect another new scheme to emerge when the next round of NPAs is upon us.

# Chapter 9

## Indian Reforms Event-Driven, Even Post-2014

Reforms in India have tended to result from incident-based responses, and this pattern has been largely party/ideology-agnostic. This was witnessed during the four or five political configurations that came to power after the 1991 elections. All the different groupings that came to power in 1991 had, surprisingly, competing narratives nestled comfortably aside complementary political agendas. The convergence of views was usually on the inevitability of reforms and their irreversible nature.

The general tendency to bring in reforms only as a reaction to an event, or more specifically, as a response to a crisis, has been pronounced across different regimes. Ever since 1991, when the economic reforms process was initiated, all successive governments (many of them coalition arrangements)—headed by Prime Ministers P.V. Narasimha Rao, Deve Gowda, I.K. Gujral, Atal Bihari Vajpayee, Manmohan Singh and Narendra Modi—readily bought into the idea of economic reforms, with varying degrees of conviction and pace of implementation. Admittedly, the political-economy compulsions were unique for each government, but there was an equal number of elements common to them all, springing from the broad societal, political and economic changes that the 1991 crisis and the attendant reforms had put into motion.

The reason behind this common tendency found in almost all political shades—to reform only when pushed to a corner—perhaps lies in the nature of India's polity. Given the developmental compulsions, the always-on election cycles, the obsession with caste and the recurring concerns over designing welfare benefits that broadly align with political exigencies, an issue like economic reforms probably ranks low as a political imperative or on the list of priorities necessary for winning elections. Apart from some sections of the middle class, and segments of industry which seek out bottom-line-focused selective reforms, the idea of standalone or continuing financial-sector reforms may have little cache among the electorate.

The political class, on most occasions, is adept at gauging public sentiment and acting on the dominant trends. In recent years, most political parties, including well-heeled senior politicians in their individual capacity, have tended to privately employ market research agencies or individuals to figure out the public mood and their list of priorities before designing, finalizing and launching their political campaigns. It is quite possible that none of the market research reports (which are private in nature) has voters listing financial sector reforms as either a burning priority or a desirable outcome. The question remains as to whether senior politicians and ministers, when they become part of the executive and are responsible for overall economic development, should allow their narrow political agenda to totally and utterly dominate all policy decisions. It would be naïve to think that they would completely jettison their political agenda because that would be betraying the electorate's trust and breaching their pre-poll promises. But it may also not be totally unrealistic to expect them to pursue some larger cause or development agenda that has not been spelt out in their pre-election campaign.

There is another way of looking at this. There is no incentive for initiating financial sector reforms if there is no popular uprising or demand for it. However, an incident in which many voters are deprived of their savings, unfairly or illegally, presents a compelling reason to act or to be seen as acting and doing something. Seen differently, financial sector reforms in India are perhaps the by-product of crises, occasionally fashioned in the teeth of public unrest and political brinkmanship. In the absence of the right circumstances, financial sector reforms do not usually get a look-in.

One good example is the steady stream of numerous papers published since 1992 on activating and deepening the corporate bond market. Some of their suggestions have been accepted, but by and large the Indian corporate bond market remains small and shallow.

The Committee on Making Mumbai an International Financial Centre, set up by the finance ministry under the chairmanship of former World Bank economist Percy Mistry, had a long list of experts. However, when the final report was submitted in February 2007, Percy Mistry's signature was missing from the report. He had resigned three days before the submission of the report. It later transpired that some of the nominees on the committee had objected to the committee's formulation that the government dilute its stake in public-sector banks. This suggestion, based on Mistry's critique of how public-sector banks worked in India, prompted criticism from the two chiefs of public-sector banks on the committee. They wanted the reference to public-sector banks dropped.

In a later interview,[1] Mistry explained why he had resigned:

The original arguments and reasoning for the recommendations were provided in a fairly forthright language. This was diluted to a point of senselessness by an extraordinary sense of overdone political sensitivity by a few members. It was not by any means a unanimous view of the committee to dilute the report. It was the view of just a few members. They represented mainly the public sector institutions, and perhaps believed that they were coming in for some unfair criticism for the state the Indian financial system found itself in.

The recommendation that the government should divest its holdings in public-sector banks has been made by many other official committees, and it has been duly ignored on every occasion. In the government's defence, shorn of their inefficiency, public-sector banks have a definite role in the country, given India's developmental stage. The vast sums of resource transfers from the government to the ultimate beneficiaries are largely undertaken by the public-sector banks because none of the private-sector banks has a comparable, deep, all-India network. Most of the public-sector banks started life as private organizations, but their social and developmental identity was forged in the post-nationalization period. That is now hardwired into their genetic architecture.

In a 2016 paper[2] published by the Indian Council for Research on International Economic Relations, distinguished fellow at the Centre for Social and Economic Progress and former diplomat Jaimini Bhagwati and his co-authors also decide to question the repeated demands for bank privatization:

Given the Rupees 6 lakh crores or more of stressed assets on the books of Indian public sector banks (PSBs), there are renewed calls for a reduction in the government's stake in PSBs to less than 50 per cent. It is surprising that repeated wrong-doing in private financial sector firms and banks in the US and UK does not convince Indian observers that it is not necessarily public ownership that results in malfeasance or negligence. As for the argument that governments do not have to repeatedly provide the same levels of tax-payer funded support in the US and UK as in India, financial sector crises have set back GDP growth rates in these and other developed countries for almost a decade since 2008.

In short, the government has so far baulked at taking as drastic a reform step as privatizing public-sector banks, not only because of the enormous political-economy complications involved but also because there has been no precipitating need for such a policy action. Indeed, privatization of government banks could have adverse political ramifications because the impact of such a move will reverberate across a broad swathe of stakeholders: employees, welfare beneficiaries, pensioners and small-scale borrowers, among others.

In the end, though, the idea of converting Mumbai into an international financial centre went nowhere. Instead, ironically, after the BJP came to power at the Centre in 2014, that same suggestion was transposed to Gujarat International Finance Tec-City, or GIFT City, near Ahmedabad.

Many other committee reports and working papers suggesting various reform measures have been authored over the past two decades, but few have found acceptance except when there was a crisis.

And, to be fair, this tendency applies equally to all dispensations. Given the recent political developments, there might also be a temptation to apportion blame for the episodic nature of financial sector reforms to a particular political party, a tendency that might even take the shape of partisan accusations. In reality, though, India's immutable predilection for episodic reforms transcends governments and also applies to the BJP-led government, which came to power in 2014.

The din of accusations and counter-accusations usually masks the broader question about the nature of conflicting interests that favours the status quo. More importantly, what kinds of conflicting interests have remained unassailable, or inordinately influential, despite more than three decades of financial sector reforms? That question remains unanswered. The sporadic reforms since 2014, predictably crisis-inspired, might hold some clues.

Two particular traits of the current government have emerged in their responses to crises over the past decade. Both the government and the RBI have used the velvet-hand-in-an-iron-glove approach. Whenever a crisis or a scam necessitated some corrective action and tightening of the existing regulatory framework, it was usually accompanied by the easing of either credit availability or liquidity norms. In case after case, it was noticed that the authorities were concerned about a possible economic slowdown and took special care to ensure that credit growth continued apace. This is markedly different from the past when regulators, at the sign of a scam or a crisis, would first clamp down tight on the entire financial system, and then subsequently ease the controls gradually.

The second feature that has surfaced is how the promise of overturning the conventional power equation among various stakeholders in the Indian financial system—especially between the borrower and the lender—was duly attempted but turned out to be short-lived. Traditionally, ever since the establishment of the BIFR and the various schemes subsequently introduced to tackle the problem of bad loans, the advantage has always rested with the debtor, or the borrower, for exploiting the system to their benefit. And when, for a brief while, the Insolvency and Bankruptcy Code threatened to overturn that power equation in favour of the creditors, it proved to be transient. The debtors have since managed to wrest control once again, making bad loans a permanent feature of the Indian financial sector.

The pernicious presence of bad loans in the economy has even prompted RBI governor Shaktikanta Das to comment,[3] during a meeting with the boards of public- and private-sector banks in May 2023, on how banks are still trying to manipulate and mask their NPA levels:

> During the course of our supervisory process, certain instances of using innovative ways to conceal the real status of stressed loans have also come to our notice. To mention a few, such methods include bringing two lenders together to evergreen each other's loans by sale and buyback of loans or debt instruments; good borrowers being persuaded to enter into structured deals with a stressed borrower to conceal the stress; use of Internal or Office accounts to adjust borrower's repayment obligations; renewal of loans or disbursement of new / additional loans to the stressed borrower or related entities closer to the repayment date of the earlier loans; and similar other methods. We have also come across a few examples where one method of evergreening, after being pointed out by the regulator, was replaced by another method. Such practices beg the question as to whose interest such smart methods serve.

## The Persistent NPA Mess

Like the reluctant reforms gene that populates the Indian political class across aisles, there is another shared characteristic that seems immutable across regimes. The niggling problem of NPAs has plagued governments of all hues equally. In almost a decade since the BJP government has been in power, neither the administration nor its regulators have been able to comprehensively address the issue of NPAs. Like a troublesome wraith that refuses to vacate a dilapidated mansion, NPAs continue to haunt the Indian financial system, in outright defiance of all remedial measures and regulatory frameworks.

Like all other past attempts, policy measures over the last decade to resolve the NPA problem have stumbled, either because of the ingenuity of the borrowing class or because administrators have wilfully blunted the relevant policies under pressure from various stakeholders.

The genesis of the current NPA problem can be found in the aftermath of the 2008 financial crisis when the government adopted an accommodative monetary policy coupled with a fiscal stimulus. The stimulus helped spike demand momentarily, impelling the corporate sector to borrow for capacity expansion. Around the same time, the steadily rising drumbeat of the need for increasing private investment in infrastructure, since government finances were limited or finite, encouraged many Corporate India players to bid for infrastructure projects and access bank loans to finance these projects. This was a double-edged problem: most companies harboured undue expectations about cash flows from infrastructure projects, and banks had used deposits, which are short-term in nature, to lend out money for intrinsically long-term projects. By 2011–12, corporates were struggling to service their debt overindulgence, and banks, overburdened with bad loans, had turned off their credit taps. The upshot was a slowdown in the economy and a serious financial sector logjam.

As India entered 2014, the year the BJP government assumed office in Delhi, the situation in the financial sector was characterized by what the former chief economic adviser Arvind Subramanian had famously described as the twin balance sheet problem. The corporate sector had overindulged on loans and the subsequent digestion problems led to all kinds of ailments, including an inability to repay the loans or undertake fresh projects. Banks, on the other hand, had over-lent in their exuberance, and the growing volume of NPAs tucked away in the recesses of their balance sheets was sucking up all the lendable capital available.

The BJP had made many campaign promises about resolving the NPA overhang and rejuvenating economic growth. Its manifesto for the 2014 general elections promised: 'NPAs have increased sharply over the past few years and the trend continues.

BJP will take necessary steps to reduce NPAs in Banking sector. Also, BJP will set up a strong regulatory framework for the non-banking financial companies to protect the investors.'

In short, the financial sector was under severe stress and, in response to the emergent crisis, the RBI did what it does best when faced with a predicament. The central bank initiated a process—called the Asset Quality Review (AQR)—during the period August-November 2015 to assess the true position of the banking system's NPAs. The RBI had suspected, and rightly so, that banks had been using multiple contrivances—such as restructuring loans or evergreening them (lending small amounts to borrowers—directly or indirectly—before the interest-due date to help them avoid default), among other tricks—to under-report the actual NPA figures. When the data from the exercise was finally released, the systemic NPA figure was found to be a staggering 15 per cent of advances, with the government-owned banks responsible for close to 90 per cent of the bad loans.

The revelation of higher-than-expected NPAs came with its own costs, of course. The RBI's annual Report on Trend and Progress of Banking in India 2015–16 acknowledged the costs of the AQR:

> AQR brought to the fore significant discrepancies in the reported levels of impairment and actual position and hence, led to increase in provisioning requirements for banks. Although aimed at better recognition of and provisioning for NPAs in the medium- to long-term, AQR resulted in an adverse impact on the profitability of banks in the short term. Hence, the banking sector's performance as captured through the annual accounts of banks showed a continued deterioration during the year when compared to the previous year.

A large part of the newly discovered NPAs resided with government-owned banks. Naturally, the higher amount of NPAs required higher provisioning, and the consequent hole left behind in their balance sheets necessitated the banks' recapitalization. That did happen, but only in dribs and drabs, and the government's contributions turned out to be inadequate.

The discovery of the real NPA situation in the AQR led to a series of retaliatory, stringent measures from the RBI and other investigative agencies. The RBI responded with 'prompt corrective action' (PCA), which essentially selected a few weak banks and bundled them into a straitjacket, disallowing them from conducting any further business till they got their balance sheets back in working condition.

Then came the sudden, infamous demonetization decision on 8 November 2016, which is also likely to have generated its own share of NPAs. On the evening of 8 November 2016, Prime Minister Narendra Modi went live on national networks to announce that the government had decided to withdraw from circulation all currency notes of Rs 500 and Rs 1000 denominations. They would be replaced with new banknotes of Rs 500 (in a new design) and Rs 2000 denominations. The government's primary reason behind demonetization was to curb the generation of black money and the secondary reason was to nudge Indians towards using digital payments systems instead of cash. The unilateral decision without any adequate preparations and the attendant economic shock aggravated the state of NPAs in the financial system.

The sudden decision to withdraw 86 per cent of the currency from the system, without providing for any replacement, resulted in hardships for everyone. There was a protracted cash shortage, leading to severe economic disruptions. Individuals had to queue up outside banks for hours—occasionally even overnight—to replace the discontinued notes with new currency. Markets—both retail and wholesale—froze, and normal business transactions stalled. Bhaskar Chakravorti, dean of global business at Fletcher

School, Tufts University, panned the move[4] in a *Harvard Business Review* article: '. . . this unfortunate crisis is a case study in poor policy and even poorer execution. Unfortunately, it is also the poor that bear the greatest burden.'

While the demonetization process was spawning its share of NPAs, in 2017, the RBI referred forty of the largest NPAs for resolution under the newly legislated Insolvency and Bankruptcy Code. This took NPAs out of the banks' control, forcing them to write down the value of the loans in their books, but without any line of sight to fresh capital sources.

The persistence of NPAs, the tightening of norms, heightened provisioning, the referring of cases to the IBC and the lack of capital top-up, on top of the unilateral demonetization move, left banks with very little appetite for lending. Firms across the corporate spectrum—whether large companies or medium-sized or small-scale units—were also in no mood to borrow, having to deal with repayment of past loans. In addition, slowing economic growth had left them with large, unutilized capacities, obviating the need for fresh borrowings.

Year-on-year credit growth had been steadily dropping, from the 21.5 per cent achieved during 2010–11 to a low of 8.2 per cent in 2016–17; this was the lowest credit growth after 1991–92 when bank credit grew by only 8 per cent, as a direct consequence of the BoP crisis (the ensuing economic slowdown after demonetization affected the appetite for loans, with the annual credit growth rate further dipping to 6.1 per cent by 2019–20, just before the full-blown pandemic accentuated the economic shock). The RBI, by then under governor Urjit Patel, had accorded NPA resolution as its priority Number One.

The central bank even issued a controversial circular on 12 February 2018, further revising the framework for the resolution of stressed assets. In a nutshell, the circular directed banks to resolve debts of over Rs 2000 crore within 180 days in the case of a default, failing which the defaulter had to be admitted to the NCLT for insolvency action within fifteen days of the expiry of the original 180 days. In addition, the circular also made it mandatory for banks to disclose all defaults, even if interest repayment was overdue by only a day. The RBI directive was designed to end the evergreening of loans, a ploy used by banks to perpetually defer the recognition of a bad loan as an NPA.

This circular created a lot of heartburn in the industry. It was also around this time that a concerted whisper campaign was launched, alleging that the RBI was throttling nascent credit growth. The RBI also increased interest rates twice during the period—once in June 2018 and once again in August 2018—reversing the three-year trend of progressively lower interest rates, set in motion in 2015. Governor Urjit Patel believed that the economy was operating close to its potential output and this could lead to elevated inflationary pressures. In the meantime, in the backdrop of industry complaining bitterly about Urjit Patel, relations between the government and the RBI governor had started souring. The government began to put pressure on Patel to ease the various restrictions and enable credit growth. There was also a public stand-off between Patel and government officials, especially former finance secretary Subhash Chandra Garg, over the transfer of the RBI's surplus reserves to the government. Patel, and his predecessor Raghuram Rajan, had been resisting government pressure to transfer the surplus reserves, arguing that it was not prudent to use central bank reserves to bridge the fiscal deficit. In the end, the government's anxiety over stagnant credit demand, growing NPAs and tepid economic growth was so violently misaligned with Patel's resolute and single-minded determination to bring NPAs down that something had to give.

Urjit Patel finally resigned on 10 December 2018, with nine months still left of his three-year term, the second governor in the RBI's history to not complete his term (the first was Benegal

Rama Rau who resigned in January 1957, in the middle of his second term, due to differences with the then finance minister T.T. Krishnamachari).

Enter Shaktikanta Das, a seasoned bureaucrat, as the RBI's twenty-fifth governor. Among his first tasks after taking over as governor was to allow a one-time restructuring of MSME loans of up to Rs 25 crore. On 31 January 2019, the RBI took the additional step of releasing three banks from the PCA strictures: Bank of India, Bank of Maharashtra and Oriental Bank of Commerce. The press release announcing the relaxations stated:

> On a review of the performance of Public Sector Banks (PSBs) currently under the Prompt Corrective Action Framework (PCAF), it was noted that a few banks are not in breach of the PCA parameters as per their published results for the quarter ending December 2018, except Return on Assets (RoA). However, though the RoA continues to be negative, the same is reflected in the capital adequacy indicator. These banks have provided a written commitment that they would comply with the norms of minimum regulatory capital, Net NPA and leverage ratio on an ongoing basis and have apprised the Reserve Bank of India of the structural and systemic improvements that they have put in place which would help the banks in continuing to meet these commitments. Further, the Government has also assured that the capital requirements of these banks will be duly factored in while making bank-wise allocations during the current financial year.

> Taking all the above into consideration, it has been decided that Bank of India and Bank of Maharashtra which meet the regulatory norms including Capital Conservation Buffer (CCB) and have Net NPAs of less than 6% as per third quarter results, are taken out of the PCA framework subject to certain conditions and continuous monitoring. In the case of Oriental Bank of Commerce, though the net NPA was 7.15%, as per the published results of third quarter, the Government has since infused sufficient capital and bank has brought the Net NPA

to less than 6%. Hence, it has been decided to remove the restrictions placed on Oriental Bank of Commerce under PCA framework subject to certain conditions and close monitoring.

A few months later, in April 2019, the Supreme Court overruled the RBI's contentious 12 February circular, questioning the central bank's jurisdiction in directing banks to take defaulters to the NCLT. In his book *Overdraft*, published two years after he resigned as RBI governor, Urjit Patel writes that he finds the developments during this period curious:

> Sowing disorder by confusing issues is a tried-and-trusted, distressingly often successful routine by which stakeholders, official and private, plant the seeds of policy/regulation reversal in India; this has been the case for as long as I can remember. It does not help that few policymakers have the patience to sift the wheat from the chaff, appreciate intricacies and focus on final outcomes. The prospect of a transparent, time-bound process on autopilot for recovering debt was unsettling.
>
> No high court granted a stay to the assorted petitioners. From July 2018 onwards, the IBC was felt, at least by some lobbies, to be constraining, that is, too strict on borrowers in terms of regulatory timelines and the consequences thereof. Lawyers who had agreed to represent the RBI in the Supreme Court (SC) dropped out at the eleventh hour, literally the night before the hearing. The SC granted a stay and postponed hearings more than once, in effect, until the following year. In April 2019, the SC pronounced the regulation to be illegal.

Patel detected a deliberate design to promote higher credit growth:

> The government's priorities in terms of lending to specific segments – say, MSME and agriculture – and bailing out systemic sectors like power generation have been perceived to be undermined by the RBI's rules on default definition and

by GBs (*government banks*) placed under the PCA framework.
Consequently, the regulator's de facto powers have been diluted
on several subjects related to, inter alia, preserving financial
stability. Circulars were reversed and the PCA framework
essentially ditched as these came in the way of stimulating the
economy through higher credit growth.

The RBI's focus turned to credit growth and economic revival,
in line with what the government had also been seeking. By the
end of August 2019, the RBI had also approved the transfer of
Rs 1,76,051 crore from its surplus reserves to the government.

As 2019–20 came to a close, and with the world and the
country entering the coronavirus pandemic, the RBI's and the
government's exertions did not seem to have borne fruit in the
short term. The year ended with only a 6.1 per cent credit growth
and a disappointing 4 per cent GDP growth. The other wrinkle
consisted of the GNPAs, which had touched 9.1 per cent by
September 2019 but would subsequently decline to 7.5 per cent
by September 2020, helped somewhat by the pandemic-induced
business lull and the introduction of regulatory forbearance which
temporarily halted recognition of NPAs. But there was another
bout of crisis management, or fire-fighting, by the RBI in the
interim, which had a salutary influence on the NPA data.

As the economy froze with the pandemic and the subsequent
economic lockdowns, the RBI went into overdrive, and with good
reason. On 17 April 2020, Governor Shaktikanta Das 'virtually'
delivered a monetary policy statement outlining the central bank's
objectives and responsibilities:

> The overarching objective is to keep the financial system and
> financial markets sound, liquid and smoothly functioning so
> that finance keeps flowing to all stakeholders, especially those
> that are disadvantaged and vulnerable. Regulatory measures that
> have been announced so far – including those made today - are

dovetailed into the objective of preserving financial stability. Although social distancing separates us, we stand united and resolute. Eventually, we shall cure; and we shall endure.

The RBI's monetary measures included a significant expansion of liquidity to allow financial markets and institutions to meet their commitments in the midst of the severe dislocation caused by the pandemic, a significant reduction in interest rates, and ensuring of monetary transmission to allow end users to benefit from the low rates. The central bank's regulatory and supervision measures included the declaration of a moratorium on term loans and a deferment of interest on working capital loans. This included a standstill for asset classification. This is a standard central bank response to a severe economic shock, and the RBI, in the glaring absence of a fiscal response from Delhi, had to pull out all the stops to keep all the boats afloat in the system. The noticeable lack of a fiscal response from the government in New Delhi, in the midst of mounting deaths and the heart-rending scenes of reverse migration of labour, was mystifying. Prudence demanded a counter-cyclical fiscal policy response, which demands increased government spending during episodes of low economic growth—a universally acknowledged macro-economy management tool.

As a logical extension, the government also suspended IBC's operations during this period. Once the moratorium was over, the RBI offered companies a restructuring programme in 2021. In another curious ruling, somewhat like the apex court's verdict on the RBI's February 12 circular, the Supreme Court on 3 September 2020 directed banks not to declare any loan as an NPA if it had not been declared bad by 31 August 2020. The Supreme Court finally vacated this stay on 23 March 2021. In effect, stressed loans got a court-sanctioned interest repayment holiday for about a year.

The pandemic brought in its wake multifaceted collateral damage. Apart from it being a severe shock to the economy, it upended many established supply chains across the world. Most multinational corporations had their supply chains spread across the globe, impelled by the need to squeeze out efficiency gains, lowering costs or leveraging low-tax jurisdictions. The raw material would be sourced in one part of the world, incorporated into an intermediate good somewhere else, assembled into the final product in a third country and finally consumed in yet another country. Once the pandemic had abated somewhat and consumption demand revived, it took these supply chains a long time to recover and resume functionality. This put pressure on prices. Then, in February 2022, Russia invaded Ukraine, sending oil and other commodity prices shooting up. The inflationary impulse across the world forced central banks across the globe to start increasing interest rates and retrench the accommodative monetary policies that had been in place since the 2008 financial crisis.

The RBI too had no option but to follow suit. The high interest rates, combined with tightening liquidity, aggravated the pre-existing stressed situation. However, with tepid credit demand and slow credit growth, the NPA problem seems to have been reined in. According to the RBI's Monetary Policy Report of April 2023, which is published once in six months, the banking system's stressed assets as of December 2022 amounted to 5.8 per cent of all advances and NPAs 4.5 per cent of advances. In the RBI's universe, NPAs plus written-off assets plus restructured assets equals stressed assets. As discussed in the previous chapter on NPAs, the RBI seems to have adopted an aggressive policy on loan write-offs to help display improved headline NPA numbers. A policy on aggressive write-offs as a one-time measure to clean up the bank's loan books would, perhaps, still be acceptable if recoveries are robust; however, as data shows, that is not the case. Part of the improvement in NPAs shown in the Monetary

Policy Report of April 2023 has also been achieved by the sale of stressed assets by banks to ARCs. Yes Bank, for example, sold Rs 48,000 crore of its stressed assets to JC Flowers ARC in September 2022. Even though the sale is believed to be in the range of 3–4 per cent of the bank's bad loans, it has brought down the bank's total NPAs to a somewhat respectable number.

As a response to the persisting NPA problem, the government has also launched its own ARC, National Asset Reconstruction Company Ltd. NARCL will pay banks 15 per cent of the acquisition cost as upfront cash and the balance as security receipts, which will be guaranteed by the government. While the balance sheets of banks will be partially cleansed of bad loans, enabling them to focus on credit growth once again as demand picks up in the economy, the jury is out on how successful NARCL will be in resolving the acquired bad loans, or on whether the next boom will see a fresh round of NPA generation. Post-pandemic, it would seem that the RBI has taken on itself the role of resolving some of the troublesome crises rather than relying on the institutional framework set in place. For example, it managed to convince SBI to buy 49 per cent of Yes Bank's restructured equity capital. When PMC failed, it again convinced the newly licensed Unity Small Finance Bank to acquire the beleaguered urban cooperative bank in January 2022. When Lakshmi Vilas Bank had reached a point of no return—it had gross NPAs of over 25 per cent, capital adequacy of below 2 per cent and losses of over Rs 1150 crore in 2020—the RBI forcibly merged it with the Indian operations of the Singapore-based bank, DBS Bank India. The only financial sector entity that was put through the IBC system was scam-hit DHFL, which was acquired by Piramal Capital in September 2021 for Rs 34,250 crore.

Once again, egregious misgovernance and the accumulation of NPAs in these institutions forced the RBI to launch the rescue operation. The truth is, NPAs never went away; they just took intermittent breaks. Here are a few examples of how NPAs continue to bedevil the financial system, blessed by borrowers who only briefly felt threatened by the banking sector's control over the IBC process and have now re-occupied their earlier pole position.

## IL&FS

The 2018 collapse of infrastructure financing NBFC IL&FS Ltd, earlier known as Infrastructure Leasing and Financial Services Ltd, had sent the entire financial system into shock, as has been discussed in the chapter on NBFCs. The company had defaulted on its numerous debt obligations in July and August 2018, and the repercussions of this were felt across the full spectrum of the financial system. Banks turned risk-averse, damming credit flow to industry and other sectors. Mutual funds which had invested in IL&FS bonds reneged on their payout to unit holders and had to segregate the investments into specific vehicles, and other NBFCs found it difficult to access funds and had to pay higher interest rates for all market-based borrowings.

The interesting bit is that neither of the two large financial sector regulators—the RBI or SEBI—was alert to the possibility of this NBFC delivering such a shock to the system, despite the presence of some indications. The RBI's Financial Stability Report of December 2017 had clearly stated:

> NBFCs were the largest net borrowers of funds from the financial system, with highest funds received from SCBs (40 per cent), followed by AMCMFs (37 per cent) and insurance companies (19 per cent). SUCBs, AIFIs, HFCs and PFs together accounted for 4 per cent of the borrowings by NBFCs within the financial system.[5]

That NBFCs emerged as the system's largest borrowers should have set the alarm bells ringing somewhere. This is not to suggest that the mere fact of NBFCs being large borrowers should have aroused suspicion, but when mutual funds become the system's second largest lenders to NBFCs, surely there should have been some soul-searching, leading to a routine examination of the funds' end-use or an assessment of the borrowing NBFCs' capital adequacy and quality of asset base.

IL&FS's total outstanding debt at the time of the default was between Rs 90,000 crore and Rs 1 lakh crore. The company had been in deep trouble for a while but had managed to evade scrutiny with the help of some deft accounting jugglery and complex round-tripping of funds among its 348 subsidiaries (while the disclosed number was only 169). Two issues then cropped up during the default, which spurred the regulators into taking some kind of rearguard action.

The first is the lackadaisical role played by the auditors and the credit rating agencies in detecting the long-festering mess in the company. Both categories of gatekeepers, entrusted with the fiduciary responsibility of protecting the interests of shareholders and lenders, green-lit the company's accounts and its numerous debt instruments without highlighting the risks that lurked underneath. This is the basic duty of both auditors and rating agencies, and both were remiss in their obligations towards the regulators and investors, provoking a former Secretary in the Ministry of Corporate Affairs, Injeti Srinivas, to comment:[6] 'We are not expecting an auditor to detect a needle in a haystack, but if an elephant is in the room, they ought to find it.' The credit rating agencies downgraded IL&FS only after the default, the post-facto action eroding the basic principle of a rating providing an early warning about the borrower's ability to repay debt.

SEBI finally swung into action in September 2019, a full twelve months after IL&FS and its subsidiaries had defaulted on their loan commitments. It notified the SEBI (Credit Rating Agencies) (Amendment) Regulations, 2019, the new amendment envisioning the addition of an enabling clause in the rating agreement between the credit rating agency and the entity getting rated. This empowered the rating agency to ask for and acquire relevant details about the issuer's existing or potential future borrowings and an update on how the borrowings are being serviced. SEBI hoped this provision would help rating agencies acquire timely credit information before assigning ratings to issuers of debt instruments. This amendment to the rules became significant in light of the forensic auditor Grant Thornton's report that many of the IL&FS officials had hidden crucial credit information from the rating agencies.

But soon after the amendment, SEBI also took an unprecedented step: it levied a penalty of Rs 25 lakh each on the three credit rating agencies involved in rating the debentures issued by IL&FS. These agencies were ICRA Ltd, India Ratings and Research and Care Ratings.

The RBI, on its part, reinforced its existing liquidity risk management framework for NBFCs. The new framework was made applicable to all non-deposit-taking NBFCs with asset sizes of Rs 100 crore and above, systemically important core investment companies (CICs) and all deposit-taking NBFCs, irrespective of their asset size. The revised liquidity management framework was probably prompted by the yawning asset-liability mismatch at IL&FS, which led to its eventual defaults and collapse. IL&FS, like most other NBFCs, was borrowing short-term money from the banking system, or issuing three-month commercial paper in the money markets, and investing those funds in long-term infrastructure projects, a mismatch that is a sure-fire recipe for disaster. The RBI guidelines were largely similar to the asset-liability management framework for commercial banks.

The response to the IL&FS crisis was a continuing stream of new regulations.

In October 2021, to bring some order to the sprawling and arbitrage-enabling regulations for NBFCs, the RBI brought in a revised framework, one differentiated on the basis of size, activity and 'perceived' riskiness of institutions. The new regulations,[7] which came into effect a year later, classified NBFCs into four layers: base, middle, upper and top. While the eligibility criteria for the base and middle layers would be rule-bound and activity-determined, the criteria for the upper layer would be determined by the RBI, based on a set of weighted parameters, and would invite heightened regulatory attention. In any case, the RBI also decided that the top ten NBFCs, in terms of assets, would always reside in the upper layer, irrespective of all other mitigating factors. The top layer would remain largely empty unless the RBI felt that the systemic risk arising from the actions of certain NBFCs in the upper layer had increased substantially. Going by the relative lack of clarity from the RBI about the exact metrics that will qualify NBFCs for the top layer, especially when compared with the detailed criteria spelt out for the other layers, it can be safely assumed that the central bank has left itself considerable elbow-room for discretionary action, if necessary. An August 2023 article[8] in the *Economic and Political Weekly* points out a number of anomalies in the scale-based regulatory framework, including the lack of specific parameters or a parametric methodology for defining 'riskiness'.

In September 2022, the central bank released a list of the sixteen NBFCs that it felt should be part of the upper layer. HDFC Ltd was a notable exclusion because it had already announced its plans for a merger with HDFC Bank. In September 2023, another list was released with fifteen NBFCs making the cut to the upper layer. At the time of going to press, the top layer continued to remain empty, indicating that the central bank does not perceive any threat to financial stability from large NBFCs yet. But, more importantly, this re-categorization of NBFCs is yet to be tested as a regulatory framework. It primarily seeks to calibrate regulation with the risk profile of NBFCs, especially in view of their growing systemic importance: the lower the risk, the lower the regulatory shackles.

This new framework also seems like a break from the past, with regulatory intensity changing with individual institutions, or a cluster of similar institutions, rather than the earlier practice of regulation being industry-focused where one rule applied to all. This is a continuation of the RBI's new, forbearing approach to the NBFC sector. This velvet-hand-in-iron-glove approach was first evident immediately after the IL&FS debacle, when the RBI also eased the path for NBFCs to access bank credit. In the monetary policy of August 2019, the RBI changed some of the extant rules so that banks could lend more to NBFCs. One, banks could now extend up to 20 per cent of their capital to a single NBFC, against 15 per cent earlier. Two, banks were also allowed to use NBFCs as conduits for achieving their priority-sector credit targets. In other words, bank credit to NBFCs, which would then be on-lent to eligible priority-credit sectors, was eligible to be counted as priority-sector credit in the banks' books.

The IL&FS crisis inspired another piece of reforms. The debacle created the necessary and sufficient conditions for including NBFCs in the insolvency and bankruptcy resolution and liquidation framework. The original insolvency and bankruptcy code had excluded NBFCs. The provisions can theoretically afford beleaguered NBFCs a breather: on admission to the resolution process, NBFCs will be entitled to a moratorium, which can give them an opportunity to regroup their finances. But, so far, only one large NBFC crisis—that of DHFL—has been resolved through the IBC process.

The RBI's pairing of the carrot and stick—facilitating credit growth alongside drafting new regulations—shows how the central bank considered the NBFC as an important cog in the wheel of the Indian financial system, not only from the viewpoint of risk but also as a partner in economic development. Increasingly, the RBI also located outsized peril in the inter-connectedness of the system and the unquantifiable risk to the system that could arise from the collapse of just one large, or even mid-sized, NBFC.

These ice-cold but conflicting realizations—the NBFC sector's economic importance as well as the systemic hazard it could pose—shaped many of the subsequent measures.

But many of these reform measures could well have been implemented earlier, without having to wait for a national crisis to erupt.

## Yes Bank and PMC Bank

The collapse of these two banks—one a private commercial bank and the other an urban cooperative bank—between September 2019 (PMC) and March 2020 (Yes Bank) had many common elements, apart from highlighting how the central bank had missed many of the early warning signals.

On 7 February 2002, the RBI granted approval and licence to banking professionals Ashok Kapur, Rana Kapoor and Harkirat Singh, along with Rabobank, for launching a commercial bank. The licence was granted primarily on the strength and reputation of Rabobank's proposed stake in the bank. The Netherlands-headquartered Rabobank was a well-known agricultural lender with a consistently top-notch credit rating, and the RBI hoped the institution would introduce some of its famed agri-related credit and risk management practices to the Indian financial sector.

The licence resulted in Yes Bank, which commenced commercial operations in August 2004. Yes Bank was one of the two private bank licensees approved by the RBI that year, the other being Kotak Mahindra Finance Company, an NBFC which was asked to convert itself into a bank, Kotak Mahindra Bank.

However, fate had different plans for the Yes Bank leadership. The first sign of what was in store for the bank came in 2003, when founding partner Harkirat Singh withdrew from the bank, claiming[9] later that he was ousted by the Kapur-Kapoor pair. The duo had appointed Ashok Kapur as executive chairman of the bank when Singh was ostensibly on vacation. Singh also claimed that the vital information that Kapur and Kapoor were related—their wives are sisters—was not shared with him.

Ashok Kapur tragically fell to terrorist bullets during the November 2008 attacks in Mumbai. Kapur was entertaining some guests at one of the premier South Mumbai hotels that was attacked when he was mowed down by the terrorists. This made Rana Kapoor the primary promoter-shareholder, and uncontested leader, of the bank. Further, in 2012, Rabobank also exited the bank by selling a large chunk of its shareholding, confirming its severing of ties in favour of launching its own NBFC in India.

From there to March 2020, when Rana Kapoor was arrested and Yes Bank was put under an RBI-monitored revival programme under the care of India's largest commercial bank, SBI—with a new chief executive and a completely overhauled board of directors—the Yes Bank saga is a snapshot of bank excesses going unchecked till affairs reach breaking point.

One of the key reasons behind Yes Bank's collapse was its precarious asset-liability position and rapidly worsening loan quality. The bank also was stretched, as it had exposure to IL&FS, housing finance company DHFL and the Reliance companies managed by Anil Ambani, among others. These companies had collapsed and were unable to repay their loans. The Enforcement Directorate suspected that many of the loans advanced by Yes Bank were allegedly round-tripped to benefit Rana Kapoor and his family members.

But here is where it gets uncomfortable. The bank's parlous state of affairs was somewhat evident as early as in 2017 and 2018, when it had to undergo the RBI-mandated AQR. The bank's cavalier attitude to loans and credit discipline had been in evidence for some time even before that, and yet Rana Kapoor was allowed to continue with his brinkmanship and bluster. The RBI stepped in only when the bank was on the brink of collapse and was a threat to systemic stability, given the financial system's extensive interconnectedness.

This raises two questions. Was the RBI stopped from acting by powerful political interests or politically connected business houses whom Rana Kapoor had assiduously cultivated for more than a decade? Rana Kapoor's earlier stints with Bank of America and ANZ Grindlays as head of wholesale banking was marked by large advances to many politically connected industry groups, some of which had even turned into NPAs. Alternatively, was the RBI slow in getting off the blocks because its alarm bells were programmed, much like in the past, to go off only when the bank reached a cliff edge?

The irony is that a multi-player scam sat between Yes Bank, PMC Bank, Reliance Capital, DHFL and HDIL. It involved a flurry of many big-ticket transactions, and yet the battle-scarred RBI once again missed the signs. It was hoped that the Central Repository on Information of Large Credits, CRILC, which was set up in 2013, would be able to provide some early warning on Yes Bank's loan profligacy. It is also no coincidence that many of the touchpoints in this five-cornered deal machine had connections with influential political figures. The merry-go-round of funds and loans stopped after the IL&FS debacle spooked markets and it became difficult for the dramatis personae to refinance their existing loans.

DHFL, for example, has been accused of defrauding seventeen banks of over Rs 34,000 crore. A forensic report submitted by audit firm KPMG says the DHFL promoters had re-routed close to Rs 30,000 crore from its bank borrowings to more than sixty related entities, mostly for re-investment in property or the securities market.

Rana Kapoor was arrested on 9 March 2020. But on 4 March, just before his arrest, the RBI had imposed a thirty-day moratorium on Yes Bank, which essentially meant the bank could not lend any money or allow deposit withdrawals over Rs 50,000 per customer. A moratorium brings the bank to a standstill to allow the central bank to take stock of the situation and devise remedial measures. It also allows the RBI to supersede the institution's board of directors. Under the proposed reconstruction scheme, SBI picked up a 49 per cent stake in the bank's restructured capital and appointed its deputy managing director, Prashant Kumar, as Yes Bank's chief executive.

Speaking in Parliament about the collapse of Yes Bank, Member of Parliament Sougata Ray (Trinamool Congress) asked the government on 16 March 2020, for a closer scrutiny of private banks:

> The Yes Bank fiasco has exposed the inability of the Government to govern and regulate Financial Institutions . . . The Government should explain how the loan book of Yes Bank saw a massive jump between 2014 and 2019 and how the loan book went up to Rs. 2.42 lakh crores in March, 2019. Anil Ambani Group, ESSEL, ILFS, DHFL and Vodafone were among the stressed Corporates, YES Bank was exposed to . . . The Government says that it will protect the employees' jobs and salaries for one year. It does explain the accusation that it had failed to monitor the bank's troubles. The arrest of Rana Kapoor, detention of his daughter and search on his premises has come too late in the day . . . I would request the Government to take immediate steps to monitor the business of private banks of the country to ensure the safety of investors of such banks and inform Parliament of the steps taken in the matter.

The similarities of this case with that of Punjab Maharashtra Cooperative Bank (PMC) are surprising. The chapter in this book on cooperative banks covered the collapse of PMC Bank in brief. The cooperative bank had been cooking its books regularly, sweeping its bad loans under the carpet along with all the other detritus. It had regularly indulged in over-lending to certain borrowers in violation of the RBI's risk management guidelines, which mandate the maximum that a bank can lend to a single entity or a single business group. It had brazenly made a hash of corporate governance norms. Yet the regulators swooped in only after the bank had reached the point of no return.

Once the initial phase of moratorium, arrests and restructuring was over, the RBI got down to the task of tightening its regulatory framework. On 6 January 2020, the central bank issued a notification tightening its extant supervisory action framework (SAF) for urban cooperative banks, which spelt out new thresholds and triggers, such as net NPAs touching 6 per cent or the bank incurring losses for two consecutive financial years or capital adequacy falling below 9 per cent. Breach of these red lines would require the urban cooperative bank concerned to initiate corrective action, which could be combined with supervisory RBI action. The RBI circular also made it clear that the central bank could initiate pre-emptive action beyond these parameters if it observed stress in other important indicators/parameters, or in the event of serious governance issues. The RBI also warned that in an extreme case, it might consider cancelling the cooperative bank's licence.

The irony is that the SAF has been in existence since 2012 and has been updated regularly, on top of the parameters being tightened frequently. Despite these forbidding warnings, the deterioration continued apace. In all fairness, it can be argued that it is not possible for the RBI to keep track of all individual banks, especially in an economy predicated on lesser controls and interference. As a compelling corollary, such a system would also require enlightened boards at companies that act in the interests of shareholders and depositors, conscientious auditors who are not glossing over misdemeanours in the hope of snagging lucrative consulting assignments, and credible credit rating agencies not beholden to debt issuers. However, given the political complexion of board-level appointments at the public-sector banks and (to a greater degree) cooperative banks, expecting directors to act as fiduciary gate-keepers or guardians of depositor interests is like asking the neighbourhood greengrocer for a cryogenic engine.

## SEBI Actions on Mutual Funds

The mutual fund industry has seen tremendous action over the past few years, with its aggressive marketing and distribution taking the industry's assets under management to stratospheric levels. According to data from the mutual fund industry body, the Association of Mutual Funds in India (AMFI), the industry's assets under management (AUM) went up from Rs 8,26,000 crore as on 30 April 2013 to Rs 41,61,822 crore as on 30 April 2023, a five-fold increase in ten years.

This represents an encouraging trend of financialization of savings in the economy, one indicating some movement of household savings away from physical savings to financial instruments. At close to 20 per cent of the aggregate deposits of all scheduled banks on 30 April 2023, mutual funds have been able to attract both wholesale as well as retail investments.

Unfortunately, regulation of the mutual fund sector has been rather episodic and somewhat reactionary, provoked by the eruption of crises. The first example is the conflicting stand on the segregation of portfolios.

In 2015, JP Morgan's mutual fund management decided to restrict redemptions in two funds (JPMorgan India Short Term Income Fund and JPMorgan India Treasury Fund) after their holding of Amtek Auto non-convertible debentures turned sour. The bonds had been downgraded by credit rating agencies and the two funds had an aggregate exposure of 20 per cent to the bonds. The fund house also decided to segregate the bonds into a separate fund, with payouts promised to unitholders as and when the bond payments materialized.

SEBI took exception to this and initiated adjudication proceedings against the fund houses and their key personnel. In September 2018, the fund house settled with SEBI, paying a fine exceeding Rs 8 crore. The mutual fund's self-regulatory organization, the Association of Mutual Funds in India (AMFI), is believed to have approached SEBI in 2016 and suggested that segregation be allowed to shield the rest of the fund from redemption pressure. SEBI rejected the suggestion on the grounds that this would induce fund managers to disregard risk and perhaps even embolden them to take unnecessary risks.

Cut to 2018, and the IL&FS collapse was seen visibly shaving valuations across portfolios and rendering many investments infructuous. As bonds issued by various NBFCs and housing finance companies entered volatile territory and mutual funds started feeling the heat of redemption pressure, AMFI once again approached SEBI and suggested that funds be allowed to side-pocket troubled investments. Surprisingly, SEBI agreed this time. In December 2018, SEBI issued a circular saying, 'In order to ensure fair treatment to all investors in case of a credit event and to deal with liquidity risk, it has been decided to permit the creation of a segregated portfolio of debt and money market instruments by mutual funds schemes.'

The next year, the Essel Group came close to defaulting on the Rs 7000 crore it had borrowed from eighty-seven schemes of nine mutual fund houses against pledged shares of group company Zee Entertainment. Kotak Mutual Fund's fixed maturity plan schemes—FMPs, which are launched for a fixed period and invest largely in debt of the co-terminus maturity—had picked up a substantial portion of the outstanding debt. Even HDFC Mutual Fund's FMPs were saddled with the same debt. Both fund houses decided to defer the maturity of their FMPs.

In August 2021, SEBI fined Kotak Rs 40 lakh and six of its senior officers a cumulative Rs 1.20 crore, which included Rs 30 lakh levied on Managing Director Nilesh Shah and

Rs 25 lakh on Chief Investment Officer Lakshmi Iyer. Interestingly, the adjudication order penalized Kotak Mutual for postponing redemption payment to its FMP investors, which amounts to segregating, but which the fund house had failed to explicitly mention in its offer documents. There was, however, no censure of the fund house's injudicious decision of subscribing to a large chunk of a single group's outstanding debt. Also, curiously and conspicuously, there was no SEBI stricture on the Essel Group for playing fast and loose with its repayment commitments, sparking off speculations of political influences coming into play.

Further contretemps were in store. In April 2020, storied fund house Franklin Templeton decided to wind down six of its debt-focused fund schemes claiming there was redemption pressure and drying up of liquidity in the bond markets. SEBI's investigations found that Franklin Templeton had not instituted proper controls or risk assessment norms; it had also miscommunicated to investors the scheme details. On closer investigation, SEBI also found that some Franklin Templeton senior officers had redeemed their investments in these schemes before the winding-down news was shared with other investors. This prompted the securities market regulator to extend its existing laws on the prohibition of insider trading to mutual funds too. It is curious why this was not accomplished before and why this precise regulation had to wait for a specific event.

## In Conclusion

The contours of India's economic reforms, financial sector reforms in particular, have been determined largely by political-economy compulsions, barring the initial burst of 1991 economic reforms. What makes financial sector reforms particularly vulnerable to political-economy compulsions is the uneven power distribution among the five main stakeholders: the government, the financial institutions, the regulators, the industrial consumers of financial products and services and the retail or household participants in the financial system. India's distorted campaign finance system invests industrial consumers with disproportionate political bargaining powers, which then tends to distort the reforms dynamics into strange shapes. Retail consumers, in contrast, lack political bargaining power and hence have very little role in influencing policy development. But come a crisis, which is usually accompanied by the spectacle of defrauded pensioners or poor families losing their savings to some trickster, and it presents the administration with a clear and present political problem. Reforms happen in quick succession then. Hence, crisis, given the nature of India's political economy, has become the mother of all financial sector reforms.

The 1991 rash of reforms was largely centred on macroeconomic adjustment and fiscal stabilization, with related pathways radiating to the financial sector and industrial policy. It did not move the needle much in the public sector (read government), leaving many of the patronage networks untouched. This may have been one of the core reasons for the persistent hesitancy in bringing about reforms, which would get amped up only in the event of a crisis or a scam.

Has the Indian financial sector been exorcised of all crises? It's difficult to predict anything either way, but some unaddressed risks lie at the heart of the financial sector even today, and changes are likely to occur only in the event of a crisis.

- The recovery process for debt is still shot through with distortions, especially penal provisions for wilful defaults. All measures taken so far have yielded sub-optimal results because of the persisting issues of poor design and implementation. Every so often a new regulatory scheme is launched with great fanfare, but gets finessed by Indian corporates in no time. Often, authorities themselves dilute the provisions.

- As a related issue, credit risk still remains an unresolved mystery in the Indian financial system. Typically, most lenders—more so private banks and NBFCs—don't lend their own money, but their incentive structures are designed to encourage ever-higher lending. But once things go south, there are no incentives for early disclosure and resolution. Accounting and sleight of hand keep things going for some time. RBI governor Shaktikanta Das has been using every public platform to discuss this flaw in the Indian banking system. Addressing[10] a conference of directors of PSU banks in Mumbai on 29 May 2023, in Mumbai, he said: 'During the course of our supervisory process, certain instances of using innovative ways to conceal the real status of stressed loans have also come to our notice . . . Such practices beg the question as to whose interest such smart methods serve.' Once the problem gets out of hand, the central bank and the government are forced to step in, reigniting the debate on moral hazard and how the sharpening asymmetry of the political economy remains a constant source of financial crises.

- Anybody and everybody is allowed to lend money, but only banks and NBFCs are subject to the RBI's ever-tightening regulatory framework. Mutual funds, which are regulated by SEBI, have also launched credit funds, which act like NBFCs but are structured like mutual funds. As somebody said, in India what is not expressly prohibited is permitted. Even private equity (PE) funds have been indulging in lending, with some disastrous results. One leading PE, for example, picked up shiploads of unviable debt paper and, when valuations melted, dumped the dud investments on a public-sector mutual fund. Lending by non-regulated institutions is a clear case of regulatory arbitrage and embeds the financial system with unquantifiable risks. Clearly, regulations across regulators have to be aligned so that anybody in the business of lending money has to comply with all the regulatory and prudential norms.

- Lack of available capital for growth has forced many financial players to pivot to foreign capital, especially PE funds. Multiple unstated problems can bubble up from the growing trend of PE investment in NBFCs or smaller, private banks. One, going by the trend observed so far, most PE investments in NBFCs have been in unlisted companies and have been routed from funds residing in tax shelters. There is very little regulatory line of sight into the provenance of these funds. Two, investment in an NBFC allows PE funds to access a vehicle that can borrow from banks for on-lending in the Indian market, something that might have been difficult for them to accomplish directly.

How the government or regulators deal with all the above incipient risks (as well as many others not listed in the preceding paragraphs) will determine the temperature for future financial sector reforms. But, at a broader level, a lot will depend on how the canvas for reforms is mounted.

Many political scientists and analysts have held that India is a weak state teeming with many strong actors. In this fervid theatre of policy mapping and implementation, usually circumscribed by the interplay between various actors with objectives not necessarily aligned with the national interest, it is necessary to ask what actually can be called a reform. World Bank's Stuti Khemani has a list of what makes for a reform in her paper *Political Economy of Reform*, but topping it is the notion that a reform can be called successful only if it generates large benefits over the costly status quo: 'Counting any type of policy or institutional change as a "reform" is not consistent with how economics research examines reforms.'

As a corollary, it is also necessary to understand who gains and who loses from a particular policy document. This will then provide some idea of whether a specific reforms measure will succeed or not. All the various policy formulations to sort out the NPA problem in India had some design flaw, which ensured that the scales were always tilted in favour of a small but influential political constituency and not the country's financial system or its citizens.

In the end, the success of financial reforms will depend on two factors. One, the political resolve to initiate reforms that not only overhaul the status quo but which are also designed to resist manipulation by narrow pecuniary interests. Finally, and importantly, it will also require the political class to implement decisions that are not solely influenced by scams or crises but are driven by the need to deliver maximum utility to a maximum number of people.

It all boils down to the quality of politics. If we focus on the classical definition of politics, which concerns itself with the distribution of material goods and services among the various stakeholders in society (and does not engage with more contemporary issues of culture and identity), it might be legitimate to ask whether the track record on the distribution of financial goods and services among Indians so far can be considered good politics. Data on financial inclusion shows there is still a long way to go.

The RBI has constructed an index on financial inclusion, incorporating details of banking, insurance, investment, postal savings and pensions with weightages assigned for access (35 per cent), usage (45 per cent) and quality (20 per cent). The value of the financial inclusion index was 60.1 for the twelve-month period ended March 2023, against 56.4 in March 2022, demonstrating an improvement in financial inclusion. But, evidently, there is still a lot of headroom and proof that a huge gap still exists in the availability and utilization of financial services by urban and rural Indians. While there has indeed been some steady progress in financial inclusion, going by whatever metric or measure is available, it is also equally true that financial inclusion cannot be accomplished without first tackling the deep-rooted problems of poverty and deprivation. The 2008 report by the government-appointed committee on financial inclusion (chaired by former RBI governor C. Rangarajan) had noted that financial inclusion, defined solely by opening of bank deposits or creating credit delivery systems, was meaningless unless the government also made conscious efforts to improve the earnings capacity of the poorer sections of society.

In the final analysis, instead of being episodic or driven largely by events, financial sector reforms will probably need to address how they can deliver tailor-made products and services to the different sections of society, depending on their income levels, and how they can empower ordinary Indians so that they can use financial products and services for improving their lives and realizing their true potential. It is that quality of politics and financial sector reforms which can deliver maximum utility to a maximum number of people.

# Bibliography

1. Singh, Dr Manmohan. Speech Introducing the Budget for 1991–92, 24 July 1991, https://eparlib.nic.in/bitstream/123456789/111/1/Budget_Speech_Final_1991–92.pdf.

2. Singh, Dr Manmohan. Convocation Speech, Indian Institute of Management, Bangalore, 1991, https://www.iimb.ac.in/node/264.

3. Ahluwalia, Montek S. *Backstage: The Story Behind India's High Growth Years*. Rupa, 2020.

4. Ahluwalia, Montek S. 'Economic Reforms in India Since 1991: Has Gradualism Worked?', *Journal of Economic Perspectives*, Summer 2002, Vol. 16, No. 3, pp. 67–88.

5. Ahluwalia, Montek S. 'The 1991 Reforms: How Home-Grown Were They?', *Economic and Political Weekly*, Vol. L1, No. 29, 16 July 2016, pp. 39–46.

6. World Bank, 'India: 1991 Country Economic Memorandum', Report No. 9412-IN, 23 August 1991, http://documents1.worldbank.org/curated/en/962181468033534646/pdf/multi0page.pdf.

7. International Monetary Fund, Annual Report, 1991.

8. Sharma, Vijay Paul and Hrima Thaker. 'Economic Policy Reforms and Indian Fertilizer Industry', Centre for Management in Agriculture; Indian Institute of Management, Ahmedabad, February 2010, https://www.iima.ac.in/c/document_library/7IndianFertilizerIndustryb053.pdf?uuid=1829f627-b799-4aa9-a2dd-fa93a88dd8fb&groupId=62390.

9. Hanson, James and Sanjay Kathuria (eds.). *India: A Financial Sector for the Twenty-First Century*. Oxford University Press, 1999.

10. Ramesh, Jairam. *To the Brink and Back: India's 1991 Story*. Rupa, 2015.

11. Sitapati, Vinay. *Half Lion: How P.V. Narasimha Rao Transformed India.* Penguin Books, an imprint of Penguin Random House, 2017.

12. Baru, Sanjaya. *1991: How P.V. Narasimha Rao Made History.* Aleph, 2016.

13. Khatkhate, Deena. 'Timing and Sequence of Financial Sector Reforms: Evidence and Rationale', *Economic and Political Weekly,* 11 July 1998.

14. Mohan, Rakesh. 'Financial Sector Reforms and Monetary Policy: The Indian Experience', WP No. 320, Center for International Development, Stanford University, April 2007.

15. Krueger, Anne O. (ed.). *Economic Policy Reforms and the Indian Economy.* Oxford University Press, 2002.

16. World Bank, https://documents1.worldbank.org/curated/en/999451468260069468/pdf/multi0page.pdf

17. Panagariya, Arvind. 'India in the 1980s and 1990s: A Triumph of Reforms' November 2003, https://www.imf.org/external/np/apd/seminars/2003/newdelhi/pana.pdf

18. Rangarajan, C. *Forks In The Road: My Days at RBI and Beyond.* Penguin Business, 2022.

19. Reserve Bank of India, *The Reserve Bank of India*, Vol. I, 1935–51, S.L.N. Simha, 1970.

20. Reserve Bank of India, *The Reserve Bank of India*, Vol. II, 1951–67, G. Balachandran. Oxford University Press, 1998.

21. Reserve Bank of India, *The Reserve Bank of India* (Vol. III, 1967–81), A. Vasudevan (ed.), 2005.

22. Reserve Bank of India, *The Reserve Bank of India* (Vol. IV, Parts A & B, 1981–97), Academic Foundation, 2013.

23. Reserve Bank of India, *The Reserve Bank of India* (Vol. V, 1997–2008), Tirthankar Roy (ed.). Cambridge University Press, 2022.

24. Subramanian, Samanth. 'Long View: India's Very First Corruption Scandal', the *New York Times*, 9 May 2012.

25. Desai, Ashok H. 'Afterthoughts on the Mundhra Affair', the *Economic Weekly*, July 1959.

26. Malhotra, Inder. 'The Mundhra Affair', the *Indian Express*, 12 December 2008.

27. Mukherji, Rahul. *Political Economy of Reforms in India*. Oxford India Short Introductions; Oxford University Press, 2014, p. 200.

28. Reddy, Y.V. *Advice and Dissent: My Life in Public Service*. Harper Business, an imprint of Harper Collins Publishers, 2017, p. 480.

29. Datta, Bhabatosh. *Indian Planning at the Crossroads*. Oxford University Press, 1992, p. 251.

30. Venkitaramanan, S. 'Regulation and Supervision Issues: Banks and Non-Banks', in James Hanson and Sanjay Kathuria (eds), *India: A Financial Sector for the Twenty-First Century*. Oxford University Press, 1999, pp. 132–163.

31. Ahluwalia, Montek S. 'Reforming India's Financial Sector: An Overview', in James Hanson and Sanjay Kathuria (eds), *India: A Financial Sector for the Twenty-First Century*. Oxford University Press, 1999, pp. 29–54.

32. Tarapore, S.S., 'Indian Banking: Preparing for the Next Round of Reform', in James Hanson and Sanjay Kathuria (eds), *India: A Financial Sector for the Twenty-First Century*. Oxford University Press, 1999, pp. 57–70.

33. Sarkar, Jayati. 'India's Banking Sector: Current Status, Emerging Challenges, and Policy Imperatives in a Globalized Environment', in James Hanson and Sanjay Kathuria (eds), *India: A Financial Sector for the Twenty-First Century*. Oxford University Press, 1999, pp. 71–131.

34. Kelkar, Vijay and Ajay Shah. *In Service of the Republic: The Art and Science of Economic Policy*. Penguin Allen Lane, an imprint of Penguin Random House, 2019, p. 425.

35. Khemani, Stuti. 'Political Economy of Reform', Policy Research Working Paper 8224, World Bank Group, October 2017.

36. Dhingra, Sanchita and Abha Shukla. 'Growing Private Equity Investment in the NBFC Sector: Analysing Risks', *Economic and Political Weekly*, Vol. LVIII, No. 18, 16 May 2023.

37. Shah, Ajay and Susan Thomas. 'Developing the Indian Capital Market', in James Hanson and Sanjay Kathuria (eds), *India: A Financial Sector for the Twenty-First Century*. Oxford University Press, 1999, pp. 205–65.

38. Rajan, Raghuram. Note to Parliamentary Estimates Committee on NPAs.

39. Rao, M. Rajeshwar. 'NBFC Regulation – Looking Ahead', speech delivered to Assocham on 6 November 2020, https://rbi.org.in/scripts/BS_SpeechesView.aspx?Id=1101

40. Report of the Study Group on Non-Banking Companies, chaired by James S. Raj, 1975.

41. Mundra, S.S. 'Asset Resolution and Managing NPAs – What, Why and How?', presentation delivered at the first CII Banking Summit in Mumbai, 11 February 2016.

42. Ray, Saon. 'Understanding the NBFC Conundrum', *Economic and Political Weekly*, Vol. LIV, No. 14, 6 April 2019.

43. Patel, Urjit. *Overdraft: Saving the Indian Saver*. Harper Business, an imprint of Harper Collins Publishers, 2020, p. 195.

44. Reserve Bank of India, Trend and Progress of Banking in India, 2015–16.

45. Shah, Ajay and Susan Thomas. Policy Issues in the Indian Securities Market; working paper no 106; August 2001; Center for International Development, Stanford University; https://kingcenter.stanford.edu/sites/g/files/sbiybj16611/files/media/file/106wp_0.pdf

46. Gent, John-Echeverri. 'Politics of Market Micro-Structure: Towards a New Political Economy of India's Equity Market Reform', *India's Economic Transition: The Politics of Reforms*, Rahul Mukherjee (ed.). Oxford University Press, 2007.

47. Chakravarty, Sukhamoy. Report of the Committee to Review the Working of the Monetary System, Reserve Bank of India, 1985.

48. Vaghul, N. Report of the Working Group on the Money Market, Reserve Bank of India, 1987.

49. Basu, Debashis and Sucheta Dalal. *The Scam*. Kensource Business Books, 2009.

50. C Rangarajan, Report of the Committee on Financial Inclusion, 2008.

51. Mehra, Puja. *The Lost Decade: 2008–18*. Penguin Random House India. 2019.

52. Balakrishnan, Pulapre. 'Markets, Growth and Social Opportunity: India Since 1991', *Economic and Political Weekly*, 14 January 2017, Vol. LII, No. 2.

53. Acharya, Viral, *Quest for Restoring Financial Stability in India*. Vintage, an imprint of Penguin Random House India, 2023.

54. Mohan, Rakesh and Partha Ray, 'Indian Financial Sector: Structure, Trends and Turns', IMF Working Paper WP/17/7, International Monetary Fund, January 2017.

55. Subbarao, Duvvuri. *Who Moved My Interest Rate?* Viking, an imprint of Penguin Random House India, 2016.

56. Varshney, Ashutosh. 'Mass Politics or Elite Politics? India's Economic Reforms in Comparative Perspective' in *India in the Era of Economic Reforms*, Jefferey Sachs, Ashutosh Varshney and Nirupam Bajpai (eds). Oxford University Press, 1999.

57. Murthy, R.C. *The Fall of Angels*. HarperCollins Publishers India, 1995.

58. Rajan, Raghuram G. *I Do What I Do*. Harper Business, an imprint of HarperCollins Publishers India, 2017.

59. Tripathi, Dwijendra. *The Oxford History of Indian Business*. Oxford University Press, 2004.

60. Patil, R.H. 'Financial Sector Reforms: Realities and Myths'. *Economic and Political Weekly*, 8 May 2010, Vol. XLV, No. 19.

61. Joshi, Vijay. *India's Long Road: The Search for Prosperity*. Penguin Random House India, 2016.

62. Awasthi, Arvind and Siddharth Shukla. 'RBI's Scale-Based Regulation for NBFCs: A Bevy of Anomalies', *Economic and Political Weekly*, 5 August 2023, Vol. LVIII, No. 31.

63. Reddy, Y.V. *India and the Global Financial Crisis: Managing Money and Finance*. Orient Blackswan, 2009.

64. Reddy, Y.V. *Lectures on Economic and Financial Sector Reforms in India*. Oxford University Press, 2002.

65. Acharya, Shankar. *Essays on Macroeconomic Policy and Growth in India*. Oxford University Press, 2006.

66. Ahluwalia, Montek S., Y.V. Reddy and S.S. Tarapore (eds.). *Macroeconomics and Monetary Policy: Issues for a Reforming Economy* (a *Festschrift* honouring C. Rangarajan). Oxford University Press, 1998.

67. Krueger, Anne O. (ed.). *Economic Policy Reforms and the Indian Economy.* Oxford University Press, 2002.

68. Boughton, James M. 'Tearing Down Walls: The International Monetary Fund 1990–1999', International Monetary Fund, 2012, https://www.elibrary.imf.org/display/book/9781616350840/978 1616350840.xml

69. Barua, Samir K., and Jayanth R. Varma. *Securities Scam: Genesis, Mechanics, and Impact, Vikalpa,* January–March 1993, Vol. 18, No. 1.

70. Frankopan, Peter. *The Silk Roads: A New History of the World.* Bloomsbury, 2015.

71. Chakraborti, Haripada. *Trade and Commerce of Ancient India (C. 200 B.C.—C. 650 A.D.).* Academic Publishers, 1966, freely downloadable from: https://ignca.gov.in/Asi_data/74357.pdf.

# Notes

## Chapter 1: In the Beginning

1 Development financial institutions were responsible for extending long-term loans for industrial development and infrastructure, while commercial banks could only lend short-term working capital.

2 The difference between an economy's total incoming and outgoing payments, which include exports and imports of goods and services, investment flows, remittances, interest payments, etc. BoP is usually divided into current account and capital account. The Ministry for Statistics and Programme Implementation defines it as a statistical statement that systematically summarizes for a specific time period the economic transactions of an economy with the rest of the world.

3 'India: 1991 Country Economic Memorandum', Report No. 9412-IN, Document of the World Bank, 23 August 1991, https://documents1.worldbank.org/curated/en/962181468033534646/pdf/multi0page.pdf.

4 The author was a professor of economics, at the University of Maryland when this paper was published in 2003. Arvind Panagariya, 'India in the 1980s and 1990s: A Triumph of Reforms', IMF Working Paper, March 2004, https://www.imf.org/external/pubs/ft/wp/2004/wp0443.pdf; p. 16.

5  https://www.discoursemagazine.com/politics/2022/07/07/
   ideas-of-india-liberalization-and-narasimha-rao/.

6  Balance of trade in goods and services, plus incomes from
   employment, investments or loans (via dividends or interest),
   remittances from workers overseas and international transfers
   (gifts). A deficit implies outflows exceeding inflows, or
   expenditure exceeding income.

7  1991 International Monetary Fund, Annual Report, https://
   www.imf.org/external/pubs/ft/ar/archive/pdf/ar1991.pdf.

8  Vinay Sitapati, *Half-Lion: How Narasimha Rao Transformed India*
   (Penguin Viking, 27 June 2016), p. 110.

9  Budget 1991-92 Speech of Shri Manmohan Singh Minister of
   Finance, 24 July 1991, https://www.indiabudget.gov.in/doc/
   bspeech/bs199192.pdf.

10 *RBI History*, 1989–1997, p. 1262.

11 Special Drawing Rights, which is not a currency but an asset
   that a nation can accumulate in its foreign exchange reserves;
   its value is based on a basket of five currencies: the US dollar,
   the Chinese renminbi, the Euro, the Japanese yen and the
   British pound.

12 Budget 1991-92 Speech of Shri Manmohan Singh Minister
   of Finance, https://www.indiabudget.gov.in/doc/bspeech/
   bs199293.pdf.

13 'Tearing Down Walls: The International Monetary Fund
   1990-99', IMF, 2012, pp. 449–450, https://www.elibrary.imf.
   org/display/book/9781616350840/9781616350840.xml.

14 Budget and RBI: New Directions (by Dr. Y.V. Reddy at
   Hyderabad on 8 March 1997), https://rbi.org.in/scripts/BS_
   SpeechesView.aspx?Id=227.

15 *RBI History*, 1989–1997, p. 1230.

16 'Autonomy of Central Banks', Tenth M.G. Kutty Memorial
   Lecture delivered by Dr C. Rangarajan, Governor at
   Calcutta on 17 September 1993, Reserve Bank of India
   Bulletin, December 1993, https://rbidocs.rbi.org.in/rdocs/

Speeches/PDFs/01SP17091993C02400881DFB454B8B4
5CE7B25576630.PDF.

17 'Mass Politics or Elite Politics? India's Economic Reforms in
Comparative Perspective'; *India in the Era of Economic Reforms*;
ed. Jeffrey Sachs, Ashutosh Varshney, Nirupam Bajpai
(Oxford University Press), pp. 222–60.

18 Stuti Khemani, 'Political Economy of Reform', Policy Research
Working Paper, World Bank Group, Development Research
Group, Macroeconomics and Growth Team, October 2017,
https://openknowledge.worldbank.org/server/api/core/
bitstreams/7fd3b2d0-223a-50a8-9a83-bb9221a24299/content.

## Chapter 2: Recurring Scams in Pre-Reforms India

1 *RBI History*, Vol. I.

## Chapter 3: The Securities Scam of 1992: A Brief Anatomy

1 Samir K. Barua and Jayanth R. Varma, 'Securities Scam:
Genesis, Mechanics, and Impact', Perspectives, Vol. 18, No.
1, January–March 1993, https://journals.sagepub.com/doi/
pdf/10.1177/0256090919930101.

2 Subsequently merged with the State Bank of India in
August 2008.

3 'Monitoring and Inspection of Brokers', Circulars, 29 May 1992,
https://www.sebi.gov.in/legal/circulars/may-1992/monitoring-
and-inspection-of-brokers_19379.html.

## Chapter 4: Equity Markets: A Historical Perspective

1 Freely downloadable from: https://ignca.gov.in/Asi_
data/74357.pdf.

2 Payment Systems in India 1998, Reserve Bank of India,
https://rbi.org.in/scripts/OccasionalPublications.aspx?
head=Payment%20Systems%20in%20India.

3 Even though the badla concept was borrowed from the LSE, the latter abolished the practice some years ago. Interestingly, the Milan Stock Exchange still uses a similar deferral product, called the riporti system.

4 Jeffrey C. Williams and Emilio Barone, 'Lending of Money and Shares Through the Riporti Market of the Milan Stock Exchange', January 1991, posted 5 March 2004. https://ssrn.com/abstract=512464 or http://dx.doi.org/10.2139/ssrn.512464.

5 Jayanth R. Verma, 'Reforming the Stock Market's *Badla* System', *The Hindu BusinessLine*, 14 August 2022, https://www.thehindubusinessline.com/india-at-75/reforming-the-stock-markets-badla-system/article65757687.ece.

6 Samir K. Barua and Jayanth R. Varma, 'Securities Scam: Genesis, Mechanics, and Impact', *Perspectives*, Vol. 18, No. 1, January–March 1993, https://journals.sagepub.com/doi/pdf/10.1177/0256090919930101.

7 Shah and Thomas 2002 argue that there are examples of this sort internationally where a new exchange has overtaken the incumbent in just one year.

8 https://eparlib.nic.in/bitstream/123456789/1094781/1/10_XV_18-12-1995_p222_p222_u3050.pdf.

9 https://eparlib.nic.in/bitstream/123456789/1095926/1/10_XVI_01-03-1996_p50_p50_u536.pdf.

10 https://eparlib.nic.in/bitstream/123456789/794805/1/10_III_30041992_p192_p201_d11.pdf.

11 SEBI Annual Report for 2017–18, p. 58; https://www.sebi.gov.in/reports-and-statistics/publications/aug-2018/annual-report-2017-18_39868.html.

## Chapter 5: Home Trade and Coop Banks

1 Vaibhav Ganjapure, 'Government Appoints Justice JN Patel to Probe NDCCB Scam', the *Times of India*, 14 July 2022, https://

timesofindia.indiatimes.com/city/nagpur/govt-appoints-justice-jn-patel-to-probe-ndccb-scam/articleshow/92860858.cms.

## Chapter 6: Controlling NBFCs

1 Report of the Sub-Committee of the Central Board of Directors of Reserve Bank of India to Study Issues and Concerns in the MFI Sector, Reserve Bank of India, 19 January 2011, https://rbi.org.in/Scripts/PublicationReportDetails.aspx?UrlPage=&ID=608.
2 Non Banking Financial Company-Micro Finance Institutions (NBFC-MFIs) – Directions – Modifications, Reserve Bank of India, 3 August 2012, https://rbi.org.in/scripts/NotificationUser.aspx?Mode=0&Id=7493.
3 Civil Appeal No. 5233 0f 2012, *Nedumpilli Finance Company Limited Versus State Of Kerala & Ors.*, https://main.sci.gov.in/supremecourt/2010/1744/1744_2010_10_1501_35747_Judgement_10-May-2022.pdf.
4 Scale Based Regulation (SBR): A Revised Regulatory Framework for NBFCs, Reserve Bank of India, 22 October 2021, https://rbi.org.in/Scripts/NotificationUser.aspx?Id=12179&Mode=0.

## Chapter 7: Banking Reforms

1 C. Rangarajan, 'Banking and Profitability', Address by C. Rangarajan, Deputy Governor, at Bank Economists' Conference on Banking for Better Profitability hosted by the Vysya Bank Limited in Bangalore on 12 January 1991, Reserve Bank of India Bulletin, February 1991, https://rbidocs.rbi.org.in/rdocs/Speeches/PDFs/02SP12011991786938DBC78C40F2B6184533A76D5578.PDF.
2 *The Oxford History of Indian Business* (Oxford University Press, 2004), p. 146.
3 https://rbidocs.rbi.org.in/rdocs/Publications/PDFs/bs72-95-1.pdf.

4 According to the IMF, Article IV consultation involves a 'regular, usually annual, comprehensive discussion between the IMF staff and representatives of individual member countries concerning the member's economic and financial policies. The basis for these discussions is in Article IV of the IMF Articles of Agreement (as amended, effective 1978) which directs the Fund to exercise firm surveillance over each member's exchange rate policies.'

5 Y.V. Reddy, *India and the Global Financial Crisis: Managing Money and Finance* (Orient Blackswan, 2009), p. 125.

6 'Reports on Currency and Finance', Special Edition, Vol. IV, p. 110–11.

7 S.S. Tarapore, 'Indian Banking: Preparing for the Next Round of Reform; India: A Financial Sector for the Twenty-First Century'; ed. James A. Hanson and Sanjay Kathuria, 1999, p. 57.

8 'RBI Releases Guidelines for Licensing of Payments Banks', Reserve Bank of India, 27 November 2014, https://www.rbi.org.in/Scripts/BS_PressReleaseDisplay.aspx?prid=32615.

9 'RBI releases Guidelines for Licensing of Small Finance Banks in the Private Sector', Reserve Bank of India, 27 November 2014, https://www.rbi.org.in/Scripts/BS_PressReleaseDisplay.aspx?prid=32614.

10 C. Rangarajan, 'Imperatives of Banking in India', Inaugural Address by Dr C. Rangarajan, Governor, at the Bank Economists' Meet 1994, organized by the Union Bank of India at Goa on 5 September 1994, https://rbidocs.rbi.org.in/rdocs/Speeches/PDFs/01SP05091994DE713A1C223C4CF0B1E724C24849C84C.PDF.

## Chapter 8: NPAs: A Problem That Refuses To Go Away

1 'Some Aspects and Issues Relating to NPAs in Commercial Banks', prepared in the Department of Banking Supervision, RBI, CO by A.Q. Siddiqi, chief general manager in charge, and A.S. Rao and R.M. Thakkar, deputy general managers, https://rbidocs.rbi.org.in/rdocs/Bulletin/PDFs/7546.pdf.

2 Raghav Ohri, 'Debt Recovery Tribunals Bogged Down by Inadequate Infrastructure and Red Tape', the *Economic Times*, 10 June 2014, https://economictimes.indiatimes.com/news/economy/infrastructure/debt-recovery-tribunals-bogged-down-by-inadequate-infrastructure-and-red-tape/articleshow/36316928.cms?from=mdr.

3 Kanchan Chaudhari, 'Place Petitions before FM: HC on Poor Condition of Debt Recovery Tribunals in Mumbai', Hindustan Times, 15 February 2020, https://www.hindustantimes.com/mumbai-news/place-petitions-before-fm-hc-on-poor-condition-of-debt-recovery-tribunals-in-mumbai/story-l1lNAt9vOjTu0MB0JZ1NgJ.html.

4 Chapter IV, Restructuring of Loans, Draft Report IPP, rb.gy/0nh52.

5 'Statement by Dr. Raghuram Rajan on Taking Office on September 4, 2013', Reserve Bank of India, 4 September 2014, https://rbi.org.in/scripts/BS_PressReleaseDisplay.aspx?prid=29479.

6 'Discussion Paper on Early Recognition of Financial Distress, Prompt Steps for Resolution and Fair Recovery for Lenders: Framework for Revitalising Distressed Assets in the Economy', Reserve Bank of India, 17 December 2013, https://rbi.org.in/Scripts/PublicationReportDetails.aspx?UrlPage=&ID=715.

7 'Early Recognition of Financial Distress, Prompt Steps for Resolution and Fair Recovery for Lenders: Framework for Revitalising Distressed Assets in the Economy', Reserve Bank of India, 30 January 2014, https://rbidocs.rbi.org.in/rdocs/content/pdfs/NPA300114RFF.pdf.

8 'Flexible Structuring of Long Term Project Loans to Infrastructure and Core Industries', Reserve Bank of India, 15 July 2014, https://rbi.org.in/scripts/NotificationUser.aspx?Mode=0&Id=9101.

9 'Strategic Debt Restructuring Scheme', Reserve Bank of India, 8 June 2015, https://rbi.org.in/scripts/NotificationUser.aspx?Mode=0&Id=9767.

10 'Scheme for Sustainable Structuring of Stressed Assets', Reserve Bank of India, 13 June 2016, https://rbi.org.in/scripts/NotificationUser.aspx?Mode=0&Id=10446.

11 'Some Ways to Decisively Resolve Bank Stressed Assets', Dr Viral V. Acharya, Deputy Governor—21 February 2017—at the Indian Banks' Association Banking Technology Conference, Mumbai, https://rbi.org.in/Scripts/BS_SpeechesView.aspx?Id=1035.

12 S.S. Mundra, 'Asset Resolution and Managing NPAs—What, Why and How?', 1st CII Banking Summit, Mumbai, 11 February 2016, https://rbidocs.rbi.org.in/rdocs/Speeches/PDFs/PPT1102166AB61D0F35C546539EF4DCD3C83B3668.pdf.

13 'Unstarred Question No-2983 Answered on 7th August / Sravana 16, 1945 (Saka)', Government of India, Ministry of Finance, Department of Financial Services, https://sansad.in/getFile/loksabhaquestions/annex/1712/AU2983.pdf?source=pqals.

14 'Framework for Compromise Settlements and Technical Write-offs', Reserve Bank of India, 8 June 2023, https://rbi.org.in/Scripts/NotificationUser.aspx?Id=12513&Mode=0.

15 For an understanding of the Code and its processes, see: https://ibbi.gov.in/uploads/whatsnew/e42fddce80e99d28b683a7e21c81110e.pdf.

16  Budget 2021-2022, Speech of Nirmala Sitharaman, Minister
of Finance, 1 February 2021, https://www.indiabudget.gov.
in/budget2021-22/doc/Budget_Speech.pdf.

17  'Lok Sabha Starred Question No. *56 Answered on
24.07.2023', Government of India, Ministry of Finance,
https://sansad.in/getFile/loksabhaquestions/annex/1712/
AS56.pdf?source=pqals.

## Chapter 9: Indian Reforms Event-Driven, Even Post-2014

1  DNA Web Team, 'Throw the Door Open', DNA, 14 September
2017, https://www.dnaindia.com/business/report-throw-the-
door-open-1094824.

2  Jaimini Bhagwati, M. Shuheb Khan and Ramakrishna Reddy
Bogathi, 'Financial Sector Legislative Reforms Commission
(FSLRC) and Financial Sector Regulation in India', Working
Paper 324, Indian Council for Research on International
Economic Relations, June 2016, https://icrier.org/pdf/
Working_Paper_324.pdf.

3  'Governance in Banks: Driving Sustainable Growth and Stability',
Inaugural Address by Shaktikanta Das, Governor, at the
Conference of Directors of Banks organized by the Reserve Bank
of India for Public Sector Banks on 22 May 2023 in New Delhi
and Private Sector Banks on 29 May 2023 in Mumbai, https://
www.rbi.org.in/Scripts/BS_SpeechesView.aspx?Id=1364.

4  Bhaskar Chakravorti, 'India's Botched War on Cash', *Harvard
Business Review*, 14 December 2016, https://hbr.org/2016/12/
indias-botched-war-on-cash.

5  SCB: scheduled commercial bank; AMCMFs: asset
management companies managing mutual funds; SUCB:
scheduled urban cooperative bank; AIFI: all India financial
institution; HFC: housing finance company; PF: pension fund.

6 Jayshree P. Upadhyay, 'Inside the Audit Lapses that Led to IL&FS Crisis', *Mint*, 21 May 2019, https://www.livemint.com/companies/news/inside-the-audit-lapses-that-led-to-il-fs-crisis-1558456079750.html.

7 'Scale Based Regulation (SBR): A Revised Regulatory Framework for NBFCs', Reserve Bank of India, 22 October 2021, https://rbidocs.rbi.org.in/rdocs/notification/PDFs/NT1127AD09AD866884557BD4DEEA150ACC91A.PDF.

8 https://www.epw.in/system/files/pdf/2023_58/31/CM_LVIII_31_050823_Arvind_Awasthi.pdf.

9 Anita Bhoir, 'History Repeating Itself at Yes Bank, Says Harkirat Singh', the *Economic Times*, 26 June 2013, https://economictimes.indiatimes.com/industry/banking/finance/banking/history-repeating-itself-at-yes-bank-says-harkirat-singh/articleshow/20771853.cms.

10 'Governance in Banks: Driving Sustainable Growth and Stability – Shaktikanta Das', 23 June 2023, https://www.rbi.org.in/Scripts/BS_ViewBulletin.aspx?Id=21856.

Scan QR code to access the
Penguin Random House India website